THE
CONGRESSIONAL
MEDAL
OF
HONOR

Text
Bill Harris

Editorial
Gill Waugh
Jane Adams
Scott Coombs

Commissioning Editor
Andrew Preston

Designed by
Design Box

Photography
United Press International/Bettmann, New York
National Archives, Washington, DC

Picture Research
Leora Kahn

Production
Ruth Arthur
David Proffit
Sally Connolly

Director of Production
Gerald Hughes

Director of Publishing
David Gibbon

THE
CONGRESSIONAL
MEDAL
OF
HONOR

BILL HARRIS

PORTLAND HOUSE

1862 – The first Medal of Honor as awarded by the United States Army – A reward for military glory to enlisted men of the Army and Voluntary Forces who "shall most distinguish themselves by their gallantry in action, and other soldier-like qualities." It remained the sole American military decoration for nearly forty years. It was instituted by Act of Congress in 1862, following the establishment of a similar medal for enlisted men of the Navy in 1861. It is the earliest American decoration now in existence.

1896 – Upon recommendation of the Adjutant General, Brigadier General George E. Ruggles, the ribbon was changed because the original had been imitated to such an extent by semi-military organizations. Stronger laws to protect the real intent and purpose of the Medal of Honor were enacted. This time also, the award of the Medal of Honor was extended to include officers and enlisted men alike.

1904 – The many existing "ambiguities" of the law regarding the practice of awarding the Medal of Honor, as were pointed out by Elihu Root, Secretary of War, resulted in this design which was patented for protection against duplication by non-military organizations. Thus, control of the design of the Medal was put into the hands of the Secretary of War, and for the first time, previously uncontrolled imitations of the Medal were halted. This medal was worn either suspended from the neck on a detachable neckband, or pinned over the left breast.

1944 – (same design as 1904) The existing option of wearing the Medal of Honor of 1904 either over the left breast or suspended around the neck on a ribbon from its suspension band created new problems. As more medals for lesser degrees of heroism and valor were issued, and when controversies developed involving the wearing of the Medal of Honor with foreign military neck decorations, consideration was given by the Army Staff toward more definitively clarifying regulations to preclude any possible displacement of the medal of Honor, and to establish for its a separate and distinct place of recognition.

Acting on a recommendation addressed to the Adjutant General in 1942 by Lieutenant Colonel W. Lee Hart, then Medical Inspector of the Seventh Corps Area, the Army Staff maintained that the Medal of Honor should be held senior to any military decoration, American or foreign, and that all American military decorations should be held senior to any foreign awards. The manner of wearing the Medal of Honor was then restricted, and the suspension band as fashioned in the patented model of 1904 was no longer authorized. As prescribed by Army Regulations in 1944, the Medal of Honor is now worn around the neck above all other decorations.

Source: The Institute of Heraldry, United States Army Cameron Station, Alexandria, Virginia

INTRODUCTION

In 1983, I had the privilege of helping to produce the events surrounding the dedication of the Congressional Medal of Honor Society's Hall of Honor at the Intrepid Sea-Air-Space Museum in New York. Among the highlights of the week was the presentation of the Society's Patriots Award to former-president Ronald Reagan. But what makes it indelible in all our memories was the opportunity to meet and talk with 150 Medal of Honor winners, nearly two-thirds of those alive at the time. Walking the streets of New York with them made us all walk a little taller; listening to their conversations made us all swell with pride to be in the same room with them. And it gave us a better definition of the word "hero." Not one of those 150 men expected us to be impressed by what they had done. Most were reluctant to give us any details of their war stories. Nearly all of them gave credit to the men who had served with them, men whose lives they had saved. And that is the thread that runs through almost every one of the 3,412 citations that have singled out America's bravest fighting men since the Civil War. The formal requirement is that the Medal of Honor be earned by "conspicuous gallantry and intrepidness above and beyond the call of duty." In practice, the vast majority of them have been won by men who put their lives on the line to protect the men fighting at their side. Of the 238 who earned Medals of Honor in the Vietnam War, sixty-three sacrificed their lives by absorbing the blasts of grenades or landmines to protect the men around them. The stories that follow are about some of the others who have earned America's highest tribute. We all owe our way of life to them.

Bill Harris

6

On July 1, 1898, Lieutenant Colonel Theodore Roosevelt, wearing a uniform he had tailor made at Brooks Brothers in New York, led a dramatic charge of hand-picked horsemen up San Juan Hill at Santiago, Cuba, and became a national hero. There were twenty Medals of Honor awarded for heroism that day to soldiers who stormed the hill and the Spanish outpost at El Caney, twin battles that led to an armistice ending the war two weeks later, but Colonel Roosevelt was not among them. Although his heroism brightened his political star, he was denied wearing the gold five-pointed star suspended beneath a blue silk ribbon that is America's highest honor.

It wasn't as though the old Rough Rider didn't try. He had been recommended for the medal, but the War Department rejected it citing the fact that there had been no eyewitnesses to any outstanding acts of bravery. Roosevelt was as quick in providing them as the Secretary of War had been in brushing him off. Among the eyewitnesses he produced was Captain Robert Howze, who had won the Medal of Honor seven years earlier fighting Indians in South Dakota and who swore on his honor that he had seen Roosevelt display personal gallantry, not once but twice during the charge. General Leonard Wood, who was also there that day, said that Roosevelt was the first man to face

Colonel Theodore Roosevelt was denied the medal after leading his Rough Riders up San Juan Hill (previous pages) at Santiago, Cuba, during the Spanish-American War. The War Department said he was too aggressive.

General Leonard Wood (left), one of the men who recommended Roosevelt for recognition, won his own Medal of Honor in 1886 in a hair-raising dash through an Apache stronghold to deliver important dispatches, and for volunteering to take command of an infantry detachment that he had served as a surgeon.

Though he had lobbied hard for the Medal of Honor, when it was denied to him Theodore Roosevelt thundered that he never really wanted "that infernal medal" anyway. There were other honors waiting in the wings, but, as Harry Truman was fond of saying, "I'd rather wear that medal than be President of the United States."

the enemy on the hill and described the Colonel's bravery as "most distinguished." General Wood was a man who knew bravery when he saw it. As an army doctor during the Indian Wars in 1886, he earned his Medal of Honor by delivering an urgent message after riding seventy miles through Apache territory and then walking another thirty after his horse was shot out from under him. Still, Secretary of War Russell Alger wasn't impressed. Saying that he felt he was being bullied, he humiliated Roosevelt with a public announcement that the recommendation had been denied and the case was closed forever.

It may be the only time in the history of military affairs that a soldier was denied a medal because he was too aggressive. But there's no denying that the assessment was probably correct. On the other hand, the Secretary neglected to point out that the Rough Rider was rough on him long before the charge up San Juan Hill. Almost from the day the "splendid little war" began with the sinking of the battleship *Maine*, Roosevelt had been criticizing the War Department for considering it a naval affair and refusing to commit army troops.

Nearly fifty years later, the name Theodore Roosevelt was added to the roll of Medal of Honor winners when it was awarded to the former-president's son, a brigadier general in World War II. Neither politics nor sentiment had anything to do with it.

Theodore Roosevelt, Jr. had served in the First World War as a field officer in the First Infantry Division. He had been the victim of a gas attack, was wounded twice and decorated fifteen times. In 1940, he rejoined the First, and two years later led his men across North Africa to victory at Tunisia. They participated in the invasion of Sicily and, before they were relieved, took eighteen cities in less than four weeks. The division, known as "Red One," became legendary but their success under Roosevelt and General Terry Allen was an embarrassment to their commanding officer, General Omar Bradley. He found the division temperamental and undisciplined, and decided the only way to give them a little humility was to reassign Roosevelt and Allen.

Roosevelt was transferred to a French unit that he led on his third amphibious landing of the war. Though he was fifty-six years old by then and had clearly served his country with distinction, he was determined to be part of the biggest amphibious landing of them all, the invasion of France on D-day. He pleaded with General Eisenhower to give him the chance, but was turned down twice before finally being assigned to lead the Fourth Infantry Division into the battle. The Fourth had never seen combat before, and the decision was based on the fact that few generals had seen as much of it as Theodore Roosevelt, Jr.

He was at the head of the first wave when it hit the beach, and as soon as he was out of the water he realized that they had landed in the wrong spot. After inspecting the area behind the beachhead, he found the road they had been scheduled to use, directing his men in an assault on German defenses that might have cut them off if they had followed the original plan. By the end of the day they were well on their way toward Cherbourg.

General Eisenhower was impressed and made a decision a few days later to reward Roosevelt with a division of his own. But the decision came too late. On July 16, 1944, Theodore Roosevelt, Jr. died in his sleep of a heart attack. Later that year, as he presented the posthumous medal to the general's widow, President Franklin Roosevelt said that "his father would have been proudest of all."

As a Colonel in the Spanish-American War, Theodore Roosevelt saved the taxpayers' money by buying his own uniform, which he had tailor-made for him at Brooks Brothers in New York. He also provided the uniforms for his Rough Riders, most of whom were cowboys from New Mexico; and for their officers, all of whom he recruited at Ivy-League colleges.

Not long after this photograph was taken, Brigadier General Theodore Roosevelt died in his sleep of a heart attack, on July 16, 1944. He was to have taken command of an infantry division a few days later.

General Roosevelt had served in two wars, winning fifteen decorations in World War I. In World War II, he saw more action than any other American general, and finally won his Medal of Honor, posthumously, following his actions on D-day, in 1944.

THE PRIDE OF THE NATION

Of all the American presidents, Theodore Roosevelt probably did more to put pride behind the Medal of Honor than any other. When the award slipped from his grasp, he said he didn't want "that infernal medal" anyway; but as President he was instrumental in having the army's version redesigned and in having both the army and navy Medals of Honor patented to prevent their use by anyone who didn't deserve them. It was during the Roosevelt administration that it became mandatory that all claims for the medal should be accompanied by official documents. Roosevelt also issued an executive order requiring that the medal should be awarded with an impressive ceremonial. Under the terms of the order, winners are sent to Washington, D.C., where the commander-in-chief can personally make the presentation. It allowed for division commanders in the field to present the medal, but in practice, since Roosevelt began the custom, almost all have been awarded in White House ceremonies. Before the Roosevelt administration, only two presidents, Lincoln and Grant, had taken the trouble. Most of the decorations were simply mailed to the winners, and quite a few were returned because the post office couldn't find the unknown addressees.

It is also significant that in less than forty-five years before Roosevelt moved into the White House, more than four times the number of Medals of Honor were awarded than in the nearly seventy years that followed.

Somehow, the idea of a medal for battlefield valor seemed vaguely un-American to the Founding Fathers. The Constitution specifically prohibited titles of nobility and there was a natural fear that any recognition raising a common man to uncommon heights was the first step away from a classless society. But their War of Independence helped them see the error of their ways. In 1776, Congress had a medal cast in France to reward General Washington for his defense of Boston. Later in the war similar medals were made for General Horatio Gates and Admiral John Paul Jones, but none were awarded again until 1780 when three militiamen were recognized for their capture of the traitor Benedict Arnold and preventing an attack on the American fort at West Point. And that gave General Washington an idea. Soon after, he issued an order to create a medal for gallantry consisting of "the figure of a heart in purple cloth, edged with lace." He envisioned it as a sign that "the road to glory in a citizen's army is open to all." But in the following sixteen months before his army was disbanded, only three of his men found the road to glory, and the decoration, now known as the Purple Heart, wasn't awarded again for almost 150 years.

Charles A. Lindbergh exchanged the confetti on his collar (previous pages) for a Medal of Honor in 1927. Lindbergh was a captain in the Army Air Corps Reserve when he made the first solo flight from New York to Paris in May, 1927. The following December, he was awarded the Medal of Honor by a special act of Congress. The citation said he displayed "heroic courage and skill as a navigator at the risk of his life ... [achieving] the greatest individual triumph of any American citizen." Not only that, but he was also something of a master mechanic (left).

In fact, more than eighty years passed before America had another decoration to award. And almost as if to make the Founding Fathers' fears a self-fullfilling prophecy, the idea for it came from the penchant of European nobility for calling attention to themselves with a chest-full of medals.

When the Civil War broke out, the government sent agents to Europe to recruit seasoned officers to lead their green troops into battle. In the early days of the war they cut fine figures in Washington where they were as sought after for teas and fancy-dress balls as for their expertise in leading men into battle. And, like the lion in *The Wizard of Oz*, they never went anywhere without their medals to remind everyone of their bravery. It impressed official Washington, but it also had an effect on the young men who wore the uniform of the Union Army. They wistfully wished that they had a chance for the same kind of recognition and when their wishes reached the ear of Adjutant General Edward Townsend he passed them on to his boss, Secretary of War, Edwin Stanton.

When they had a meeting to discuss it, Gideon Wells, the Secretary of the Navy, also happened to be in the room. Wells knew that General Winfield Scott was violently opposed to medals in any form, and though the general was retired by then, he still wielded tremendous influence with the army. The thought appealed to Wells's instinct for inter-service rivalry. He began that very afternoon to have a bill prepared for congressional approval to create a medal for the navy. "General Scott shall exert no undue influence over sailors," he said.

The bill passed in less than a month, and in December 1861 President Lincoln signed the law creating a navy Medal of Honor. He formalized a Medal of Honor for the army the following July. But it wasn't until more than a year later that Congress got around to appropriating the money to actually buy any medals and none could be awarded until then. They haggled over the price, as congressmen often do, and eventually kept the cost under two dollars apiece by using the same basic design for both medals. The army, whose inverted five-pointed star was topped with an eagle, placed an order for two thousand. The navy ordered two hundred of its version, with an anchor above the star.

The original design was created by the Philadelphia Mint and manufactured by the firm of William Wilson & Sons. The star contained a bas relief of Minerva, the Roman goddess of wisdom, representing the Union. She held a shield in her left hand against an attacker with fork-tongued serpents; and in her right hand, the ancient Roman symbol

of authority, an axe bound in wooden staves known as a fasces. The figure was surrounded by thirty-four stars, representing the number of states at the time.

Before the war ended, the army had issued twenty-one hundred Medals of Honor and the navy had honored 327 sailors and marines. And, according to the original legislation, the story should have ended there. Though Congress had gone along with the idea, they weren't convinced their constituents would respond with enthusiasm and inserted wording in the law that the medals would be awarded only "during the present rebellion." But even congressmen can be wrong. The public's enthusiasm was overwhelming. Long after the war was over, veterans were submitting their own applications, many of which were accepted without question. Veterans organizations routinely awarded Medals of Honor to their members. And the military continued granting the award, the only medal they could present, even though the law establishing it had expired. The Medal of Honor was clearly an idea whose time had come. But it took official Washington until 1897 to clear up the confusion. New legislation placed the War Department in charge of awarding the medal and gave it strict guidelines to follow.

The guidelines were refined in 1904 after a new design for the army medal was created in Paris and quickly approved in Washington. The figure of Minerva was replaced by a bust of the goddess surrounded by the words "United States of America," and the gilded star was surrounded by an open laurel wreath enameled in green, as were oak leaves within each of the star's five points. The star was suspended by an eagle supported by a bar, containing the word "valor," from a blue silk neck ribbon with thirteen white stars representing the original states. The back of the star was left blank to contain the name of the winner, and the back of the bar contained the words "The Congress to...." Probably because of that inscription, and the fact that the original medal was created with congressional approval, the decoration has become known as the "Congressional Medal of Honor." But winners are chosen by their peers and not by Congress, and its official name is simply the "Medal of Honor."

Congress has voted on a few occasions to honor individuals with the medal. In 1927, it honored Colonel Charles Lindbergh with the army medal for his solo trans-Atlantic flight. It also awarded the navy's Medal of Honor to Admiral Richard E. Byrd and to machinist Floyd Bennett in recognition of the first flight to the North Pole in 1926. Ensign Henry Drexler and Boatswain's Mate George

Cholister, who gave their lives saving their shipmates in a 1924 fire aboard the U.S.S. *Trenton*, also received the medal through a special act of Congress. And in 1933, Congress voted to present the award to Lieutenant Richmond Hobson for heroism at Santiago Harbor during the Spanish-American War. But the most dramatic congressional action in awarding the Medal of Honor came in 1921 when it was designated for the World War I unknown soldiers of Britain, France and United States, followed by the unknowns representing Italy, Belgium and Rumania. The tradition continued in 1948 when the Medal of Honor was voted for the American unknown soldier of World War II and later for the unknowns of Korea and Vietnam.

In 1935, Congress voted a Medal of Honor for Major General Adolphus Greely, who had worked his way up through the ranks from an ordinary private during forty-five years of army service. According to his citation, that was reason enough. But what Congress neglected to say was that Greely was a bona fide hero. It was just that his heroics were a little bit embarrassing to official Washington. The strange story began in 1881 when Greely volunteered to lead an exploration into the Arctic. Short of the Pole, but further north than any man had ever been, his party was cut adrift on an ice floe. They radioed for help, but the army said rescue at sea was the navy's job, and the navy argued that Greely's twenty-four men were all army personnel and that rescue attempts should be kept in the family. The debate raged for an incredible three years. The Greely party managed to float down to Greenland and they were able to fend for themselves after a fashion. But by the time Congress got around to settling the debate and dispatching a ship to pick them up, there were only six survivors. For reasons lost to history, the tabloid press began running stories that they had survived by resorting to cannibalism, and Greely became the subject of an official investigation. The government wasn't able to uncover any proof of the allegations, which the men steadfastly denied. But it made good copy for the newspapers, and reporters didn't bother asking why it took so long for a ship to sail to Greenland. It took more than fifty years for the government to make amends. But Congress could never bring itself to set the record completely straight.

Among the men who pricked at the congressional conscience in Greely's behalf was former Major General Billy Mitchell, who ten years earlier had been court-martialed for accusing the navy and the War Department of incompetence. His crime had been to warn the government of the role bombers would have in future wars, and for

Major General Billy Mitchell was awarded a special posthumous medal by Congress in 1948 in recognition of the "foresight in the field of American military aviation" that he had shown over twenty years before, to the irritation of the authorities at the time. However, Mitchell was proved right by events in World War II – hence the special award.

20

President Franklin D. Roosevelt presented the Medal of Honor to Navy Commander Richard E. Byrd on his return from the first flight over the North Pole. The President's wife, Eleanor, is smiling in the background.

saying that battleships were a thing of the past. In spite of the fact that he proved the latter prediction by sinking a captured German battleship with seven bombers in fifteen minutes, or possibly because of it, the court-martial stripped him of his rank for a period of five years. But Mitchell made the sentence moot by resigning from the army and becoming a private citizen and even more irritating to official Washington. Six years after he died, the Japanese proved his theories right in their attack on Pearl Harbor. In fact, his prophecies came true almost every day during World War II; and when the war ended, Congress put its collective mind to work to find a way to tell the world that it didn't hold anything against Billy Mitchell any longer. A medal was the answer, and because it was awarded by Congress, Mitchell's name is on the Medal of Honor Roll. But Mitchell's medal isn't the same as the others. The award presented to the former flyer's son in 1948 contains Mitchell's name and his likeness on the front and an eagle on the reverse side. It is fitting. The award was made in recognition of a man who dared to be different. According to the citation, it was presented for his "outstanding pioneer service and foresight."

Congress has also been involved in taking away some Medals of Honor. In 1916, the conferees took a hard look at the country's system of rewarding outstanding valor and found it wanting. They formed a special board to investigate each and every one of the 2,625 medals that had been awarded, and charged it with the responsibility of deciding if any had been given for any cause other than distinguished conduct involving actual conflict with an enemy. A few months later, 910 names were removed from the list and the holders of the medals were warned that wearing them would be considered a misdemeanor. The most famous among the disqualified was Colonel William F. Cody, better known as "Buffalo Bill." The majority were 864 members of the Twenty-seventh Maine Volunteer Infantry who had been given their medals following a direct order from President Lincoln.

The men of the Twenty-seventh Maine had signed up for a nine-month tour of duty in 1862, and served all of their time with their sister outfit, the Twenty-fifth Maine, as garrison troops in Washington. A few days before their enlistments expired, they began getting ready to go home, and the president was appalled. The Confederate Army was marching on Gettysburg at the time, and every man was needed. An appeal went out to the men to re-enlist, and every man of the Twenty-fifth refused. But 309 men of the Twenty-seventh stepped forward and volunteered to stay.

After his flight over the North Pole in 1926, Commander Byrd was promoted to admiral.

As it turned out, they stayed less than a week, and none
went into battle. But Lincoln was overcome with gratitude
and promised that each of the volunteers would be given a
Medal of Honor. The men smiled respectfully as they
boarded the train that would take them back to Maine. As
often happens in government affairs, records were mixed up
and when it came time to make good on the presidential
promise, nobody knew which men had volunteered. Three
years later, the problem was solved with a decision to give
the award to the entire regiment. When the medals arrived,
they were turned over to Colonel Mark Wentworth, the
senior military officer in the Pine Tree State, who was
ordered to make the presentation. But Wentworth didn't
obey the order. He himself had dodged bullets in the war
and it went against his grain to hand out decorations to
troops who had never heard a shot fired in anger. He gave
medals to the men he knew had volunteered, but stored the
rest of them in his barn. Later, other veterans of the
regiment broke into the barn and took their medals, and by
the time Wentworth died all the remaining ones were gone.

The 1916 board had its work cut out for it, and its final
report said that hundreds of Medals of Honor had been
rewards "greater than would now be given for the same
acts." But it conceded there was no question that the
majority had been given for distinguished conduct in action.
And in establishing the medal in the first place, Congress
had directed that the navy award could be earned for
gallantry in action "and other seamanlike qualities." The
army was empowered to grant the medal for gallantry in
action "and other soldierlike qualities." Both left plenty of
room for interpretation and allowed giving the Medal of
Honor for acts not at all connected with heroism. It's
amazing they were awarded with such restraint. But the
loopholes were plugged and the meaning of the medal
enhanced through new legislation in 1918.

The new law also created lesser awards, the
Distinguished Service Medal and the Distinguished Service
Cross for combat gallantry. It also instituted a citation
called the Silver Star, which became a formal decoration in
1932. A year later, Congress approved a similar system of
recognition for the navy and established its Distinguished
Service Medal and the Navy Cross. This was the beginning
of what is known as the "Pyramid of Honor," with the
Medal of Honor at its apex. Over the years the number of
decorations has increased to fifteen for the army and air
force and fourteen for the navy and Marine Corps. In both
cases, last on the list is the Purple Heart, the country's
original medal, now awarded for wounds received in action.

In one of the strangest tales in the history of inter-service rivalry, a band of U.S. Army men, who had trudged farther north on the polar ice pack than anyone before them, were left stranded at the U.S. station at Fort Conger on Ellesmere Island while the War Department debated about whose responsibility it was to rescue them. The expedition had been stationed at Fort Conger between August 1881 and August 1883 as part of the joint program of scientific research set up for the first International Polar Year. Their mission ended in tragedy, only six men out of the original twenty-five surviving the dreadful ordeal.

The U.S. Army expedition to Ellesmere Island was commanded by Adolphus Greely, who was promoted to brigadier general in 1887. He took command of the Presidio at San Francisco, where he distinguished himself during the 1906 earthquake. Greely was awarded the Medal of Honor by a special act of Congress in 1935, officially in recognition of his rise from the rank of private in a Signal Corps career that began in 1844 and lasted for forty-five years.

William F. Cody, who preferred being called Buffalo Bill, was awarded the Medal of Honor for his services as a scout during the Indian Campaigns. In a review of past winners made in 1917, the year Bill died, an Army board rescinded his medal and those of four other scouts, because they were civilians.

As much as he enjoyed being called Buffalo Bill by others, Cody called himself colonel, and always wore the eagles of that rank on the shoulder of his buckskin jacket. The Medal of Honor he lost was reinstated in 1989 along with those of the four other scouts.

THE GREAT LOCOMOTIVE CHASE

The first Medals of Honor were awarded to a half-dozen survivors of one of the most incredible actions of the Civil War, or any other war for that matter. It was a top-secret mission behind enemy lines that turned out to be a complete failure; but what became known as "The Great Locomotive Chase" will always be remembered for its high drama as well as the heroism of the men behind it.

The original assignment fell to a civilian, James J. Andrews, whose career as a spy for the Union Army was less than spectacular. He had ventured into enemy territory twice, once to gather information, which he couldn't locate, and soon after to destroy a railroad bridge, which was still standing long after he got back into friendly territory. But he pleaded for a chance to redeem himself, and came up with a wild plan to destroy all the railroad bridges between Atlanta and Chattanooga. The Union strategists liked the idea. Their army was heading for a confrontation at Shiloh, and the idea of cutting off reinforcements from the South seemed like excellent insurance. Andrews was given the go-ahead and empowered to gather volunteers to go deep into enemy territory to help him pull off his wild scheme. But he was warned, as were the volunteers he signed up, that the mission was strictly unofficial, that it must be performed out of uniform and with such secrecy that if they were caught, the Union would deny ever having heard of them. They were also told that the denial probably wouldn't do any good and if they were caught they'd be hanged on the spot as spies. In spite of it all, twenty-four men volunteered.

Three of the men lost their way in rainstorms on the way to a rendezvous at Marietta, Georgia, and Andrews decided to get on with the plan without them. Then he told his men for the first time what they were doing in Marietta. The plan was for each of them to buy a one-way ticket to different towns along the line of the Western & Atlantic Railroad between there and Chattanooga, but once aboard the train, they would seize control of it and proceed to burn every bridge along the way once they had crossed it. At that point, Andrews lost two more of his volunteers, and when the train pulled away early the next morning, twenty-four hours behind schedule and in a driving rainstorm that would make burning bridges a highly unlikely proposition, there were nineteen Andrews Raiders aboard.

Seven miles up the line, the train pulled into a siding to allow engineer Jeff Cain and conductor William Fuller to enjoy a twenty-minute breakfast at Big Shanty. All of the other passengers, except the nineteen Raiders, decided to join them. There was a Confederate encampment at Big Shanty, but none of the soldiers thought it was at all strange

to see Andrews and two of his men uncouple the passenger cars from the train or to watch some of the passengers scramble from them into one of the boxcars. The first one to notice anything odd at all was engineer Cain who looked up from the breakfast table and saw his beloved engine, the *General*, highballing up the pike without him.

Andrews kept up a full head of steam for the next twenty miles, stopping occasionally to toss logs across the tracks behind him and to cut telegraph wires. But by then he was convinced his scheme was working and he slowed his pace. What he didn't know was that conductor William Fuller was on his heels. Fuller had begun the chase on foot but within a mile or two he found an abandoned handcar and used it to gain ground even faster. Then Andrews handed him an even better way. The Raiders had passed a locomotive on a siding but steamed right on by without destroying it. It was a gift from heaven as far as Fuller was concerned, and he was soon bearing down on the Raiders at full-throttle with other men he had picked up along the way.

Andrews and his men, meanwhile, lost an hour's lead when they pulled off into a siding to let a couple of southbound trains pass them. The trains were loaded with supplies being moved out of the way of a Yankee advance further up the line, which made Andrews's cover story a little odd. He had been stopped a time or two along the way and explained himself out of the tight situations by saying he was rushing supplies northward.

The Raiders were hard at work removing rails when they looked over their shoulders and discovered they were being chased. Fuller had been delayed by the same southbound trains, but rather than sit it out as Andrews had done, he took advantage of his knowledge of the railroad to find and commandeer a second locomotive to keep heading doggedly northward. When he was stopped by a ripped-up section of track, he abandoned the engine and began running again. After running three miles, he met yet another southbound train Andrews had let pass. After taking charge, he put it in reverse, uncoupled its cars at the first siding, and kept moving backwards in the direction of the stolen train as fast as a full head of steam could move him.

When Andrews finally saw him coming, he moved ahead as fast as the *General* could run, covering more than sixty miles in an hour, while his men tossed logs from the rear car to try to slow down the engine that was bearing down on them in reverse. At one point they uncoupled their rear car and set fire to it in the middle of a wooden bridge. But still Fuller kept coming, roaring through the smoke and flames, and pushing the burning car off the bridge where it

couldn't do any more damage. When they saw they weren't likely to stop him, the Raiders began to jump off their train and head for the woods. Then, within five miles of Tennessee and the Union lines, the *General* ran out of fuel and out of steam. They had traveled ninety miles. Ironically, if the Raiders hadn't left so many logs behind them on the tracks, they might have had enough fuel to get to safety. But as it turned out, all of them were rounded up and put into prison within a week.

Less than a month after he bought his train ticket at Marietta, James Andrews was hanged, and over the next two weeks, seven of his men followed him to the scaffold. The two men who backed out at the start of the adventure were among those hanged, leaving fourteen men to ponder their fate.

They also used the time to compare notes. They heard about the capture of Private Jacob Parrott, of how he had been beaten with a rawhide whip and threatened with hanging if he didn't tell everything he knew, which, in fact, was very little. The story ended with his rescue by a Confederate colonel, who led him off to an unknown prison. The survivors got more details from Alf Wilson, the engineer of the stolen locomotive, who was captured along with fellow Raider Mark Wood. He told the others how they had managed to elude the cavalry patrols for a week, finding their way through the unfamiliar countryside with an atlas they calmly bought in a Georgia bookstore. He also told them about their interrogation by General Danville Leadbetter, the Confederate commander at Chattanooga, who flatly told them, "I'll be damned if I don't hang every last one of you."

Eight men had already been hanged, of course. There had been no court martial but the justification was that Andrews and one of his men had escaped and needed to be rounded up a second time. But the survivors decided that escape represented their only chance, in spite of the example.

They planned it for nearly six months, and then one night when the guard delivered their dinner, they grabbed him from behind and took his keys. Once in the woods outside the prison, they broke into pairs and ran for their lives. Eight of them made it back to the Union lines, but the other six were recaptured and clapped in irons. They were exchanged for Confederate prisoners five months later and taken to Washington for a debriefing.

Their first stop was the office of Secretary of War, Edwin Stanton. When they arrived they were swept through a waiting room full of people to the secretary's office where

Locomotives such as these (previous pages) were part of a strange Civil War adventure that earned the first Medals of Honor ever presented. Known as "The Great Locomotive Chase," the adventure was a complete failure as a mission, but is nevertheless remembered for its high drama and for the heroism of the men involved.

Edwin McMaster Stanton (right), Secretary of War in President Lincoln's Cabinet, made the first formal presentation of a Medal of Honor, following "The Great Locomotive Chase," and was also a key figure in the actual creation of the award.

Pioneer photographer Mathew Brady was on hand to record the scene at a U.S. military railroad depot in Virginia (overleaf), one of many that were of key importance in fighting the Civil War.

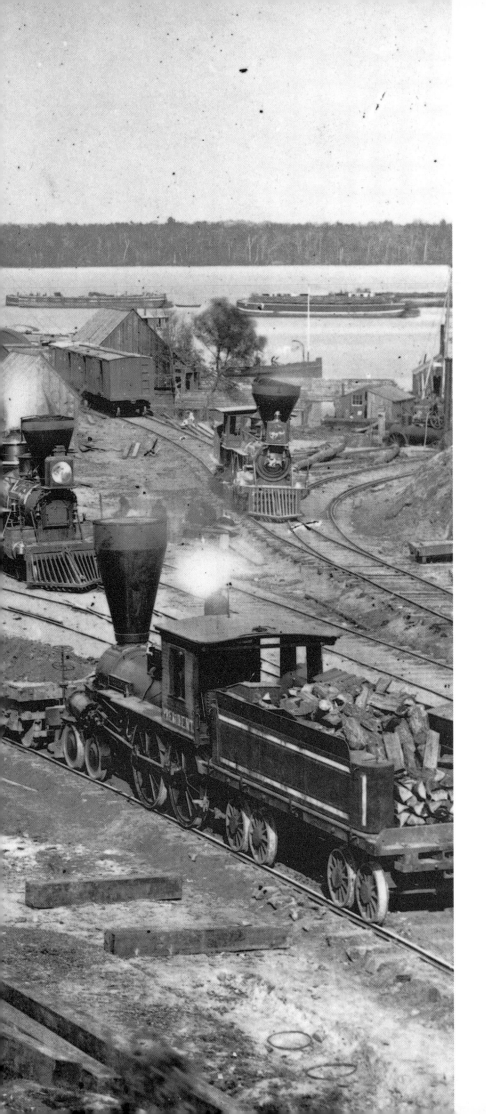

they found themselves in the presence of not only Stanton, but Secretary of the Treasury, Salmon Chase, and Tennessee Governor Andrew Johnson, who would soon become President of the United States.

Stanton was quite impressed by the six young men, especially nineteen year-old Jacob Parrott, who turned down his offer of an appointment to the U.S. Military Academy at West Point because he said he was anxious to get back to his old outfit and into the fight again. Promising them promotions to first lieutenancies, the secretary reached into his safe and produced one hundred dollars for each of them to spend during their time in Washington. Then, as the soldiers were turning to leave, he put his hand on Parrott's arm and said, "there is one more thing I want you to have."

As he walked slowly to his desk, he told them that Congress had authorized a special medal for heroism, but that none had been given to any soldier. Then he reached into a drawer and took out a leather case which he handed to Parrott. It contained the new Medal of Honor. Jacob Parrott and five former Andrews Raiders became the first to receive it that afternoon, March 25, 1863. In the months that followed, the other survivors of the Great Locomotive Chase also received the medal and those who gave their lives were honored posthumously. But three of the Raiders were denied the opportunity. James Andrews didn't qualify for it because he was a civilian. Nor did civilian William Campbell, who had gone along to be with his friend, Private Philip Shadrach. Shadrach was one of the seven hanged in retaliation for Andrews's escape, but his family never received his medal. He had enlisted under an assumed name.

William Fuller, the railroad man who led the chase, never received a medal either. He was a civilian, first of all, but in any case, as a rebel he wouldn't have been eligible. The Confederate Congress at Richmond instituted a decoration similar to the Medal of Honor with legislation directing that it should be awarded for one outstanding act in securing every important victory and specifying that it should be granted after a majority vote of all the survivors of the battle. But the medal itself was never struck and it was eventually replaced with an order establishing a Roll of Honor, to be published in newspapers within each of the Confederate states.

"SPARE YOUR COUNTRY'S FLAG . . ."

When Stonewall Jackson led his rebel troops into Frederick, Maryland, in 1862 he was was forced to deal with a redoubtable old woman named Barbara Fritchie who it was said defiantly waved the Stars and Stripes from her window and challenged him to do something about it. For generations after, schoolboys who had trouble spelling her name swelled with patriotic pride in quoting the poem that immortalized her with the words, "'Shoot if you must this old gray head/ But spare your country's flag,' she said."

There is hardly a schoolboy left who quite understands the meaning of risking one's life for something as abstract as a flag. But during the nineteenth century, it was the most important thing a man could do. And by far the vast majority of Medals of Honor awarded during the Civil War were for the capturing or recapturing of flags. Many of the citations also refer to the capture of a general or vital equipment, but the flag was the prize that mattered most.

Though Jacob Parrott was the first soldier to wear the medal, he was not the first to earn it. That honor belongs to Private Francis Brownell of the Eleventh New York. He earned it during the capture of a Confederate flag at Alexandria, Virginia on May 24, 1861, seven months before President Lincoln signed the act creating the navy's medal and more than a year before the Medal of Honor was authorized for the army. Brownell didn't actually get his medal until sixteen years after the capture of the flag, after having nominated himself, having his request turned down and taking his case to his congressman. And he wasn't the man who actually took the flag. Credit for that went to his commanding officer. But in those days only enlisted men were eligible for the Medal of Honor. Officers were rewarded for gallantry by the granting of brevet promotions, which earned them a higher rank, but not higher pay. The law was changed, and made retroactive, to include army officers in 1863. (Naval officers were disqualified until 1915.) But the honor never went to Colonel Ephraim Ellsworth for what happened that day in Alexandria.

The Eleventh New York had taken the city and were marching through its streets when the colonel noticed the rebel flag flying from the top of a hotel that was the tallest building in town. Ellsworth leaped from his horse and rushed into the building, followed by his aide, Private Brownell. A few minutes later, he emerged on the roof, scaled the flagpole and grabbed the symbol of resistance. With that, a shot rang out and Colonel Ellsworth, still clutching the flag, fell dead. Brownell reacted quickly. He shot the killer and then finished him off with a bayonet.

Before the creation of the Pyramid of Honor, which

83837-J

restricted awarding of the Medal of Honor to any one person more than once, the decoration was won twice by eighteen fighting men. The only Civil War soldier among them was Second Lieutenant Thomas Custer who leaped his horse over the enemy's position at Sailor Creek, Virginia, and captured not one, but two regimental flags, though his horse was killed and he himself wounded. Two weeks later he captured another flag, and his second Medal of Honor, at Namozene Church. His brother, General George Armstrong Custer, made a name for himself, but not a place on the Medal of Honor roll, nine years later at Little Big Horn in Southern Montana. The navy had two dual winners in the war. The first was Coxwain John Cooper who earned the medal when he stayed at his post in the face of enemy fire during a battle in Mobile Bay, and helped turn the tide of battle. Eight months later, he earned his second medal on the same ship and in the same place for, in the words of his citation, risking "being blown to pieces by exploding shells" to rescue a wounded man. The other was Boatswain's Mate Patrick Mullen whose first Medal of Honor was awarded for loading and accurately firing his howitzer though forced by enemy fire to lie on his back. His second was for rescuing an officer from drowning.

Among the famous names that were added to the Medal of Honor roll during the Civil War was that of First Lieutenant Arthur MacArthur, who won the award during the battle of Missionary Ridge for his action in planting the colors of the Twenty-fourth Wisconsin Infantry on the ridge's crest. His son, General Douglas MacArthur, received the medal in 1942 for his leadership in defending the Philippines.

Not as well known is Dr. Mary Edwards Walker, but if her name is sometimes forgotten, it isn't because she didn't try to leave her mark on history. She is remembered as the only woman ever to receive a Medal of Honor. She should also be recalled as the only person to have had the honor taken away and restored. The fact is, Mary E. Walker worked harder to wear the Medal of Honor than many other winners worked to earn it.

As soon as the Civil War broke out, Dr. Walker applied for an army commission as a surgeon, but her request was rejected out of hand because women didn't do such things in 1861. But they allowed her to sign on as a nurse, and some say that was the army's first mistake. Dr. Walker insisted on dealing with doctors as equals, frequently giving them advice and always refusing menial jobs like scrubbing floors and changing sheets. She also insisted on wearing trousers and the insignia of a surgeon rather than a nurse's

The decks of Union gunboats were the stage for hundreds of acts of Civil War heroism. The gun crew of U.S.S. Miami *(previous pages) are on maneuvers on the James River, Virginia.*

Second Lieutenant Thomas W. Custer (left) earned two Medals of Honor in the Union Army. His brother, General George A. Custer, would make a name for himself in the Indian Campaigns nine years later, but would not win a Medal of Honor.

President Lincoln often visited the front during the Civil War, under the watchful eye of his bodyguard, Major Allen Pinkerton, head of the famous detective agency. The general, whose camp President Lincoln is looking over, is George B. McClellan, Commander of the Army of the Potomac.

Heavy Artillery battalions, such as Company M of the 9th N.Y. Heavy Artillery, produced their share of Medal of Honor winners during the Civil War.

However much apparent glamor was attached to other soldiers, the backbone of the Union Army comprised the foot soldiers who marched from camps, such as the winter quarters at Fort Brady, James River, Virginia (right), into enemy artillery fire.

skirts. She eventually got surgeon's status by fiat when the last of the male doctors assigned to the Fifty-second Ohio Infantry was killed. But the medical board had pronounced her unqualified for the job, and she was listed on the record as a volunteer. The men she tended after the battle of Chickamauga were grateful she was there, but everyone was just as happy when she was taken prisoner, apparently during a spying mission behind enemy lines.

After she was parolled four months later, she began a feud with the War Department over back pay, and while she was waiting for them to see things her way, took an assignment as warden of a female prison in Kentucky. When the war ended, a government board ruled that she didn't qualify as a doctor anyway and sent her a check for $766 for services rendered over a five-year period.

Next she applied for a brevet promotion to the rank of major, but the Secretary of War pointed out that she had never held a commission to begin with. So Dr. Walker did the next best thing. She took her case directly to President Andrew Johnson. The President, realizing that this wasn't a problem that was likely to go away, finally made a decision to present her with a Medal of Honor for "valuable service to the government." The citation also noted, with just a touch of ironic humor, that her efforts "have been earnest and untiring in a variety of ways."

After the medal was pinned to her jacket in 1866, she never went anywhere without it. She never went anywhere dressed in anything but men's clothes, either, and on at least one occasion was hauled into court on charges of impersonating a man. She was found not guilty. She gave up her medical career in favor of traveling with carnivals and tent shows making speeches against smoking and in favor of women's rights. Finally in 1916 her medal was taken away along with the others found unworthy at the time. But though she was warned that wearing the Medal of Honor constituted a crime, she never stopped and began making regular appearances, medal and all, on Capitol Hill where her appeals for reinstatement fell on deaf ears.

She finally died at the age of eighty-six in 1919, still wearing the Medal of Honor. But officially she didn't have the right. That was restored to her posthumously in 1977. Her family never gave up the fight.

General Arthur MacArthur won his Medal of Honor as a first lieutenant, planting his regiment's colors on the crest of Missionary Ridge, Tennessee, during the bloody battle there in 1863.

Dr. Mary E. Walker, the only woman ever to receive a Medal of Honor, lived to see the honor taken away, in 1916, though she always refused to stop wearing the medal itself. It was restored posthumously in 1977.

General Douglas
MacArthur followed in
his father's footsteps,
also winning the
Medal of Honor. It
was awarded for his
leadership in the
defense of the Bataan
Peninsula in the
Philippines in 1942,
and for his triumphal
return to the islands
two years later. He is
seen wading ashore at
Leyte during the
landings in the
Philippines in October
1944.

General Douglas MacArthur, who was commander of army forces in the Far East during World War II, was elevated to the unusual rank of five-star general in 1944. Corncob pipes were the general's favorite.

TO THE PLAINS AND BEYOND

When American fighting men began jumping out of
airplanes into battle, they did it with the name of Geronimo
on their lips. It was a fitting battle cry. Of the 423 men who
won Medals of Honor fighting Indians, more than half won
them fighting the Chiricahua Apaches led by the legendary
Geronimo.

And the action that finally brought Geronimo to his
knees in the Sierra Madre Mountains of Mexico resulted in
the first army medals for action on foreign soil. Seventeen
navy men had won the Medal of Honor after a Civil War
encounter between the U.S.S. *Kearsarge* and the
Confederate raider *Alabama* at Cherbourg, France, during
the Civil War.

Geronimo's first encounter with the U.S. Cavalry came
in 1876 when he refused to go along with a federal order
sending his people to a reservation in the Arizona desert.
The army took him there in chains. Not much was heard
from him again until 1881 when he expressed his
dissatisfaction over the beefing-up of the garrison at nearby
Fort Apache by killing several of the white men, including
the police commissioner. Before the killings could be
avenged, he led a band of Chiracahuas across the border
into Mexico. Over the next four years, he became the
scourge of the Southwest terrifying white men and Indians
alike with lightning raids that resulted in horrible deaths for
anyone who got in their way.

Mexico had been considered a safe haven by the Indians
of the Southwest, until the Great White Father in
Washington negotiated a treaty with the Mexicans allowing
American troops to cross the line to round up renegades. It
came as a surprise to the Indians. As often happened with
treaties in those days, no one had bothered to tell them
about it. Though it was a complete surprise, the first cavalry
foray south of the border was also a complete failure. But it
put Geronimo on notice that the Long Knives had long
arms, and no place he could run was beyond their reach.
The idea didn't frighten him, but it did make him angry. He
took his anger out on his own people by sending a raiding
party back to the Arizona reservation to massacre the
Apaches who had refused to follow him. They struck like a
whirlwind, killing nearly sixty people and then vanishing
into the night. The army knew something had to be done,
but the raiders had come more than a thousand miles
through heavily patrolled territory and then rode back the
same way they had come. But not a single soldier had seen
them and the most experienced trackers couldn't find as
much as a broken twig to mark their trail.

The unit that was put together to go after Geronimo after

The Apache chief,
Geronimo, may not
have been too fond of
the White man himself,
but he enjoyed some of
the White man's
pleasures, such as
wearing silk hats and
driving horseless
carriages (previous
pages). Geronimo was
one of the toughest,
and most elusive,
enemies the horse
soldiers ever faced in
the fight to win the
West. An indication of
his fierce strength of
character can be seen
in the photograph
(left), which was
actually taken after
the Indian chief's
surrender in 1886.
Fighting the
Chiricahua Apaches
led by Geronimo
prompted the award of
many Medals of
Honor to the U.S.
soldiers involved.

The coffins of many of the U.S. casualties in the Spanish-American War await burial at Arlington National Cemetery, which was carved from the confiscated estate of Confederate General Robert E. Lee in 1864.

the raid was made up entirely of Indians, with four cavalry officers and a surgeon. After four rugged weeks, they found Geronimo's camp, but the wily chief escaped before they could attack. They had no sooner burned the village to the ground when a unit of the Mexican army, also made up of Indians, rode up and, thinking the American scouts were Geronimo's braves, began firing. During the confusion, the American commander, Captain Emmett Crawford was shot through the head. Then, as the second in command, Lieutenant Marion Maus, was trying to restore order, an Indian woman rode up with a message from Geronimo. He wanted to talk, she said.

Maus agreed, but he knew he was at a serious disadvantage. His ammunition was almost gone, he wasn't certain of the loyalty of the men under his command, he was

hundreds of miles inside enemy territory and his captain was on the verge of death. But when Geronimo asked him why he had come, he calmly said his mission was to destroy or capture the Apaches and he intended to follow his orders. It impressed the chief, who then agreed to insure him safe passage back to the border and to follow in a few weeks for a peace conference. He was as good as his word, but when he arrived back in Arizona, he drank too much at his welcoming celebration and escaped again with a company of new recruits to his cause.

A second company was sent to bring him back, but they found the trail almost impossible to follow. After three weeks of a hard march, they discovered that Geronimo had led them around a great circle and they were less than thirty miles from their starting point. Two months later they were

still looking for the elusive Apaches. But the trek was as hard on the pursued as the pursuers, and to makes matters worse for Geronimo, the Mexican army was scouring the hills for him, too. He finally agreed to surrender to the Americans, sensing that their terms would be easier to live with. He may have been right. In 1886, Geronimo and the remainder of his tribe were resettled on a reservation in Florida. Among the legacies he left the horse soldiers on the Plains were twenty-three Medals of Honor for bravery among the men who were sent to track him down. Ten of them were awarded to Apache scouts.

Once the West was open for expansion, America began turning its attention abroad. In 1871, a two-day engagement in Korea produced fifteen Medal of Honor winners and between 1898, when the United States went to war with Spain, and the outbreak of World War I in 1914, American heroes earned the medal in theaters of war from Peking to Veracruz.

Among them were Marine Colonel David Porter, and his second in command, Captain Hiram Bearss, who led an assault on a guerilla base on the Philippine island of Samar in 1901. Their mission was to find and destroy the battle-hardened Moros rebels who two months earlier had completely wiped out Company C of the Ninth Infantry to

the last man. After a successful surprise attack, the marines scaled a two-hundred-foot cliff with bamboo ladders and destroyed an ingenious series of booby traps, platforms filled with tons of rock set to be dumped on the trails below, which would be used by the marines who were following them. Then, using jungle trails laced with concealed spear-filled pits, they crossed a valley and climbed the cliffs on the opposite side, completely routing the insurgents who later told them they had considered themselves safe in fortifications it had taken them three years to build and conceal.

The insurrection in the Philippines, which cost a thousand American lives, was a post script to the Spanish-American War. It began after the United States decided to annex the formerly Spanish-held islands and the natives rebelled. Like the Vietnam War, it was unpopular back home, and though nearly seventy thousand American troops were sent there between 1899 and 1913, only seventy army Medals of Honor were awarded and the navy and Marine Corps shared nineteen. Among those, the medals earned by Colonel Porter and Captain Bearss were not presented until more than thirty years later.

The problem was the regulation prohibiting the navy's award for officers. It was the same problem that haunted

Navy Lieutenant Richmond Hobson, whose heroism may have been the most dramatic of the Spanish-American War.

If the importance of an action can be measured by the number of Medals of Honor awarded to its participants, the incredible assignment of cutting the Spanish underwater communications cable at Cienfuegos, Cuba, in 1898 would dwarf all of the other acts of the war. Forty sailors and twelve marines earned Medals of Honor by volunteering to row into the harbor armed with hacksaws, which they used to cut the cable strand by strand in the face of heavy fire from shore. But inspiring as that was, a month later seven sailors were recommended for the medal after following Lieutenant Hobson on a mission that was not only dangerous, but was, in the opinion of the commander of the Atlantic Squadron, Admiral William Sampson, foolhardy. Sampson had no alternative, though; and under cover of darkness, Hobson and his seven volunteers steered the old ironclad *Merrimac* under the Spanish guns and into the narrow entrance of Santiago Harbor.

The plan was to scuttle the old ship and block the harbor, bottling-up the Spanish fleet inside. Hobson had refitted the former freighter with torpedoes, which he planned to fire as he and his crew made their escape. But before they could get past the Spanish shore batteries, heavy fire broke out and the *Merrimac*'s rudder was shot away. There was no way to turn the ship across the narrow channel, where it was needed to make an effective barrier. Hobson ordered the torpedoes blown anyway, but only two of the ten charges went off. The ship began to drift into the harbor where more shells from shore and floating mines threatened to break it into ineffective pieces. Worse, the shelling sunk the only lifeboat and the *Merrimac*'s little crew seemed doomed to go down with the ship. They put on their life jackets and leaped overboard, and several hours later were rescued by the Spanish admiral himself, who personally took them prisoner after congratulating them on what they had done. They were repatriated a few weeks later, and though Hobson wasn't allowed to share the Medal of Honor with his men, he discovered that he had become a national hero. Three years later he became a congressman from Alabama and thirty-five years later, during his famous first hundred days as President, the former-assistant secretary of the navy, Franklin D. Roosevelt presented the Medal of Honor to former navy lieutenant Richmond Pearson Hobson.

Previous pages: many of the cavalry units that fought in the Indian Campaigns also saw service in the Spanish-American War.

Color Sergeant Wright (left), who rode up San Juan Hill with the Rough Riders, did not earn a Medal of Honor for planting the Stars and Stripes at the top, although others who carried the flag into battle would be singled out for the medal.

The floor of a Civil War hospital in Washington, D.C.

The Yanks Are Coming

In the summer of 1914, after the shooting of Austro-Hungarian Archduke Ferdinand, Austria-Hungary went to war with the Serbians. The Russians joined the fight against the Austro-Hungarians, and Germany declared war on Russia. As Russia's ally, France entered the fight; and when the Germans marched across Belgium to attack the French, Great Britain went to her defense. In less than two weeks, nearly every country in Europe was at war.

The American government under President Woodrow Wilson decided to sit it out, claiming that it was a war that didn't touch the United States. But the Germans reached out and touched public opinion across the Atlantic in 1915 when one of its U-boats torpedoed the British liner *Lusitania*, killing 128 Americans. Wilson managed to overcome the resulting groundswell for going to war by extracting a promise from the Germans to keep their submarines on their own side of the ocean. But the promise was short-lived and, after several American freighters went to the bottom, Wilson called for a declaration of war, which was approved by Congress on April 6, 1917. In less than a month, a half-million American troops were in France.

Before it was over over there on November 11, 1918, 128 Americans won the Medal of Honor, including two who earned them in flying machines. The airplane was a new-fangled invention back then, but its uses as a war machine seemed obvious even to people with no imagination. In the early days of the war planes were used by observers, but they rarely got involved in actual fighting. Pilots were armed with handguns, which they sometimes used against each other, but they had their hands full just keeping their planes in the air. Machine guns could improve their fighting power, but if a pilot made the mistake of aiming directly in front, he shot up his propeller and shot himself down. The Germans provided the solution by synchronizing the guns with the turning of the propeller and the idea of aerial dog fights was born. By the time the Americans arrived, both sides had the technology, and early in 1918 American planes began meeting the enemy in the air. It created a new elite of fighting men, young officers who went off alone to fight the enemy one-on-one as medieval knights had done. It was especially true of the Ninety-fourth Aero Squadron of the First Pursuit Group, whose symbol, a top hat decorated with stars and stripes set into a ring, had become one of the most famous icons of the war. Most of the men who flew its Spads behind enemy lines were recent graduates in Ivy League colleges, on an adventure they considered the 1918 version of the traditional Grand Tour of Europe. Others among the 180

American pilots in France had gone abroad before American involvement in the war and volunteered to serve the French air force in a unit known as Escadrille Américaine, which became the Lafayette Escadrille, the first squadron of the U.S. Air Service. But there was one man among them who had different ideas about fighting a war in the air. And in September 1918 he became commanding officer of the Ninety-fourth.

Eddie Rickenbacker's background didn't include college fraternities and the other rites of passage that most fliers considered important steps on the way to becoming a hero in the air. As an orphan, he had gone to work at the age of twelve as an automobile mechanic and by the time he reached college age, he had passed a correspondence course in mechanics and had a job as a test driver for new car models. Before he was nineteen he was earning more than $40,000 a year as a race car driver. When America became involved in the war, he proposed the creation of a flying group made up of drivers like himself who understood machines and had developed skill in using them under pressure. The army didn't see the merit of his idea, but gave him a kind of consolation prize with the offer of an assignment in France as personal driver for General John J. Pershing, the Commander of the American Expeditionary Forces. Rickenbacker took the job, thinking it would give him access to the general's ear. He was right, but Pershing, convinced that flying was a young man's game, wouldn't listen to the ideas of a twenty-seven-year-old he thought should know better. Fate stepped in when a car belonging to Colonel Billy Mitchell, the head of the air service, broke down. Rickenbacker happened along, fixed the car and became Mitchell's friend. In return for the repair job, he was reassigned to the air service as chief mechanic. He turned it to an opportunity for flight training and within a few months became the oldest pilot in the Ninety-fourth.

Within two more months, he had shot down five enemy planes to become an ace, the highest honor a flyer could earn, short of the Medal of Honor. That was to come the day after he took command of the Hat-in-the-Ring Squadron. He said he was flying that day to show his men what he expected of them. But fate stepped into his life again. As he was flying his Spad toward enemy lines, he noticed a pair of German observation planes below him flying in the opposite direction. Experience told him that they'd be accompanied by Fokker fighters, and it wasn't long before they flew into view. He was high above them in the sun where they couldn't see him, and after they passed he cut his engine and swooped down on the last fighter in line.

One burst of his machine gun was all it took to send the enemy down in flames. The other German pilots panicked and broke formation, leaving the pair of observation planes unprotected. Rickenbacker dove for them. The gunners on board gave a good account of themselves, and after several passes the Spad's wings were riddled with bullet holes. Finally, with a burst from his guns, Rickenbacker shot down one of the big planes and headed back into the sun just as the Fokkers regrouped and were heading toward him. Then, as he put it, "I put on the gas and headed for home." He had engaged seven aircraft alone, far behind enemy lines, on a mission no one had asked him to make. In 1931, he was presented with the Medal of Honor for the action.

Even if he had stayed on the ground that day, Captain Eddie Rickenbacker would probably have gotten the medal anyway. Over the next five months, he bagged two enemy planes in single sorties five times. By the time the war ended, he had downed twenty-eight. The former race car driver had a strong competitive spirit and he also had a formidable competitor to keep him on his toes. It was Second Lieutenant Frank Luke, who became an ace during his first week in the air by shooting down the required five enemy planes and eight more for good measure. Like Rickenbacker, he had come up the hard way, and before the war he had cultivated his competitive instincts in a promising career as a prize fighter. But while Rickenbacker's skill was in his handling of an airplane, Luke was handier with a gun, a skill he developed as a youngster in the Arizona desert where he had also honed the instincts of a hunter.

German artillery observers directed the fire of their big guns from posts dangling under huge balloons tethered behind the lines. It was hazardous duty, to say the least, but it was also hazardous to attack them. Shooting one down required directing fire into a small area near the top of the gas bag where a concentration of hydrogen kept it aloft. The balloons were also protected against allied planes by rings of anti-aircraft guns and wherever a balloon was lofted, pursuit planes on the ground kept their engines running waiting to attack any plane whose pilot was foolhardy enough to go near the gas bag. Frank Luke liked the challenge.

He got his first balloon early in September 1918. Diving from above with his machine guns blazing, he was less than one hundred feet from the ground when the the bag finally exploded. His plane was bouncing across the sky, but he managed to pull out of the dive and head for home, unscratched and eager for more of the same kind of

Captain Eddie Rickenbacker (previous pages) was America's first air ace. He went on to become commander of the famous Hat-in-The-Ring Squadron, before finally receiving the Medal of Honor for bravery behind enemy lines in the First World War.

Second Lieutenant Frank Luke was designated an ace after shooting down five enemy planes, plus eight more for good measure, during his first week in the air over France in World War I.

Frank Luke made a specialty of shooting down German observation balloons. Before he himself was shot down, he claimed eleven of them, and also destroyed eighteen enemy fighter planes – all in just seventeen days.

Luke's plane was shot down by machine gunners on the ground. He survived the crash, but was killed by a German patrol after he opened fire on them rather than be taken prisoner.

Major Charles W. Whittlesey was in command of a detachment, the famous "Lost Battalion," which was pinned down in the Argonne Forest in October, 1918. Major Whittlesey earned the Medal of Honor for his leadership in the fighting that ensued.

Major Whittlesey's co-commander, Captain George McMurtry, was awarded the Medal of Honor along with the major for keeping the unit together in the face of fifty per cent casualties during the detachment's five-day siege in the Argonne Forest.

adventure. The next day he exploded a second balloon and narrowly escaped being caught in the flames. Two days after that he got two more, seriously damaging two Spads in the process. After limping home from his second run, he asked for a third plane to go out again. But his request was rejected. It gave him time to think, and he developed a plan to attack just after sunset when the big balloons were still visible in reflected light, but his little biplane was virtually invisible. The landing fields were also nearly invisible by the time he came back from his hunting trips, but Frank Luke wasn't a man to let little details like that get in his way. On his first night flight, he lit up the sky with fires from three balloons and the next night he got two more.

But Luke didn't do it alone. On September 18, 1918, as he was engaged in a dog fight that cost the enemy five planes in ten minutes, his wingman, Lieutenant Joseph Wehner, was hit and his plane went down in flames. Luke avenged him by shooting down three more Germans. Then, when he got back to his base, he requested a car to drive out to the front lines to bring his friend back. Instead, his commanding officer grounded him. But the next day, Luke was airborne again and shot down his fifteenth German plane. There was no holding him back. His commanding officer finally gave up trying, but after Luke left the aerodrome on September 29 for another unauthorized hunt, he said that "when Luke gets back, I'm going to court-martial him first and then recommend him for the Medal of Honor."

But Luke didn't come back that night. After downing three German balloons, his plane was badly damaged from ground fire and he was forced to crash land. In the process, he kept firing at ground troops, killing more than a dozen of them. He was no sooner on the ground than he found himself surrounded by a German patrol, but rather than surrender, he pulled out his pistol and killed three of them before they killed him. In just seventeen days he had eighteen confirmed victories in the air, and ten more that were unconfirmed. He had also blown eleven balloons from the sky.

The lone eagles of the air service captured the public imagination like little else during World War I. But when word trickled back home that a doughboy had captured the whole German Army single-handedly, spirits soared. Actually, it wasn't the whole German Army. It was just a battalion.

The doughboy was Alvin C. York, late of Pall Mall, Tennessee. Before the war he had supported himself by hunting foxes and had developed a skill with the long rifle so he could shoot the animals cleanly through the head to preserve the valuable pelts. But he was a leader in the Church of Christ in the Christian Union, and it was against his religion to use his gun on fellow humans. When a wartime draft was instituted, he applied for an exemption as a conscientious objector. The draft board rejected the request on the grounds that his church wasn't an organized religious sect, and though he appealed the decision in a letter to President Wilson, the rejection stood and he was assigned to the Eighty-second Infantry Division.

During his basic training, he made no bones about warning his superiors that he would follow their orders in battle, except orders to kill. Otherwise he was a model soldier. His battalion commander, who could quote scripture with the best of them, took York under his wing and finally cleared his conscience, with words from the Bible and a considerable amount of praying between them. And by the time his unit left for France, York knew what he had to do. He earned a battlefield promotion to corporal with his amazing marksmanship and by the time the Eighty-second headed for the Meuse-Argonne offensive, Corporal York was already considered one of the most valuable soldiers in the army. But there was more to come. Much more.

On October 18, 1918, his platoon was in front of an advance on a hill where the Germans were dug in. In the resulting firefight, all but seven of the Americans were killed, leaving Corporal York as the only noncommissioned officer. He ordered his men to advance, and they succeeded in capturing a machine gun nest and its crew. Then, as some of his men were organizing the prisoners for a march to the rear, York moved forward to have a look around. A few yards up the hill he found himself pinned down by a line of thirty-five machine guns, and quite alone. He dropped to the ground, realizing that if the German machine gunners were going to get him, they'd have to raise up their heads to take aim. When they did, he dispatched them as cleanly as he had ever killed a fox back home. After twenty-two machine gunners fell dead, a half dozen soldiers leaped out of the trench and headed for York with fixed bayonets.

The corporal knew that the body of the first man he killed would become a shield for the other five, so he took aim at the last man in line and one-by-one shot them down. Between each shot he called out for the others to surrender, and by the time the sixth man dropped with a bullet hole in the center of his forehead, a German major climbed out of the trench waving a white flag. Later he said, in what may have been the understatement of the war, "such

Sergeant Alvin York, who began the First World War as a confirmed conscientious objector, ended it as one of its most famous heroes when he took on an entire battalion single-handedly.

Sergeant York was responsible for the capture of 132 German prisoners of war, all of whom were happier to be his prisoners than his target.

In 1918, America's doughboys crawled across France on their bellies (overleaf), and walked a little taller when the job was done.

marksmanship is bound to have a demoralizing effect."

Corporal York, just as happy the killing had come to an end, called his six soldiers forward and together they followed the German officer back into the trench where the crews of thirty-five machine guns were just as happy to be York's prisoner and not his target. But the seven American soldiers weren't out of the woods yet. They had ninety German prisoners, but they were well behind enemy lines and the only way out was through a front-line trench filled with German fighting men. Corporal York decided to take a chance. Thrusting a pistol between the major's ribs, he ordered him to march forward with a warning that the pistol would go off at the sign of any false moves. Then he marched up to the trench and calmly ordered the Germans to surrender. Just as calmly, they did.

After he and his six men turned their 132 prisoners over to another battalion, they headed back to rejoin their own outfit as though nothing had happened. If it had been up to Corporal York, none of the officers above him would have known anything did happen. The story began to come together when intelligence started questioning the new German prisoners. They also learned that the battalion York had captured had been poised for surprise counterattack. Corporal York was rewarded with a promotion to sergeant and the awarding of the Medal of Honor, and by the time he went home the following spring, he was better-known to most Americans than the President himself.

About a week before Sergeant York's name went into the history books, the Meuse-Argonne campaign produced another piece of military history in the incredible stand of what became known as the "Lost Battalion."

The detachment involved included six rifle companies, forming the First and Second Battalions of the 308th Infantry, complemented by two companies of the 306th Machine Gun Battalion and a company of the 307th Infantry. It included many more men than the four companies that traditionally make up a battalion, but then again, it wasn't "lost," either.

The group, under the command of Major Charles Whittlesey, was ordered to move through the center of the Argonne Forest where the First Army had been sitting ducks for German snipers and machine gun nests for weeks. A bold move was needed to break the German defenses, and Whittlesey's men were elected. It was to be a three-pronged attack, but within an hour or two, the flanking units fell far behind, and the men in the middle found themselves in a ravine far ahead of their supporting troops, surrounded by the enemy. There was nothing to do but dig in for a siege,

even though they were armed with light weapons for an assault. They had no warm clothing to protect them from the freezing rain that was falling, and only one day's rations. The nearest water was a half-mile away and the only way to get at it was across open ground in the face of enemy fire. Planes that were sent to look for them were shot down and supplies they dropped fell into the hands of the enemy. There were no medics, though casualties were incredibly high. And volunteers who tried to get back to the American lines never made it past the German machine guns.

The Germans sent a captured soldier with a message to them on the fifth day of their ordeal. It asked for their surrender, explaining that "the suffering of your wounded men can be heard over here…and we are appealing to your human sentiments." Whittlesey ignored the request, and when the enemy launched the heaviest assault of the action a few hours later, even the most severely wounded fired back and drove the surprised Germans away. Later that same day, an American patrol found them and their agony was over. Of 600 men who walked into the ravine, 170 were dead, and nearly 200 wounded. Among the wounded were Captain George McMurtry and Major Whittlesey, both of whom earned Medals of Honor for leadership that prevented the total loss of the "Lost Battalion."

By the time they were rescued, the American artillery had started firing again. The guns had been silent after it was discovered that their shells were landing among the trapped soldiers. But by the last day, the gunners had a way to unlock the secret of the Argonne Forest. During the siege, dozens of planes were sent to drop supplies to the men, but none was able to get the sorely needed food into the ravine. But one plane, piloted by Lieutenant Harold Goettler, came close. He spotted the Americans, but was driven off by hostile fire. A few hours later, he came back convinced that if he flew lower he might succeed in helping them. But that made him an easier target and his plane was hit. He managed to fly back into friendly territory, but by the time rescuers reached the plane, both he and his observer, Lieutenant Erwin Bleckley, were dead. During the two flights, Bleckley had drawn an accurate map of the sector, and it was found clutched in his hand. It was exactly what the artillery needed, and a few hours later their shells were landing where they could do the most good. Both Bleckley and Goettler were awarded the Medal of Honor posthumously.

During World War I, the navy awarded its special Tiffany Cross version of the Medal of Honor to twenty-one

sailors and seven marines, five of whom also received the army's Medal of Honor for service with the Second Division under General Pershing. The other two marines, Lieutenant Ralph Talbot, and Sergeant Robert Robinson, earned their medals as members of the Marine Air Division. When their plane was cut off from its squadron, and attacked by a dozen enemy planes, Talbot outmaneuvered his attackers, while Robinson fired at them, downing one. The sergeant was wounded in the arm during the attack, and at the same time his gun jammed. As Talbot climbed toward safety, Robinson fixed the gun with one hand and began firing again. He was hit twice more, and as he lay unconscious over his gun, Talbot fired his guns and shot down another plane. His own plane was damaged in the action, and he headed for home, coming down just a few yards inside Allied lines. Then, after leaving Robinson in the care of a field hospital, he took off again to get the plane repaired and back into the fight.

A large part of the navy's mission in the war was protecting convoys taking supplies across the North Atlantic; and though the assignment was filled with danger and hundreds lost their lives battling U-boats and the sea itself, there were few tales of derring-do among the men who served by standing lonely watches at sea. But then on the night of May 31, 1918, a strange drama began to unfold when the crack German raider U-90 hit the troopship *President Lincoln*, amidships with three torpedoes. It was the *Lincoln*'s third crossing and she was on her way home after delivering five thousand soldiers to France. Gunnery officer Lieutenant Edouard Izak was on deck when the blasts went off, and minutes later he found himself in the water with a handful of other survivors. His ship had vanished under the waves.

It wasn't long before the U-boat surfaced and Izak was taken prisoner. The German captain explained it was his custom to capture senior officers, and since Izak's dog tag identified him as a lieutenant, and no one else was in easy reach, he was elected. Apart from explaining that he was not the captain of the *President Lincoln*, Izak said nothing to his captors. He pretended to be in a state of shock and spent the next three weeks wandering aimlessly around the submarine in a state the Germans concluded was the advance stages of *Dummheit*. The captain paid no attention to him at all and let him poke around anywhere he pleased. After all, there was no way anyone could escape from a submerged U-boat, especially someone as deranged as this prisoner seemed to be.

But it was all an act, of course. Izak, who was fluent in

German but never let them know it, was making mental notes about everything he saw and heard. He memorized charts and schedules, noted shipboard routine and made mental notes of the ship's layout. When he thought he had seen and heard enough, he decided it was time to escape. One night, while the U-90 was riding on the surface, Izak put on a life jacket and went up on deck for a breath of fresh air. But as he approached the rail, the captain approached him and he was confined to his bunk until they reached their base a few days later.

He was transferred to prison ship and kept in solitary confinement until he could be moved to a land-based prison. Once he was there, he took some of the other Allied prisoners into his confidence, telling them of the important information he had stored in his head and of his desperate need to escape. They agreed to help, and by the time Lieutenant Izac was led to a train for transfer to yet another prison, he had a compass and a map and a small supply of food hidden in his clothes. He was under heavy guard, but managed to escape from the train by forcing a washroom window open and leaping for freedom. But he sprained an ankle in the attempt and was quickly outrun by his German guards who took him back into custody. They beat him unconscious for what he had done, then tossed him back into solitary confinement. He was released two weeks later, more convinced than ever that he had to get out of there.

Once again he organized his fellow prisoners and after short-circuiting the prison's electrical system, he led a dozen of them through a barbed wire fence under cover of darkness. They split up into groups of twos and threes and headed in the general direction of neutral Switzerland. The Germans were after them with bloodhounds, but they had anticipated that and covered their tracks with red pepper they had managed to buy in the prison black market. Nine days later, after crossing the mountains in the dark, former prisoner of war Edouard Izac walked through the door of the American Legation at Berne. Not long after, he was in Washington writing his report. It was a vital addition to Allied intelligence about the German U-boats. But before his report could be circulated, the Allies had the U-boats themselves. Just before Izak put his signature on the document, French Marshal Ferdinand Foch and a delegation of Allied officers had met representatives of the German government in a railway car in the Compiègne Forest in Northern France and signed an armistice agreement. It was finally over over there.

The German U-boats (previous pages) proved a great threat to Allied convoys crossing the Atlantic in World War I. Navy Lieutenant Edouard Izak carried the secrets of a U-boat in his head on an incredible dash for freedom from a German prison during that war. His subsequent intelligence report was predated by the signing of the armistice agreement in the Compiègne Forest. But his achievement nevertheless earned him the Medal of Honor.

In 1918, in addition to the men they captured, American and French troops also rounded up hundreds of guns, which had been used against them by the enemy they called "the Hun." Left: some of the booty.

In 1921, the Congressional Medal of Honor was awarded to the Unknown Soldier of France, and was delivered to the Arc de Triomphe in Paris by General John J. "Blackjack" Pershing on December 10 of that year. A month earlier, on Armistice Day, a Medal of Honor had been pinned to the flag-draped coffin of America's Unknown Soldier at Arlington National Cemetery by President Warren G. Harding.

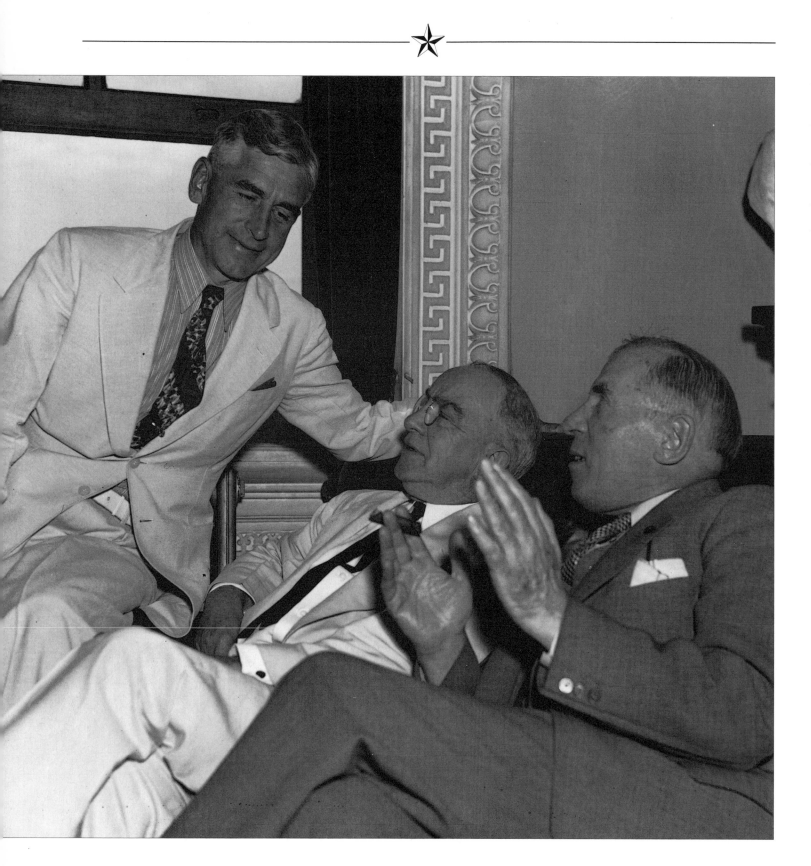

In later years, Edouard Izak (far left) became a Representative for California and is seen in 1939 waiting with Luther Johnson of Texas and Sol Bloom of New York to see Secretary of State Cordell Hull at the State Department in Washington.

Lieutenant Izak, the Congressmen ... all Americans, in fact, were happy to see the end of the First World War, but none of them were nearly as happy as the boys in the trenches.

THE YANKS COME BACK

Through most of World War II, young girls swooned at the sight of an airman, mothers swelled with pride over their sons in the navy, and the commonly accepted mark of a real man was Marine Corps dress blues. Everyone respected the G.I.'s in the infantry, of course. But they were a little short on glamour. They didn't even have a song to sing until 1945 when Frank Loesser wrote one for them. Its opening lines summed it all up: "Oh, they've got no time for glory in the infantry, Oh, they've got no use for praises loudly sung... ." It was number one on the hit parade for months and the infantry especially created its first band to play it. It was written in honor of a skinny little kid from Ohio who couldn't see without his thick glasses and had requested a demotion from sergeant to private because he was worried about his deafness. His name was Rodger Young. As the song says, he "fought and died for the men he marched among," and in the process won the Medal of Honor.

Young's platoon was involved in the fighting in the Solomon Islands in 1943. They had gotten well ahead of the main battalion and were moving back through the dense jungle when they were pinned down by a concealed machine gun. Young was wounded by the first burst, but he shouted to his buddies that he could see the machine gun nest and would take care of it. With that he crawled away, swallowed up in a tangle of vines and branches. The Japanese saw him coming and wounded him again, but he kept creeping forward firing his rifle and drawing the enemy fire away from the platoon behind him. When he got close enough, he began lobbing hand grenades toward the pillbox. Then, seconds before the nest exploded, Rodger Young was hit a third time and fell dead. He had saved the lives of twenty men.

Thanks largely to the song, Private Young became one of the most famous heroes of World War II with the possible exception of another infantryman named Audie Murphy. Murphy was a skinny kid, too, rejected by the marines and the paratroops because he was underweight. And when he fainted in the hot sun during basic training, his sergeant recommended a transfer to cooks school. But the kid had a temper and when the sergeant got a taste of it, he agreed to let him stay. After that, his 125-pound body and his baby face almost relegated him to spending the war running a stateside P.X., but his temper got him released from that assignment and he was shipped to North Africa.

He went from there to Sicily and then on to Italy. By the time he hit the beach at Anzio, he had earned two battlefield promotions and when his outfit, the Third Infantry Division, went to France he was promoted to second lieutenant. By

the beginning of 1945 he was a battle-hardened veteran, and commander of the unit he had fought in as a private. On January 25, they were attacked by a half-dozen tanks and waves of infantry. Murphy ordered his men to withdraw into the woods while he stayed in a foxhole directing artillery fire with a field telephone. Behind him, one of his tank destroyers took a direct hit and was burning when the enemy tanks came abreast of him. Murphy leaped from the foxhole and climbed up on the tank destroyer, even though it was in danger of blowing up. Then, a perfect target for the German tanks, he began firing the tank destroyer's machine guns at the advancing troops. In the confusion, the tanks began to drop back.

They kept firing, though, and hit the tank destroyer twice, but Murphy kept right on firing back. At one point during the hour-long battle, a German patrol got to within ten yards of him, and he killed them all. Finally, when his ammunition ran out, he got back to his telephone and directed the big guns onto his own position where the last of the Germans were closing in. He had been wounded in the leg, but managed to scramble back into the woods just as the artillery barrage came screaming over. When the smoke cleared, the Germans had retreated, leaving more than fifty dead. The Medal of Honor he won that day was one of thirty-five won during World War II by men of the Third Division. They fought the Germans on every front from North Africa to Germany itself, and Audie Murphy was with them every step of the way. On the way he also won the Distinguished Service Cross, the Legion of Merit, the Silver Star and a cluster, the Bronze Star and three Purple Hearts, and became the most decorated American in World War II. After the war his fame took him to Hollywood where he starred in more than forty movies, including *To Hell and Back*, his own life story.

Another lieutenant of the Third Division, Frank Burke, won his Medal of Honor just after the Third moved into Germany in the spring of 1945. As a transportation officer looking for a site for a motor-pool, Burke was one of the first Americans to enter Nuremberg. As he rounded a corner, he spotted ten German soldiers getting ready for a counterattack and rushed back to an American patrol to borrow a machine gun. The Germans didn't see him until he opened fire on them a few minutes later. They returned his fire with machine guns, rocket launchers, rifles and pistols. Then a machine gun nest behind him opened fire. He wheeled around and killed its crew, at which point his original quarry, the ten soldiers, turned and ran for their lives. Picking up one of their abandoned rifles, he began

running down the street where he was met with intense fire from snipers in an abandoned building. He managed to kill several of them, but he realized his gun wasn't going to do the job. Then he noticed that the fleeing Germans had dropped two grenades. He picked them up, pulled the pins and tossed both of them at once. At that same moment, one of the snipers was getting ready to throw a grenade at him. All three went off at the same time and the guns were silenced. But there were still four Germans left, and Burke rushed into the building after them. After cutting them down, he walked back to his platoon, fought beside them in a half-hour gunfight, then went to the aid of another platoon engaged in a fierce fight with an enemy group armed with a 20mm gun. When the day ended, Frank Burke's expedition in search of a motor-pool had resulted in his killing eleven of the enemy and wounding three others, and assisting in two actions that eliminated twenty-nine more Germans from the battle.

The first Medals of Honor in World War II were won on the first day, December 7, 1941, when fourteen navy men were singled out for heroism at Pearl Harbor. Lieutenant John Flynn was one of them. As soon as the Japanese planes appeared overhead, he rushed to a 50-calibre machine gun on a completely exposed training stand at the edge of an airport parking ramp. As the enemy planes came in low to strafe the airfield, Flynn fired back. He was hit several times, but kept right on shooting. A nearby gasoline dump exploded, showering him with fire, but he stayed at his self-appointed post. Finally he was ordered to leave to get first aid treatment, but as soon as he was bandaged he went back to his squadron and spent the rest of the day supervising the rearming of returning planes.

Ensign Francis Flaherty and Lieutenant James Ward won their Medals of Honor at Pearl Harbor aboard the U.S.S. *Arizona* where each stayed behind in burning gun turrets holding flashlights so their shipmates could escape through the thick smoke before the ship capsized. The repair ship *Vestal* was moored next to the *Arizona*, and when the battleship blew up, her skipper, Commander Cassin Young, was blown overboard from his perch behind an anti-aircraft gun. He swam back to his ship, which had also been hit and was burning, and calmly directed the *Vestal* across the harbor where she was beached and saved, along with her crew, to serve again.

The war in the South Pacific burned some new exotic place names into the American consciousness. Among the first was Guadalcanal in the Solomon Islands. The first Medal of Honor won there went to General Alexander

When the Americans reached France in 1944, M-36 tank destroyers were a common sight on the streets of cities such as Metz (previous pages).

It may not look like the face of a man who's been "to hell and back," but that's where Audie Murphy said he'd been. In the process, he became America's most-decorated hero in World War II, with awards ranging from the Purple Heart to the Medal of Honor. A career in Hollywood followed.

The explosion of a magazine on the destroyer Shaw is one of many dramatic images of the Japanese attack on Pearl Harbor on December 7, 1941. The attack brought the United States into World War II, and also produced fourteen winners of the Navy's Medal of Honor.

By April 1945, the war had been carried to German soil, and First Lieutenant Frank Burke was awarded a Medal of Honor for turning a walking tour of Nuremberg into a rout, killing eleven of the enemy and wounding three others.

The battleship Arizona was one of the major casualties of the Pearl Harbor attack. Two of her crewmen, Ensign Francis Flaherty and Lieutenant James Ward received the Medal of Honor for guiding their shipmates to safety through the thick smoke.

Airfields sheltering Navy planes, such as the one on Ford Island, were also Japanese targets in the Pearl Harbor attack. Lieutenant John Flynn earned his Medal of Honor by exposing himself to strafing enemy planes and an exploding gasoline dump to answer Japanese fire with a 50-calibre machine gun. After having his wounds treated, he went back out onto the airfield to load his squadron's planes.

Major General Alexander A. Vandegrift, who commanded the marines' assault at Guadalcanal in the Solomon Islands, was awarded the Medal of Honor for leading the attack, known as Operation Watchtower. He was later promoted to lieutenant general, and became the second highest ranking officer in the Marine Corps.

Vandegrift, who personally led the First Marine Division ashore. But it was far from the last. And, as often happened with Medal of Honor winners, two were men whose assigned roles in the battle were over long before the engagement that earned them. They were part of a crack marine outfit, known as Edson's Raiders, who had begun preparing for assaults like the landing at Guadalcanal long before the United States entered the war. They had trained with British commandos and honed their skills in the peaceful American countryside as early as 1939. But nothing could have prepared them for the horrors of the beachhead at Guadalcanal.

After a few weeks of fierce fighting and stunning casualties, the 800 surviving Raiders under Colonel Merritt Edson were reassigned to hold a ridge behind the airfield. It was far removed from the battle zone and considered secure, a perfect place for weary troops to unwind. But before they could get their first night's sleep, three thousand Japanese troops broke through the front lines and came screaming out of the jungle in an effort to recapture the airport. Infiltrators had already cut the telephone lines, so Edson's Raiders were on their own. Colonel Edson was in the thick of the fight, withdrawing his forward units without losing a man, and then taking part in the hand-to-hand fighting that raged through the night. One of his company commanders, Major Kenneth Bailey, also took part in the ten-hour battle with bayonets and knives, rifles, pistols and grenades, and was killed before it ended. In the morning, when they finally withdrew, the Japanese left a thousand dead behind. Both Edson and Bailey were awarded the Medal of Honor for winning a battle at a time the top brass had expected them to be resting.

No one got any rest during the battle for Guadalcanal, least of all Sergeant John Basilone, who was in the first wave of marines to go ashore. He was in charge of two sections of heavy machine guns, one of which was put out of action in a heavy Japanese frontal assault. He had only two men left to carry on and still the enemy kept blasting them with grenades and mortar fire. Moving an extra gun into position, Sergeant Basilone personally manned it and, as bullets whizzed past him, he repaired another. The battle continued all night long. At one point, when their ammunition was nearly gone, Sergeant Basilone braved enemy fire to get urgently needed shells to his men. When the sun came up the next morning, an entire regiment of the enemy had been virtually annihilated. Basilone, who had served with the army in the Philippines before the war, and looked every inch the war hero he was, went home after that

and embarked on a tour selling war bonds. But it wasn't his style. In 1944 he asked to be sent back into the fight, and on February 19, 1945, he was killed by a mortar blast on the black sandy beach at Iwo Jima.

The marines had island-hopped across the South Pacific, with each victory bringing mainland Japan more and more within the range of American bombers. The capture of the Marianas with the fall of Tinian in August 1944 finally made it possible for B-29s to bomb Japan itself. But there were other islands to cross on the way. And as the marines advanced on them, the Japanese became fanatically determined to stop them. The fight for Iwo Jima would be one of the bloodiest of the war.

It is a tiny island, about eight square miles of volcanic rock and thick jungle. By the time the marines landed, the Japanese had spent two years building defenses that included more than eight hundred pillboxes, three miles of underground tunnels and even deeper concrete shelters. Every inch of beach was covered with guns, there were strategically based guns behind the beaches and the 21,000 troops backing them up were armed with twenty-thousand rifles and machine guns and twenty-two million rounds of ammunition. Before the invasion, navy ships bombarded the rock for three days, but the defenders waited it out below ground and when the marines landed the Japanese force was at full strength. Intelligence had underestimated that strength by a long shot and they had also not taken the enemy's mood into account. With their homeland threatened, they fell back on ancient traditions that death was better than surrender and the most honorable death was to take as many of the enemy as possible along with them. In the battle that followed, they took nearly 6,000 American marines with them and wounded another 17,000. The battle for Iwo Jima lasted twenty-six days, and marines won twenty-six Medals of Honor during the fighting. Throughout the entire three years and nine months the U.S. was involved in World War II, only fifty-five other marines received the medal.

During the first day of the fight for Iwo Jima, the First Battalion of the Twenty-sixth Marines lost all of its officers except two second lieutenants and Captain Robert Dunlap, the commanding officer of Company C. He and his men were trapped on the beach, but he managed to lead them inland into even hotter fire from caves that honeycombed a cliff face dead ahead. The Japanese poured shrapnel and bullets into the valley with increasing accuracy, and Dunlap elected himself to do something about it. He managed to slip forward to the base of the cliff where he could locate

Major General Alexander A. Vandegrift (left) and Colonel Merritt Austin Edson (right), both of whom earned Medals of Honor at Guadalcanal, confer with Colonel Gerald Thomas (center) on a beach on the island, which had been evacuated by the Japanese just hours before.

Marine Sergeant Mitchell Paige (right) who was later promoted to the rank of lieutenant, was awarded the medal for a single-handed assault that prevented a Japanese breakthough on Guadalcanal. He was honored along with General Vandegrift (left) and Colonel Edson (center).

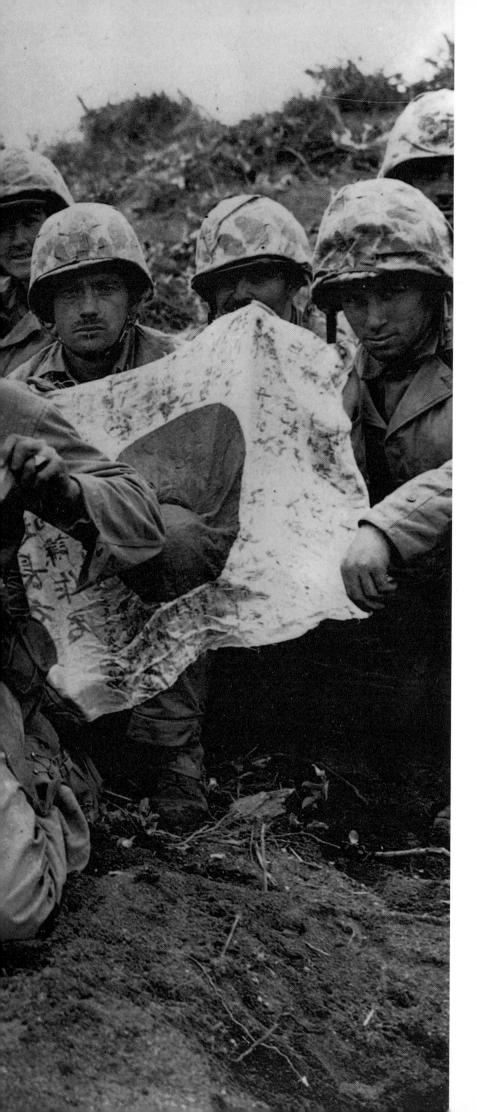

the exact positions of the guns. Then he went back to his own lines to telephone the information to the navy's big guns. Once the shells began roaring in, he moved back into the open, jumped into a shell crater and began directing the artillery fire. He stayed there for two days and two nights constantly under enemy fire. When it was all over, and the Japanese guns were destroyed, he walked back to his men, weary but unscratched.

The capture of Iwo Jima and of Okinawa the following month by the Tenth Army and the Sixth Marine Division cost the Americans nearly 50,000 casualties and the Japanese 110,000. But it put the Americans within 350 miles of Japan and paved the way for massive bombing raids of the homeland itself. They had come a long way from April 1942, when fifteen B-25s took off from the deck of the carrier *Hornet* to deliver their 500-pound bombs to the heart of Tokyo. The squadron was led by General Jimmy Doolittle, whose terse Medal of Honor citation said the volunteer mission carried "the apparent certainty of being forced to land in enemy territory or perish at sea." But the outcome wasn't quite that grim. After their famous "thirty seconds over Tokyo," Doolittle's Raiders set a course for China. They ran out of fuel just short of the coast. Two of the planes crash landed in Japanese-held territory, three of the eight survivors were executed and the others taken prisoner. One landed in Russia and was confiscated after its crew was taken prisoner. Doolittle's own plane crashed in China and its crew managed to parachute to safety. All the others crash landed in friendly territory.

When a haven was established at Iwo Jima, air raids on Japan took on a different look. B-29s began low-level runs at night loaded with incendiary bombs as well as high explosives. It was a technique that had stood the Americans in good stead earlier in the war, half a world away. But night raids were still in the future on August 1, 1943, when three Eighth Air Force bombing groups and two from the Ninth Air Force took off from a base in Libya to fly nearly fifteen hundred miles to Rumania where their mission was to take out the oil refineries at Ploesti. There were 178 B-24s involved, but no fighter escort, and each of them was expected to perform on a tight pre-arranged flight schedule coordinating five separate formations. Five men won Medals of Honor during the operation, but only two lived to tell about it.

Second Lieutenant Lloyd Hughes, was the pilot of one of the planes in the last formation. By the time he reached the target, the enemy had long since been alerted and its anti-aircraft fire was at its heaviest, and as he approached the

Members of the Fifth
Marine Division,
famous for raising the
American flag on Iwo
Jima's Mount
Suribachi, collected a
few enemy flags
(previous pages) on
their way up the
mountain.

Major General Jimmy
Doolittle (left)
electrified the country
with his bombing raid
on Tokyo in April,
1942, for which he
was awarded the
Medal of Honor.

In 1943, Lieutenant John C. Morgan was presented with the medal by his commanding officer, General Baker, for saving a Flying Fortress in an action over Europe in July of that year that can be considered as nothing short of miraculous.

The Eighth and Ninth Air Forces' 1943 bombing raid on the Rumanian oilfields at Ploesti employed 178 B-24s and produced five Medal of Honor winners.

The squadron of fifteen B-25s that took Major General Doolittle's raiders over Tokyo in April, 1942, were delivered to within striking distance on the flight deck of the carrier Hornet (right). When the Japanese politely asked where the planes had come from, President Roosevelt answered, "Shangri La."

area, flames from burning oil tanks were leaping higher than his bombing level. His B-24 took several direct hits causing gasoline to escape from the bomb bay and one of the wings, and Hughes knew that flying into the inferno ahead of him would mean almost certain death. But he also knew that if he crash-landed or turned back the entire formation would be jeopardized. He went in over his target, dropped his bombs and destroyed it, but in the process, his plane caught fire and crashed before he could bring it down in a wheat field just ahead.

Colonel Leon Johnson led the fourth wave over Ploesti, but before reaching Rumania his group went off course avoiding cloud formations over the mountains. By the time they regrouped and reached Ploesti, their assigned targets were already in flames and the sky was filled with fighter planes. But Johnson chose to go in on his low-level run anyway, and managed to finish the job that had already been started. The refinery was totally destroyed by their direct hits.

Twenty-three of the thirty-eight Medals of Honor awarded in the Army Air Corps went to bomber pilots, and of those the majority went to pilots of the Eighth Air Force. But one of the Eighth's men won his medal for fighting a private battle with the pilot of his B-17. Second Lieutenant John Morgan was the co-pilot of a B-17 that left England for a bombing mission over Europe in July 1943. Their formation was hit by enemy fighters before they reached the coast of France, and a cannon shell that crashed through the windshield hit the pilot in the forehead, leaving him in a crazed condition. He slumped over the wheel and sent the plane into a steep dive. When Morgan tried to take over the controls, the half-conscious man only held on tighter. But by sheer strength, Morgan succeeded in prying him loose and set the Flying Fortress back on course. Meanwhile, the plane's internal communications system had been blown out, and Morgan wasn't able to call for help. Then, as he was still battling with the pilot, who showed no signs of giving up, the top gunner fell though the hatch above them with his arm shot off. The waist, tail and radio gunners had all lost consciousness after the oxygen system failed, and, not hearing them, Morgan assumed they had bailed out. The navigator stayed at his post, completely unaware that anything serious was wrong. But though there was no way of getting help, Morgan made the decision to stay in formation and continue the mission. After improvising a tourniquet to stop the bleeding from the gunner's arm, he continued fighting off the pilot for two long hours while flying the plane with one hand. Finally, the navigator went into the cockpit and, discovering what was going on, helped remove the crazed pilot, revived the unconscious gunners, and they completed their mission safely. The citation that came with Lieutenant Morgan's Medal of Honor called the action "miraculous," but it was something more than that. It was, as most citations begin, an example of "conspicuous gallantry and intrepidity above and beyond the call of duty."

Some Medal of Honor winners are more conspicuous that others. Among them was a marine fighter pilot who equaled Eddie Rickenbacker's record by shooting down twenty-six enemy planes in the Pacific. Major Gregory Boyington did better than that. He had six kills to his credit before the Japanese attacked Pearl Harbor.

The hard-drinking, hard-brawling marine everyone knew as "Pappy" became a marine pilot in 1935, but early in 1941 he resigned his commission and became a soldier of fortune with Claire Lee Chennault's Flying Tigers in China. When the marines went to war he offered to rejoin them, but they had breathed a sigh of relief when he left in the first place and refused his offer. The Army Air Force wanted him; they had inducted the entire Flying Tigers outfit, in fact. But he didn't want any part of the army. He took his case to the Secretary of the Navy, who finally agreed to bury the hatchet and Pappy Boyington went to work gathering other anti-establishment flyers into a squadron he called, appropriately, the Black Sheep. Before long, just the sight of their Corsairs sent enemy planes running. And Boyington and his men liked nothing better than running after them.

Pappy won his Medal of Honor in 1944 when he led a formation of twenty-four fighters supporting a bombing strike of the island of Kahili in the central Solomon Islands. As the bombers dropped their loads, the Black Sheep circled the airfield challenging the Japanese fighters to do something about it. Not one left the ground. The next day, the Black Sheep came back, this time without the bombers, but Pappy kept up radio chatter to make the Japanese think the bombers had come back. When they finally took the bait, the squadron shot down twenty of them without losing a single plane of their own.

Boyington was shot down himself a few weeks later and taken prisoner. It wasn't until then that the recommendation for his medal was filed. It was assumed he was dead because the Japanese had never reported his capture and the award was intended to be posthumous. He almost didn't make it back, but when he did, he said he had stayed alive just to embarrass the brass.

The navy's first ace was Lieutenant Butch O'Hare, a fighter pilot based on the carrier *Lexington*. On February 20,

His mother may have named him Gregory, but Major Boyington, the marine ace, much preferred being called "Pappy." A former Flying Tiger, Boyington had bagged six Japanese planes, one more than was necessary to qualify as an ace, even before the attack on Pearl Harbor.

At a review in the high school stadium at Butte, Montana, Colonel A. Robert Ginsburgh (center) introduces Medal of Honor winner Lieutenant Commander Edward O'Hare (right) to another war hero, Army Air Force pilot, Captain Hewitt T. Wheless (left).

1942, when a formation of heavy bombers were spotted heading toward the ship, its fighters scrambled for them. All but two of the American planes flew off after the first wave, but when the guns jammed on one of remaining fighters, Lieutenant O'Hare was left alone between nine twin-engine bombers and his ship. He attacked at close range and, making every bullet count, shot down five of the enemy planes and crippled a sixth before they could reach the *Lexington*. The action lasted about four minutes, enough time for other planes of the *Lexington's* squadron to get back and finish off the others. He had single-handedly saved his ship and all the men aboard. Lieutenant O'Hare was killed the following year over the Gilbert Islands, but his name lives on in the name of Chicago's international airport.

Of the sixteen million Americans who went to war in the 1940s, more than four hundred thousand, like Butch O'Hare, didn't come back. Four-hundred thirty-three won Medals of Honor, and many of those, whose names were household words during those war years, are largely forgotten nearly half a century later. Among them was another Irish-American, Corporal Charles Kelly, a one-man army everyone called "Commando" Kelly. He had never been a model soldier and during his basic training he spent as much time in the guard house as on long hikes. The infantry cadre was just as happy to see him leave when he requested permission to join the paratroops. But he had no sooner finished his airborne training than he went AWOL, and when he finally went back, he was court-martialed, given a month's restriction and thrown out of the unit. Back in the infantry, he was assigned to the Thirty-sixth Division, made up mostly of Texans who welcomed the kid from Pittsburgh into their ranks with open arms.

In fact, Kelly felt that the men of the Thirty-sixth were his family and in his determination to help them he constantly violated the unwritten rule of every soldier: "Don't volunteer for anything." Kelly volunteered for everything; the more dangerous, the better. On September 13, 1943, not long after participating in the landing at Salerno, Italy, he volunteered to join a patrol assigned to locate and destroy enemy machine gun positions. When the patrol finished its mission, he volunteered to make contact with a battalion pinned down about a mile away, a job that involved exposing himself to enemy fire nearly every step of the way. When he returned with information about enemy strength, he volunteered to join yet another patrol, which destroyed two machine gun nests. When he ran out of ammunition, he asked for permission to go to a nearby

ammunition dump for more. When he got there, he found the storehouse under heavy enemy attack, and he joined the battle which lasted through the night. The next morning he took over positions that had been manned through the night by three men, and fired his automatic rifle until it overheated and locked. He picked up another and kept firing until it, too, overheated. By then, the enemy was poised to overrun the position, but Commando Kelly was in no mood to let that happen. He went back into the storeroom and came out with two 60mm mortar shells, which he used as hand grenades, killing a half-dozen of the approaching enemy. It slowed the German advance long enough for the sergeant in charge to order an evacuation, and Kelly, running true to form, volunteered to cover their withdrawal. He was able to hold the enemy at bay with a rocket launcher as thirty of his buddies escaped through the back door of the house that had been converted into an ammunition dump. And before the smoke cleared, Commando Kelly was right behind them. The next time he went home to Pittsburgh, the former AWOL soldier was wearing the Medal of Honor.

*Sergeant Charles E.
Kelly, better known as
Commando Kelly, was
the first Medal of
Honor recipient in the
Italian campaign in
1943.*

Edward "Butch" O'Hare was the navy's first ace. He received the Medal of Honor for stopping five enemy bombers headed for his ship, the carrier Lexington.

THE FIRES OF THE COLD WAR

The laws regulating the awarding of the Medal of Honor
have been changed and rechanged dozens of times. As
recently as 1978, they were amended to increase winners'
special pensions from $100 to $200 a month. It was a big
step. Until 1961, the pension had been just $10 a month. As
in most legal matters, words are more important than deeds,
and every time they updated the law, the legislators
managed to be consistent in authorizing the Medal for
"action involving actual conflict with an enemy." If they
had used the word "war," none of the 131 Medals of Honor
earned during the fighting in Korea between 1950 and 1953
could have been awarded. It was often called a "conflict,"
and President Harry S. Truman preferred to call it a "police
action." But if technically it wasn't a war, it had all the
earmarks. Five-and-a-half million Americans fought there,
thirty-five thousand died there.

One of the first of the heroes in Korea was awarded the
Medal of Honor posthumously. But it was a mistake. There
was no question that Major General William Dean deserved
the honor, but he was very much alive when President
Truman gave the Medal to Dean's wife in 1951.

Big Bill Dean's Twenty-fourth Infantry Division was
one of the first American outfits sent into Korea after
fighting broke out between the two halves of a country
divided after the fall of Japan in 1945. The Twenty-fourth
had been one of the first into Japan at the end of World War
II, and in the years since then it had been part of the army of
occupation. But its weapons were obsolete, its regiments
had been reduced to two battalions instead of the usual three
and few of its men had ever seen combat. General Dean had
led the Forty-fourth Division across France and Germany
five years earlier. But when the North Koreans began an
artillery barrage of the United States position near the city
of Taejon on July 19, 1950, a few weeks after the
Americans had arrived, Dean said he had never seen such
heavy fire during his seven months in the European theater
of operations.

By the time the attack began, Dean had already moved
most of his men a dozen miles south and had stayed behind
with a small staff of officers and drivers and a hand-picked
group of infantry men. On the morning of the 20th, the
small combat team was facing two full regiments of the
enemy. They entered the city with a column of tanks and
Dean organized bazooka crews to stop them. He himself
went after one of the tanks with a 75mm recoilless rifle, but
none of his shots hit their mark. He was about to toss a hand
grenade into the tank's open hatch when two more tanks
came into view and he was forced to run for cover.

One of the toughest enemies in Korea was the weather. More than once, the flight decks of carriers such as the U.S.S. Leyte (previous pages) needed to be cleared of snow before the planes could take off. Bitterly cold Korean winds also made the going tough for GIs on the move. Huddling together on a tank (left) helped make the journey more bearable.

General William F. Dean, whose Medal of Honor had been awarded posthumously, suddenly emerged, very much alive, from a communist prison ready to claim the medal for himself.

Rounding up several bazooka men, he jumped into an abandoned jeep and went back into the battle. But the tanks were on the move by then and out of range. Later in the morning, they were able to get one of the tanks by firing from the second floor of a building. But by then, General Dean knew that his small force wasn't going to save Taejon, and he ordered an evacuation convoy, which moved out with the general's jeep the last vehicle in line. Before long, they were bogged down by wreckage of other vehicles and set out on foot in the direction of the rest of their army. The last time anyone saw General Dean, he was on his way to get water from a stream for a wounded man. But it was only the beginning of his story, though it was assumed that the two-star general was dead when his bullet-riddled helmet liner was found in a rice paddy a few days later.

When he slid down an embankment to get to the stream, he slipped and fell and was knocked unconscious. No one saw him as the column moved south, leaving him alone in the darkness. When he awoke early the next morning, he was in pain from a broken shoulder, injured ribs and a mild concussion. But he was alert, and rolled quickly behind a rock when he heard footsteps coming toward him from the road. Fortunately, the sounds were made by a man from his own outfit and the pair took off in the direction of the U.S. lines. Early in their march, they reached a village and found food and shelter in one of the houses, whose occupants spoke English. But in the middle of the night, they woke to find the house surrounded by enemy soldiers. They made a dash for it and escaped into a rice paddy where they were separated. Dean hid out there for the rest of the night, but never saw his companion again.

The next morning, which was his fifty-first birthday, Dean slipped away and began wandering through the hills in the general direction of the American lines. During the next twenty days he lived on water alone and lost sixty pounds. Finally he came upon a house and was invited to come inside by the seemingly friendly Koreans, who assumed he was a Russian attached to the North Korean army. They fed him well, but he became violently ill and lost four more days recovering. In all, he would spend thirty-six days searching for friendly troops.

He thought he had found friendly civilians when two of them joined him and hid him from enemy patrols. But after several days, one of them led North Korean soldiers to his hiding place, and ordered him to surrender. Dean pulled out his pistol, but he was knocked to the ground and within a few minutes he was their prisoner. Dean had long since destroyed all of his identification, but the soldiers knew who he was, recognizing him from pictures they had seen back in 1947 when he was Military Governor of South Korea.

He was taken to a prison at Pyongyang, where he was stripped and kept in solitary confinement in an unheated, unfurnished room. For weeks he was interrogated around the clock and finally threatened with torture. Concerned that he might break under it, Dean stole a gun from an unwary guard and attempted to shoot himself. But the gun was defective and death was denied. His attempt put his captors on notice that they were in danger of losing a prize prisoner, and they began to treat him better, though not exactly like a king, for the next three long years. He had actually participated in the war for just twenty days. But his stand at Taejon was a delaying action on a grand scale that was later

credited with preventing the turning of Korea into another Bataan and saving the Americans from the experience of another death march.

Long before Dean's capture, the American force in Korea was beefed up and, as the Twenty-fourth Divison kept the enemy busy, the new units combined to defend the bulge around the southwestern port of Pusan between the Naktong River and the Sea of Japan. By the end of August most of them had tangled with the enemy, but few of them were ready for the North Korean offensive that began under a heavy fog cover on the night of August 31. By the time the fog cleared, the enemy had advanced more than ten miles into the American perimeter. In the process, they discovered something they hadn't known before. The Americans knew how to fight. One of the first to show them

The U.N. force in Korea included men from many nations, including a Canadian tank squadron (previous pages) that had originated on the Great Plains as a cavalry outfit, "Lord Strathcona's Horse."

The American Eighth Army found it easier to move to the front in Korea aboard their supporting tanks (left) rather than to march behind them.

An M-46 tank is menacing enough painted olive drab. But add a snarling tiger and it becomes a war machine to remember.

The war in Korea became a whole new ball game when Chinese troops swooped down across the Manchurian border. Lieutenants Allen and Grewe interrogate a group of prisoners from among the first Chinese troops to be taken into custody while fighting in North Korea.

Between battles, there was always work to be done reloading tanks with fuel and ammunition ready for the next stage in the fighting. Even as armistice talks were progressing in 1953, tanks were still preparing to leave for the front (right).

was Sergeant First Class Ernest Kuoma of the Seventy-second Tank Battalion. As the infantry men began to withdraw, the tanks came in to cover their movements and Kuoma's vehicle was cut off. He found himself alone and out in the open directly in the path of five hundred screaming enemy soldiers. But he held his ground and directed his tank crew's fire all night long. When the enemy threatened to overrun his tank, he leaped onto the rear deck and fired the machine gun point-blank at them. When the gun ran out of ammunition, he fired at them with his pistol, and when it was empty, he began throwing hand grenades at them, all the while completely exposed to enemy fire. After nine hours of steady battle, he turned to rejoin his unit, but took time to destroy three enemy machine gun nests on the way back. When it was all over, he had killed more than

250 of the North Korean soldiers. He had been wounded in the process, but after his tank was rearmed, he requested permission to get back into the fight. Permission was denied. Kuoma had done enough for one night.

Meanwhile, the Red onslaught had cut off Company H of the Ninth Infantry Regiment, and Private First Class Joseph Ouellette volunteered to slip through the line to the top of a nearby hill for an estimate of enemy strength and to see how near friendly troops might be. After reporting back with the grim news that help was far away, an airdrop of water was made nearby, and Ouellette volunteered to retrieve the cans, even though he had to wade through enemy fire to do it. The cans were broken and empty, but though the unit had been without water for three days, Ouellette's attitude was a morale booster. But if their

morale was high, their ammunition was low. Ouellette had an answer for that, too. In his forays he had spotted enemy dead, and once again volunteered to go back outside the perimeter to collect their weapons and ammunition. On the way back, loaded with all he could carry, he was stopped by an enemy soldier. Dropping his collection of guns and grenades, he killed the enemy in hand-to-hand combat, added his weapons to the collection and crawled back to his unit. Later he was forced from his foxhole six times escaping exploding grenades, exposing himself to small arms fire in the process. Finally, he stopped one of the bullets and fell dead.

His unit was pinned down for nearly four days. The enemy attack, alternating between infantry waves and heavy artillery shelling, kept up around the clock. By the time the thirty survivors, who hadn't had food, water or any sleep for ninety-six hours, decided to make a break for it, the man who had directed their defenses, Master Sergeant Travis Watkins, refused to join them. Like Ouellette, he had gone outside the perimeter to retrieve enemy weapons and killed five North Koreans in the process. He was wounded himself and paralyzed from the waist down, but he kept up the fight, killing six more enemy armed with grenade launchers. Through it all, he refused all offers of food and aid, saying his men needed it more. In the end, he chose to stay behind, saying that he would slow them down if they tried to carry him out. His men made it, and Watkins died smiling with pride. They had killed more than 500 of the enemy, and two of the men they left behind had earned the Medal of Honor.

The North Korean breakthrough across the Naktong River above Pusan was one of the war's bloodiest battles, but when it was over the enemy had been driven back and the Americans had a dramatic victory to their credit. The Eighth Army had gone on the offensive and the stage was set for an amphibious invasion at Inchon and a drive on the occupied capital of Seoul. Then, as the United Nations Forces marched north toward the Manchurian border at the Yalu River, they met three hundred thousand Chinese troops coming the other way.

The Eighth Army swept up the west coast behind the retreating North Koreans, the Seventh Division took the center and Seventh Marine Division moved up the left flank to take what was anticipated to be a quiet sector. The Leathernecks had heard rumors of Chinese activity ahead, but air reconnaissance and intelligence discounted them. No Chinese soldiers, much less an army, had been spotted. And besides, the Chinese weren't in this fight. They weren't, that is, until the night of November 1.

The marines who found themselves pinned down at Sudong included reservists who had been activated less than a month before. They had seen fighting in the battle to retake Seoul, but even the most battle-hardened among them had never experienced anything quite like the night attack at Sudong. Among the greenhorns among them was Staff Sergeant Archie Van Winkle. But if he was green, he was a marine, and he was ready. His platoon was surrounded when the sun came up the next morning. He set up an observation post at the crest of a hill, but though he had no idea or any way of finding out where the enemy's main force might be, he decided toward the end of the day that it was time to fight their way out. He was wounded in the charge and lost the use of an arm, but he kept going. He was hit by a grenade that broke all his ribs, but that didn't stop him either. Enemy fire was coming at them from every direction, but Van Winkle kept up the assault, finally carried from his position unconscious. When the battle ended the following day, his platoon was reorganized and the enemy had been driven back. But the fight had barely begun.

The Eighth Army was taking a beating on the other side of the peninsula, but was pressing northward to fullfill General MacArthur's plan of finishing the war by Christmas. But the plan didn't include fighting the Chinese. They struck in force during the last week of November and the war took on a grim new character.

An army task force on the western edge of the advance northward included Company E of the Twenty-seventhth Infantry, commanded by Captain Reginald Desiderio. As they pushed deeper into enemy territory, they encountered light resistance and then on the night of November 25 all hell broke loose. One of Captain Desiderio's platoons was almost completely wiped out, another had moved too far forward and was cut off nearly two thousand yards within enemy territory. Desiderio walked out into the darkness under heavy fire to get the men into defensive positions, and then guided them back to their own lines without a single casualty. Then just before dawn, the enemy attack stopped and the only sounds were made by the cold winter wind blowing down from Manchuria. But there was more to come.

Late the following afternoon, Company E got its orders to move back south. They had spent most of the day picking up their dead and tending to the wounded. The order to retreat was welcome news, and they dug in well behind the American lines where they were sure their only enemy would be the biting cold. But they had no sooner eaten their

Marine Major William E. Barber, who held his ground at Chosin Reservoir, thereby allowing 8,000 marines to escape a death trap, was obviously happy to be alive himself when he arrived in Washington to be presented with the Medal of Honor by President Truman.

first hot food in days when the Chinese troops struck again. The captain, meanwhile, had gone back to headquarters and rejoined his men with five new tanks just as the attack began. The enemy fought doggedly for two hours, rushing the tanks and sustaining heavy losses. Then, as had happened the night before, they suddenly broke off the attack and all was quiet again.

Desiderio had lost more than a dozen men, and as he was contemplating his next move, the attack began again as suddenly as it had stopped. It began with a grenade-armed patrol that got to within a few yards of the Americans without being seen. Once they made their presence known, they were followed by foot soldiers firing from the hip with deadly accuracy. A mortar round hit Desiderio, but he was on his feet in seconds moving from man to man to make sure that each of them was ready for the next wave. He was wounded a second time, but still kept going. Toward morning, the enemy began the most savage attack of all, knocking out two of the tanks. The wounded captain ran to the other three and directed their fire. But Company E's position was overrun and the battle turned to hand-to-hand fighting. Desiderio waded in, firing his rifle as he went. When it ran out of ammunition, he picked up another and kept on firing, killing nine and wounding another five before he himself was killed. His men were inspired and at a time they might have retreated, they counterattacked and the enemy broke and ran.

At the same time, miles to the east, six Chinese divisions attacked marine and army troops at the Chosin Reservoir and had them trapped in a mountain pass. Lieutenant Colonel Don Faith was in command of the Thirty-second Infantry Regiment, which had sustained heavy losses and became a prime target. Faith had fought beside his men and led them in counterattacks when their position was overrun. But he knew he had to get his men out there, and reconnoitered an escape route across the frozen reservoir. After the last of the survivors were safely on their way, Faith followed them. They joined a group of marines on the other side, and together formed a joint task force that began blasting its way through the enemy lines. When they reached a roadblock at a bend in the road, he organized an attack, and then placed himself at the head of another group of men leading them directly into enemy fire. He was wounded in the attempt and died soon after. But the attack succeeded and his men took the roadblock and were able to continue their march to safety.

No one was safe in those mountain passes and on the long march back to sea, the bitter cold weather and the

At the White House, on December 18, 1945, President Harry S. Truman presented the Medal of Honor to an assemblage of heroes (previous pages) that included, from left to right, Army PFC Mike Colalillo, Marine Captain Robert H. Dunlop, Navy Lieutenant Richard M. McCool, Army T-Sergeant Vernon McGarity and Army First Lieutenant Frank Burke.

In a White House Medal of Honor ceremony, Marine Majors Reginald Myers (left) and Carl Sitter (right) were honored by President Truman for their gallantry at Korea's Chosin Reservoir.

Seen in the photograph after making two successful attacks on enemy aircraft in one day, Air Force Major George A. Davis would destroy a total of nine MIGs and three bombers, before he was himself killed in action in 1952, while attacking fifteen MIGs in his F-86 Sabrejet. This feat earned him a posthumous Medal of Honor.

Among the planes
based on the carrier
U.S.S. Boxer *during
the Korean War were
pilotless drones that
were guided to their
targets by AD-2s,
giving them a deadly
accuracy.*

Major George A. Davis, whose actions in Korea earned him a posthumous Medal of Honor, had already enjoyed the status of ace during World War II.

constant threat of surprise attack took a terrible toll. But it may have been worse without three marine officers who won Medals of Honor helping to pave the way.

Captain William Barber was one of them. Assigned to defend a three-mile mountain pass, essential to the safe retreat from the reservoir, the 240 men under his command dug in. They were immediately attacked by a force of regimental strength, which completely surrounded their position. After successfully fighting them off, Captain Barber requested countermanding an order to withdraw, telling his superiors his men could hold the position if supplies could be airdropped to them. The lives of eight thousand marines were at stake, and permission was granted. Barber was wounded the following day, but he directed his men from a stretcher through five days and six nights of repeated enemy attacks. They claimed more than a thousand enemy lives, but not without a price. When they were relieved, his force of 240 had been reduced to eighty-two who could still walk. But they held the position and kept the pass open.

When the Chinese captured a key escape route, Captain Carl Sitter's Company G, Third Battalion of the First Marine Division was assigned to join British Royal Marines to retake it. It wasn't going to be an easy job. Leading a supply convoy, they inched their way through roadblocks, machine gun positions and hidden pockets of enemy troops. In the first five hours of their mission, the task force had moved only two miles. Sitter and his British counterpart, Colonel Douglas Drysdale, decided to change their plans. Eight tanks were dispatched to lead their column, and in the next two hours they logged three more miles. Then the going got tough. The enemy's tactic had been to let the tanks pass and then open fire on the troops marching behind them. Interspersing the tanks among the trucks following them helped speed things up, but it took them more than twelve hours to open the less than fifteen-mile stretch of road and to reach the relative safety of the American-held town of Hagaru-ri. But it wasn't as safe as they had anticipated.

Sitter's men were weary from the hard fight they had been through and weakened by the bone-chilling cold. But there was a hill to be taken and they were elected. It had been taken by the Chinese and then retaken by the Americans who were holding on by their fingernails. Sitter's company was ordered to break through enemy territory to reinforce them. They suffered twenty-five percent casualties in the attempt. When they broke through, Captain Sitter led them up the snow-covered hillside

After the tough
withdrawal from
northeast Korea, the
GIs and their tanks
gave a good account
of themselves at the
Hungnam beachhead.

through withering enemy fire. During the night, the enemy attacked in full force lighting up the hillside with mortar, machine gun and small arms fire. Though severely wounded himself, Sitter directed the defense, encouraging men without any experience in infantry tactics. By the time the battle ended, the enemy had lost more than fifty percent of its fighting force, and the hill was secure. In spite of his wounds, Captain Sitter stayed there for three more days before his men were relieved. When they marched out, his task force was reduced from 270 to just ninety-six men.

The men they rescued on the hill were a composite unit of marines and army personnel, mostly non-combatants, described by their commander, Major Reginald Myers, as "cooks and candlestick-makers." Myers had assembled them himself from among men he had found at Hagaru-ri. Many had not held a gun since their basic training, but Myers turned them into a fighting force on the spot. They caught the spirit, and fortunately for everyone concerned, the Chinese didn't know they weren't battle-hardened soldiers. Meyers kept up the appearance by running up and down the line shouting encouragement here and advice there. Their casualties were heavy, and by the time they reached the top of the hill, their original strength of 275 men had been reduced to seventy-five. But they took the hill and held it through the night until Sitter's men arrived.

Experience usually makes all the difference on a battlefield. And there was plenty of it backing up a brand-new fighting force in Korea, the United States Air Force. Many of the pilots who flew into the Korean fight had gained their skills in World War II. But in those days, their heroism was rewarded with the army's Medal of Honor. When it became a separate branch of the armed forces in 1947, the air force still used the army's medal, but in 1965, a new design was created just for fliers. Like the army's Medal of Honor, it has a five-pointed star with oak leaf-filled arms and a green wreath surrounding it. But the representation of Minerva was replaced with the head of the Statue of Liberty, and the eagle above the star replaced with thunderbolts and wings adapted from the air force's new coat of arms. The medal itself, suspended from a blue silk ribbon as are the army and navy versions, is about half again as big as the other two. Four of them were awarded for service in Korea. All of them were posthumous.

The first was earned by Major George Davis, who had won the Distinguished Flying Cross in World War II and had been made commanding officer of the 334th Fighter Squadron of the Fourth Fighter Group. Davis, like the other fliers in Korea, was among the first to fly jet aircraft in combat, but he handled his F-86 Sabrejet as though he had been flying it all his life. In less than a month he shot down nine MIG fighters and three bombers and earned his second Distinguished Flying Cross. In February 1952 Davis was leading a patrol flight near the Manchurian border when his leader ran out of oxygen and was forced to turn back along with his wingman. Almost as soon as they disappeared over the horizon, Davis spotted a dozen MIGs heading toward a sector where he knew American bombers were attacking. After positioning his two remaining planes, he dove on the MIG formation, destroying one of them in his first pass. The enemy planes unleashed their firepower on him, but he pressed on, downing a second minutes later. As he was honing in on a third, he himself was hit and crashed into a mountainside. But his attack broke up the formation and allowed the bombers time to complete their mission.

The battle took place in an area known as MIG Alley, just south of the Chinese border. American pilots were forbidden to engage the enemy in Chinese airspace, and most of the action took place in the relatively small strip between the Yalu River and the Yellow Sea. But not all the air battles were dog fights between jet fighters. Captain John Walmsley of the Eighth Bombardment Squadron, Third Bomb Group was flying a B-26 on the night of September 14, 1951 in a mission to develop new tactics, when he saw an enemy supply train below him. Taking advantage of the situation, he attacked and before his ammunition was exhausted, and the train was disabled. He radioed for another B-26 and then guided it to the target with his plane's searchlight. The light made him a perfect target for enemy anti-aircraft fire, but he flew in low over the train without taking any evasive action. The following plane completely destroyed the supply train, but the enemy guns brought down Walmsley's aircraft, which crashed into the mountains.

The war dragged on for nearly two more years after that until a truce ended it on July 27, 1953. A dozen weeks earlier, President Dwight D. Eisenhower announced at a press conference that the United States had given $60 million to France to help fight another war to protect its colonial interests in another corner of Asia. Few Americans noticed or even cared.

BALANCING THE DOMINOES

When he approved the funds to help France maintain its toehold in the region it had conquered in 1884, President Eisenhower said that if French Indochina was lost to the forces of communism, all of Southeast Asia would fall "like a set of dominoes." Exactly one year to the day after he said it, on May 8, 1954, the French were defeated by Ho Chi Minh's Vietminh guerillas at Dien Bien Phu and the French domino came crashing down. The name of Vietnam slowly but inexorably became burned into American consciousness. But it would be another ten years before America knew it was at war again.

The first Medal of Honor winner in Vietnam was Captain Roger Donlon, commander of a Green Beret outfit sent to Nam Dong in 1964 as advisors to a unit of the army of Vietnam. As advisors, Donlon's unit was technically not permitted to give orders nor to lead men into combat. But in practice they were doing most of the fighting themselves, and when the Vietcong launched a pre-dawn attack on their camp they had their work cut out for them. The first round of mortar fire set their mess hall ablaze, and the flames quickly reached the command post. As Donlon fought the fire and tried to rally the Vietnamese soldiers, his own men manned defensive mortars, hurled hand grenades and fired rifles at the enemy, who had their camp surrounded. When a demolition team breeched the main gate, Captain Donlon raced through a hail of exploding grenades and killed them. On his way from there to a mortar position, he took a hit in the stomach, but made his destination in spite of it. Then, as he was helping a wounded man from the gunpit, an exploding shell hit him in the shoulder. But still he kept going, carried an abandoned mortar to a new location, applied first aid to the wounded men he found there and then went on to move a recoilless rifle to a new position. Then, as he was carrying ammunition to the gunners, he was hit a third time and sustained a leg wound. Throughout the five-hour battle, Donlon ignored his wounds and continued moving from position to position, hurling hand grenades at the enemy and shouting encouragement to his men. Just before daylight, he was wounded again. But the battle was over and the enemy was in retreat. One hundred fifty-four Vietcong had been killed, compared to nine American casualties. It would have been hard to convince anyone who was there that night that America was not at war. That would come a month later.

On August 2, 1964, the U.S. Navy destroyer *Maddox* was attacked by North Vietnamese PT boats off the coast of Vietnam. Two days later, she was joined in the Gulf of Tonkin by a second destroyer *Turner Joy* . When they saw

blips on their radar, they opened fire into the darkness, not sure what caused the blips, nor whether any of their shells hit any unseen target. In retaliation for the incident, President Lyndon Johnson ordered air strikes against the communist PT boat bases and secured congressional endorsement allowing him to order more such strikes. Six months later, on February 2, 1965, a Vietcong attack on a combat aviation base near Pleiku resulted in the first American attack in North Vietnamese territory. Involvement came slowly after that, limited largely to air strikes and defensive action by the Green Berets in outposts in the Central Highlands. Then on March 29, 1965, a car bomb exploded outside the American Embassy in Saigon and a few days later, there were more than twenty-seven thousand American fighting men in Vietnam. The restraints

had been removed and they weren't considered advisors any longer.

Marine Corps Second Lieutenant Frank Reasoner's company was assigned to a routine patrol of the area near the airbase at Da Nang when the five-man point team he was leading was cut off by an attack by a large group of Vietcong. The fury of the enemy fire made it impossible for the main body to come to the advance party's aid, but Reasoner deployed his five men and directed their fire to hold back the attack. Their radio operator was wounded and became a convenient target for the enemy who directed their fire on him as he crawled toward cover. Reasoner rushed toward the wounded man through thick machine gun fire and was himself killed in the attempt. But he had inspired his men, who continued fighting for another half

Ho Chi Minh, Premier of North Vietnam, was still largely unknown in America when he made an official visit (previous pages) to Poland in 1957.

Vietnam became a shooting war for Americans when the U.S. destroyer Maddox (left) was attacked without provocation by North Vietnamese PT boats in the Gulf of Tonkin in 1964.

Within days of the so-called "Tonkin Incident," American leathernecks were dodging mortar fire in foxholes and would continue to do so for many years. In September 1967, the marines (right) were defending Con Thien, a key link in the 5,500-man line holding back the North Vietnamese invasion troops.

Outside the U.S. Special Forces camp at Ben Het, in June 1969, a GI bandages a wounded colleague's head, while keeping an eye out for the enemy. Of the thousands of acts of heroism in Vietnam, some would be remembered only by those men whose lives were saved by their buddies.

On September 12, 1972, an allied airstrike in support of government troops caused havoc inside the Citadel at Quang Tri, South Vietnam. None of the men and women who served in Vietnam can forget the death and destruction that rained down around them almost without stop.

Helicopters were used extensively in Vietnam, and, for the first time in American military history, television cameramen were on hand to cover every detail of the war, including repair jobs, for the evening news. The helicopter is being repaired by U.S. soldiers following an accidental raid in 1967 by two U.S. F-4 phantom jets on the government-controlled village of Lang Vie.

Cameramen provided television viewers with graphic pictures throughout the Vietnam War, including the crash, and subsequent rescue of the crew, of a helicopter that crashed during an attempted landing on the carrier, U.S.S. Blue Ridge. *The incident occurred at the time of the final U.S. evacuation from South Vietnam in 1975.*

hour, finally defeating the enemy who had them outnumbered by almost ten to one.

After the fury of the communist Tet Offensive in 1968, it was painfully apparent that this war was different than any the Americans had seen before. The enemy was spread out in the countryside and hidden in the jungles, attacking suddenly and disappearing quickly. Sustained action was rare, but on May 1, 1968, two marine companies were battered by a Vietcong regiment near the village of Dai Do and the battle to rescue them lasted five days. Two Marine officers won Medals of Honor during the action.

Two companies of marines were sent on riverboats to regain control of the village, and were pounded by heavy fire before they landed. As Company G, led by Captain Jay Vargas, moved across the open fields toward the village, Bravo Company, on their flank, took the brunt of the fire and most of its officers were killed. An inexperienced man was left in charge and panicked, shouting into his radio that he was going to withdraw. Vargas, realized that a Bravo retreat would endanger his own men, got on the radio himself and soothed the officer down and led both companies into a successful battle that drove the Vietcong into range of American gunboats nearby. But the enemy counterattacked and pushed the marines out of the village, forcing them to take cover in a cemetery, where they pulled corpses from new graves to improvise foxholes. They were surrounded as night fell, and Vargas ordered his men to stay low and shoot anything that moved. They made it through the night, and when the sun came up, Vargas made contact with another company commanded by Captain James Livingston and together they retook the village.

But they had no sooner established themselves among the burned-out houses than the Vietcong came back for more. The marines were low on ammunition and the battle was reduced to hand-to-hand combat. Vargas was hit by shrapnel, his third wound in the fight, but he kept on going. When a fellow officer was wounded a few hours later, he carried him on his back to the safety of a nearby rice paddy, but on the way he was challenged by a Vietcong soldier. Vargas killed him with his pistol and kept moving. It was his first trip to the medics that day, but before the sun set, he carried six more wounded men to safety, returning the battle each time in spite of his own wounds, and killing eight more enemy soldiers in the process. By the end of the day, the Vietcong had lost eight hundred men. They also lost the town of Dai Do.

Captain Livingston's company concentrated on the targets of heaviest resistance during the battle. Livingston

As the Vietnam War dragged on, the face of Premier Ho Chi Minh (left), which many Americans would not have recognized when he became the new ruler of several million Indo-Chinese in 1954, became as familiar to them as that of President Lyndon Johnson.

The face of the Vietcong, such as this suspect (right), captured near Da Nang in South Vietnam on August 5, 1970, became familiar to Americans, too, and it made many of them uneasy about the war.

The Vietnam War provided America with moments of inspiration, too, in the faces of men like Medal of Honor winner, Father Charles J. Watters, a chaplain who bravely ministered to wounded men under fire in the battle for Dak To, despite being unarmed himself. He was killed by friendly fire during the same battle.

was wounded twice, but refused to leave the assault, personally leading his men to the destruction of more than one hundred enemy bunkers. When he was wounded a third time, he couldn't walk any more, but still he refused to be carried out of the line of fire until he had redeployed his men and made sure that all the casualties were evacuated.

The Americans in Vietnam were contained within the Vietnamese borders, which gave the enemy sanctuary behind them. Usually they vanished through the jungle, but in November 1967 the Vietcong decided to make a stand just a few miles from the Cambodian border. The battle for a hill near Dak To lasted four days.

The job of taking the hill fell to the men of the 173d Airborne Brigade, an outfit that included machine gunner Private First Class Carlos Lozada. He was part of a four-man early warning squad positioned several yards from the main line. They had no sooner established themselves when they were attacked by a horde of enemy soldiers. Lozada spotted them coming first and began firing. He broke up the advance by killing twenty of the enemy. His buddies shouted at him to take cover during the lull but Lozada turned a deaf ear to them and kept on firing. At the same time, the enemy launched an attack in another quarter in an effort to cut off a nearby company from its battalion, and Lozada decided it was up to him to stop them. He was surrounded on three sides but stayed behind his gun. He was killed in the attempt, but his fire covered the American retreat, and four days later the men he had saved took the hill.

Many of the Medal of Honor citations that summarize the heroism of men like Carlos Lozada report that their actions had inspired the men around them. Some men on the battlefield are charged with little more than providing inspiration. They are the chaplains. Over the years seven of them have won Medals of Honor. Of the three who won them in Vietnam, Father Charles Watters earned his in the battle for Dak To. Chaplain Watters was with a company that was attacked suddenly with unusually heavy casualties, and though unarmed, he rushed forward in the face of heavy fire to give aid to the wounded and to help in moving them to safety. When the paratroopers pulled back for a counterattack, he was ministering to a fallen man and stayed in place to help even more wounded even though he was exposed to fire from both sides by then. When he was ordered back, he noticed even more wounded, and in spite of pleas from the officers and men around him, he went forward three more times to help the wounded. Once he was satisfied that all the injured men were safe, he began

assisting the medics and delivered food and water to his men. He was killed by friendly fire during a last-ditch assault that brought death to nearly fifty other men, including the entire company command.

There were fifteen Medals of Honor awarded to navy men during the 1960s. But one of them was for action on the other side of the world from Vietnam. The Pentagon had ordered the U.S.S. *Liberty,* loaded with sophisticated electronic monitoring devices, to gather intelligence from both sides during the Six Day War between Israel and her Arab neighbors.

When Israeli planes spotted the *Liberty*, an order was prepared to get the ship out of the area. But in spite of the fact that the ship was loaded to the gunwales with communications equipment, the order was never received and the ship continued cruising toward the Sinai Peninsula where the battle was raging. When she got within sight of land, three Israeli Mirage fighters dropped from the sky and began firing. The American gunners were shot before they could respond, then two more Israeli jets appeared, spraying the *Liberty's* decks with napalm. Eight men were killed in as many minutes, and the commander of the American Vessel, William McGonagle, was hit by shrapnel. In spite of his wound, Commander McGonagle stayed on the bridge for the next seventeen hours. The jets had no sooner flown off than three Israeli PT boats appeared on the scene and began firing. One of their torpedoes found its mark, completely disabling the ship and knocking out her communications system. At that point, one of the Israeli boats signaled "Do you need help?" Though his ship was dead in the water, McGonagle signaled back, "Go to hell!" By then thirty-four of his men were dead.

They finally managed to get the ship moving again and the commander stayed at his post in spite of his wound until they were able to make contact with an American destroyer and transferred the dead and wounded. The Israelis later said that they thought they had been attacking an Egyptian freighter. Possibly because of an official apology, Commander McGonagle's Medal of Honor citation describes the attack but not the attackers, simply stating that the incident took place in "international waters, Eastern Mediterranean."

In other times, Vietnam may have been a popular resort, but in the Mekong Delta in 1966, taking a dip wasn't anybody's idea of a good time. As the war grew ever tougher in South Vietnam, an allied operation was launched along the Cambodian border in the Mekong Delta, in which the 173rd U.S. Airborne Brigade was supported by groups from Australia and New Zealand.

In October 1966, the marines began a fifteen-mile sweep south of Da Nang.

129

POSTSCRIPT

The last Medal of Honor awarded to an American fighting man was presented by President Ronald Reagan on February 24, 1981. In spite of the rule that no recommendation for the medal can be considered more than two years after the event, the rule was lifted in the case of Master Sergeant Roy Benavidez and the presentation took place thirteen years after his incredible action at Loc Ninh on May 2, 1968.

Benavidez was at a forward operating base at Loc Ninh supporting a special forces team on an intelligence-gathering mission inside Cambodia. When they ran into heavy enemy fire, they called for helicopters to get them out, but none of the three Hueys could land through the heavy fire they encountered. When they went back to the base to get help for wounded crew members, Benavidez left his radio post and boarded one of the helicopters as it was taking off for a second try. The enemy fire was even heavier when they got back into the battle zone and Sergeant Benavidez jumped from the helicopter, saying he was going to try to reach the trapped men on foot, and would direct the helicopters from the ground.

As he ran toward them, he was hit several times, but kept moving. When he reached the trapped team, he found four of them dead, including the leader. Taking classified documents from the leader's body, he positioned the survivors for the helicopter pickup, dragging and carrying the wounded in spite of his own multiple wounds. Then he marked the position with smoke cannisters and provided protective fire by running alongside the helicopter as it picked up the men. At that moment, the pilot was hit and the helicopter crashed, and Benavidez was hit in the abdomen by small arms fire and in the back by grenade fragments. Still he kept going. Pulling the wounded from the burning Huey, he guided the survivors to a defensive line and then distributed water and ammunition to them. Then he got on his radio to call in air support and guide the fire of nearby gunships, which suppressed the enemy fire and made another helicopter rescue attempt possible.

As the rescue ships hovered over the area, eight of them were shot down, but finally, more than eight hours after the first call for help had gone out, one got close enough to pick up the men. As Benavidez was helping them on board, he was struck from behind by an enemy soldier and when he turned to face his enemy, he saw a bayonet inches from his stomach. He grabbed the blade and deflected the blow, and then stabbed the man, turning back to continue the rescue mission. Before all the men were safely aboard the aircraft, Benavidez was attacked twice more and both times killed

130

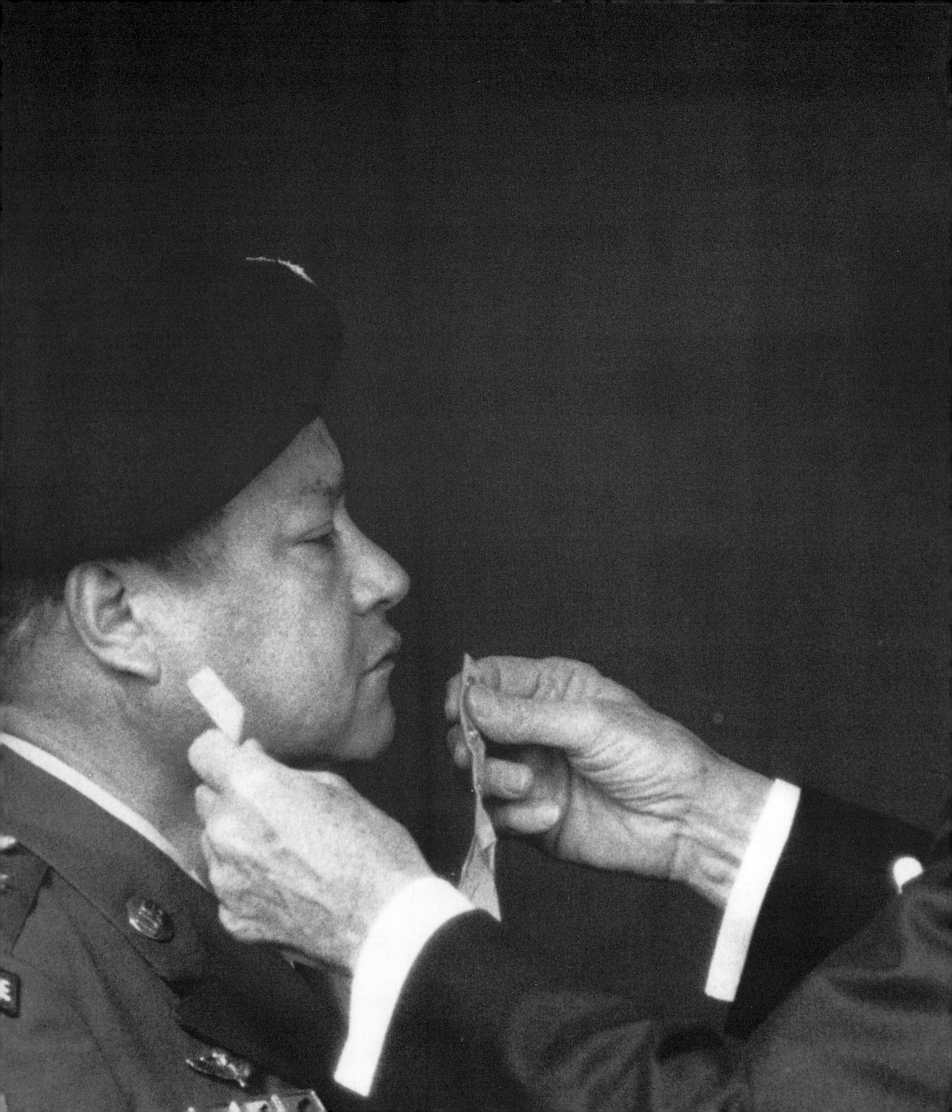

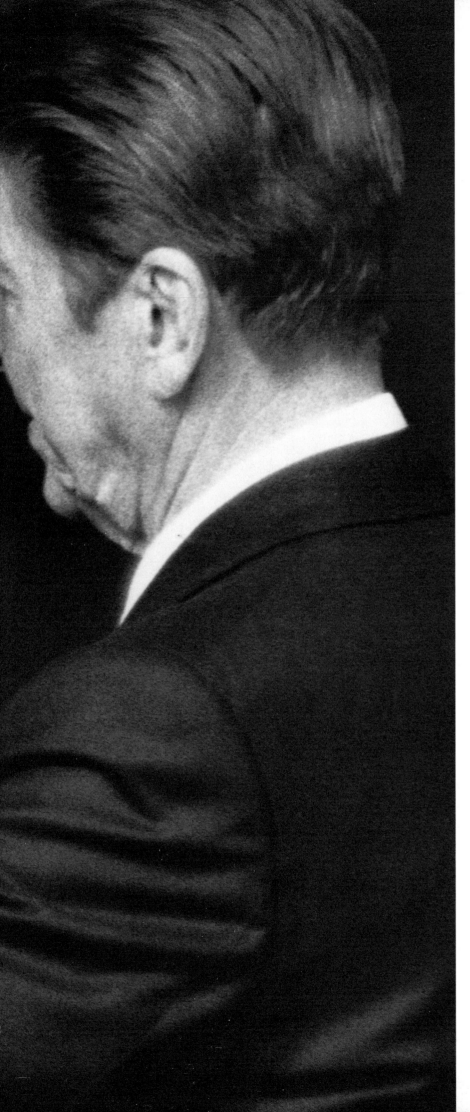

his attackers. He was the last man aboard the helicopter as it began its flight back to Loc Ninh, and because of his total exhaustion and loss of blood, wasn't able to move when they landed behind the American lines. He was pronounced dead, in fact, and possibly would have been buried if he hadn't summoned up enough strength to spit in the face of the doctor who had certified him a dead man. He was flown from there to a hospital, and that was the last any of the men he had saved saw of him. Among those who knew he had left Loc Ninh alive, nobody thought he had a ghost of a chance of survival. His commanding officer recommended him for a Distinguished Service Cross, and Sergeant Benavidez became a legendary memory among the men of the special forces.

But he didn't die. It took long months to recover, to be sure, and the Vietnam War was long over before he was discharged with an eighty percent disability and some memories of his own. When one of his men found out that he was alive, he submitted a recommendation for the Medal of Honor for his former sergeant. But the rules require that any recommendation needs the backing of at least two eyewitnesses. There were men who could confirm that he had boarded the helicopter bound for Cambodia, but as far as anyone could tell, all the men he saved had since died. The case was closed until a newspaper account of it reached the one man of the eight rescued that day who was still alive. His testimony made the awarding of the Medal of Honor possible.

It is possible that there may never be another winner of the Medal of Honor. Winning one requires actual combat with an enemy. No one who wears the medal, nor any of the American people who have proudly honored them, wants that to happen again.

GLOSSARY

Adj.	Adjutant
Adm.	Admiral
BM	Boatswain's Mate
Brig. Gen.	Brigadier General
CB	Chief Boatswain's Mate
CWO	Chief Warrant Officer
Capt.	Captain
Cmdr.	Commander
Col.	Colonel
Comm.	Commissary
Cpl.	Corporal
GM	Gunner's Mate
Gen.	General
Gy. Sgt.	Gunnery Sergeant
LCpl.	Lance Corporal
Lman	Landsman
Lt.	Lieutenant
Lt. (j.g.)	Lieutenant (junior grade)
Maj.	Major
MSgt.	Master Sergeant
NOR	Place of action not on record
Ord. Sman	Ordinary Seaman
Pfc.	Private First Class
Pvt.	Private
QG	Quarter Gunner
Reg'tal	Regimental
QM	Quartermaster
SQM	Signal Quartermaster
SSgt.	Staff Sergeant
Sfc.	Sergeant First Class
Sgt.	Sergeant
Sman	Seaman
Sp4c/5c	Specialist Fourth Class/Fifth Class

*** posthumous award**
+ second award (first award earned in earlier conflict)

THE CIVIL WAR
1861–1865

ARMY

Adams, Pvt. James F. (Nineveh, Va)
Adams, 2d Lt. John G. B. (Fredericksburg, Va)
Alber, Pvt. Frederick (Spotsylvania, Va)
Albert, Pvt. Christian (Vicksburg, Miss)
Allen Cpl. Abner P. (Petersburg, Va)
Allen, Pvt. James (South Mountain, Md)
Allen, Cpl. Nathaniel M. (Gettysburg, Pa)
Ames, 1st Lt. Adelbert (Bull Run, Va)
Ammerman, Pvt. Robert W. (Spotsylvania, Va)
Anderson, Pvt. Bruce (Fort Fisher, NC)
Anderson, Pvt. Charles W. (Waynesboro, Va)
Anderson, Sgt. Everett W. (Crosby's Creek, Tenn)
Anderson, Pvt. Frederick C. (Weldon Railroad, Va)
Anderson, Capt. Marion T. (Nashville, Tenn)
Anderson, Pvt. Peter (Bentonville, NC)
Anderson, Cpl. Thomas (Appomattox Station, Va)
Apple, Cpl. Andrew O. (Petersburg, Va)
Appleton, 1st Lt. William H. (Petersburg & New Market Heights, Va)
Archer, 1st Lt. & Adj. James W. (Corinth, Miss)
*Archer, Sgt. Lester (Fort Harrison, Va)
Archinal, Cpl. William (Vicksburg, Miss)
Armstrong, Pvt. Clinton L. (Vicksburg, Miss)
Arnold, Capt. Abraham K. (Davenport Bridge, Va)
Avery Lt. William B. (Tranter's Creek, NC)
Ayers, Sgt. David (Vicksburg, Miss)
Ayers, Pvt. John G. K. (Vicksburg, Miss)
Babcock, Sgt. William J. (Petersburg, Va)
*Bacon, Pvt. Elijah W. (Gettysburg, Pa)
Baird, Brig. Gen. Absalom (Jonesboro, Ga)
Baldwin, Capt. Frank D. (Peach Tree Creek, Ga)
Ballen, Pvt. Frederick (Vicksburg, Miss)
Banks, Sgt. George L. (Missionary Ridge, Tenn)
Barber, Cpl. James A. (Petersburg. Va)
Barker, Sgt. Nathaniel C. (Spotsylvania, Va)
Barnes, Pvt. William H. (Chapin's Farm, Va)
Barnum, Col. Henry A. (Chattanooga, Tenn)
Barrell, 1st Lt. Charles L. (Camden, SC)
Barrick, Cpl. Jesse T. (Duck River, Tenn)
Barringer, Pvt. William H. (Vicksburg, Miss)
Barry, Sgt. Maj. Augustus (NOR)
Batchelder, Lt. Col. & Chief QM Richard N. (Catlett-Fairfax Stations, Va)
Bates, Col. Delavan (Cemetery Hill, Va)
Bates, Sgt. Norman F. (Columbus, Ga)
Baybutt, Pvt. Philip (Luray, Va)
Beatty, Capt. Alexander M. (Cold Harbor, Va)
Beaty, 1st Sgt. Powhatan (Chapin's Farm, Va)
Beaufort, Cpl. Jean J. (Port Hudson, La)
Beaumont, Maj. & Asst. Adj. Gen. Eugene B. (Harpeth River, Tenn & Selma, Ala)
Bebb, Pvt. Edward J. (Columbus, Ga)
Beckwith, Pvt. Wallace A. (Fredericksburg, Va)
Beddows, Pvt. Richard (Spotsylvania, Va)
Beebe, 1st Lt. William S. (Cane River Crossing, La)
Beech, Sgt. John P. (Spotsylvania Courthouse, Va)
*Begley, Sgt. Terrence (Cold Harbor, Va)
Belcher, Pvt. Thomas (Chapin's Farm, Va)
Bell, Sgt. James B. (Missionary Ridge, Tenn)
Benedict, 2nd Lt. George G. (Gettysburg, Pa)
Benjamin, Cpl. John F. (Sayler's Creek, Va)
Benjamin, 1st Lt. Samuel N. (Bull Run-Spotsylvania, Va)
Bennett, Pvt. Orren (Sayler's Creek, Va)
Bennett, 1st Lt. Orson W. (Honey Hill, SC)
Bensinger, Pvt. William (Georgia)
Benyaurd, 1st Lt. William H. H. (Five Forks, Va)
Betts, Lt. Col. Charles M. (Greensboro, NC)
Beyer, 2d Lt. Hillary (Antietam, Md)
Bickford, Cpl. Henry H. (Waynesboro, Va)
Bickford, Cpl. Matthew (Vicksburg, Miss)
Bieger, Pvt. Charles (Ivy Farm, Miss)
Bingham, Capt. Henry H. (Wilderness, Va)
Birdsall, Sgt. Horatio L. (Columbus, Ga)
Bishop, Pvt. Francis A. (Spotsylvania, Va)
Black, Lt. Col. John C. (Prairie Grove, Ark)
Black, Capt. William P. (Pea Ridge, Ark)
Blackmar, Lt. Wilmon W. (Five Forks, Va)
Blackwood, Surgeon William R. D. (Petersburg. Va)
Blasdel, Pvt. Thomas A. (Vicksburg. Miss)
Blickensderfer, Cpl. Milton (Petersburg, Va)
Bliss, Capt. George N. (Waynesboro, Va)
Bliss, Col. Zenas R. (Fredericksburg, Va)
Blodgett, 1st Lt. Wells H. (Newtonia, Mo)
Blucher, Cpl. Charles (Fort Harrison, Va)
Blunt, 1st Lt. John W. (Cedar Creek, Va)
Boehm, 2d Lt. Peter M. (Dinwiddie Courthouse, Va)
Bonebrake, Lt. Henry G. (Five Forks, Va)
Bonnaffon, 1st Lt. Sylvester, Jr. (Boydton Plank Road, Va)
Boody, Cpl. Robert (Williamsburg & Chancellorsville, Va)
Boon, Capt. Hugh P. (Sayler's Creek, Va)
Boquet, Pvt. Nicholas (Wilson's Creek, Mo)
Boss, Cpl. Orlando (Cold Harbor, Va)
Bourke, Pvt. John G. (Stone River, Tenn)
Boury, Sgt. Richard (Charlottesville, Va)
Boutwell, Pvt. John W. (Petersburg, Va)
Bowen, Cpl. Chester B. (Winchester, Va)
Bowen, Pvt. Emmer (Vicksburg, Miss)
Box, Capt. Thomas J. (Resaca, Ga)
Boynton, Lt. Col. Henry V. (Missionary Ridge, Tenn)
Bradley, Sgt. Thomas W. (Chancellorsville, Va)
Brady, Pvt. James (Chapin's Farm, Va)
Brandle, Pvt. Joseph E. (Lenoire, Tenn)
Brannigan, Pvt. Felix (Chancellorsville, Va)
Brant, Lt. William (Petersburg, Va)
Bras, Sgt. Edgar A. (Spanish Fort, Ala)
Brest, Pvt. Lewis F. (Sayler's Creek, Va)
Brewer, Pvt. William J. (Appomattox, Va)
Breyer, Sgt. Charles (Rappahannock Station, Va)
Briggs, Cpl. Elijah A. (Petersburg, Va)
Bringle, Cpl. Andrew (Sayler's Creek, Va)
Bronner, Pvt. August F. (White Oak Swamp, Va)
Bronson, 1st Sgt. James H. (Chapin's Farm, Va)
Brosnan, Sgt. John (Petersburg, Va)
Brouse, Capt. Charles W. (Missionary Ridge, Tenn)
Brown, Sgt. Charles (Weldon Railroad, Va)
Brown, Cpl. Edward, Jr. (Fredericksburg & Salem Heights, Va)
Brown, Sgt. Henri L. (Wilderness, Va)
Brown, Capt. Jeremiah Z. (Petersburg, Va)
Brown, 1st Sgt. John H. (Vicksburg, Miss)
Brown, Capt. John H. (Franklin, Tenn)
*Brown, Capt. Morris, Jr. (Gettysburg, Pa)
Brown, Pvt. Robert B. (Missionary Ridge, Tenn)
Brown, Pvt. Uriah (Vicksburg, Miss)
Brown, Pvt. Wilson W. (Georgia)
Brownell, Pvt. Francis E. (Alexandria, Va)
Bruner, Pvt. Louis J. (Walker's Ford, Tenn)
Brush, Lt. George W. (Ashepoo River, SC)
Bruton, Capt. Christopher C. (Waynesboro, Va)
Bryant, Sgt. Andrew S. (New Bern, NC)
*Buchanan, Pvt. George A. (Chapin's Farm, Va)
Buck, Cpl. F. Clarence (Chapin's Farm, Va)
Buckingham, 1st Lt. David E. (Rowanty Creek, Va)
Buckles, Sgt. Abram J. (Wilderness, Va)
Buckley, Pvt. Denis (Peach Tree Creek, Ga)
Buckley, Sgt. John C. (Vicksburg, Miss)
Bucklyn, 1st Lt. John K. (Chancellorsville, Va)
Buffington, Sgt. John E. (Petersburg, Va)
Buffum, Pvt. Robert (Georgia)
Buhrman, Pvt. Henry G. (Vicksburg, Miss)
Bumgarner, Sgt. William (Vicksburg, Miss)
Burbank, Sgt. James H. (Blackwater, Va)
Burger, Pvt. Joseph (Nolensville, Tenn)
Burk, Pvt. E. Michael (Spotsylvania, Va)
Burk, Sgt. Thomas (Wilderness, Va)
Burke, 1st Sgt. Daniel W. (Shepherdstown Ford, Va)
Burke, Pvt. Thomas M. (Hanover Courthouse, Va)
Burns, Sgt. James M. (New Market, Va)
Burritt, Pvt. William W. (Vicksburg, Miss)
Butterfield, Brig. Gen. Daniel (Gaines's Mill, Va)
Butterfield, 1st Lt. Frank G. (Salem Heights, Va)
Cadwallader, Cpl. Abel G. (Hatcher's Run & Dabney's Mills, Va)
Cadwell, Sgt. Luman L. (Alabama Bayou, La)
Caldwell, Sgt. Daniel (Hatcher's Run, Va)
Calkin, 1st Sgt. Ivers S. (Sayler's Creek, Va)
Callahan, Pvt. John H. (Fort Blakely, Ala)
Camp, Pvt. Carlton N. (Petersburg, Va)
Campbell, Pvt. James A. (Woodstock & Amelia Courthouse, Va)
Campbell, Pvt. William (Vicksburg, Miss)
Capehart, Maj. Charles E. (Monterey Mountain, Pa)
Capehart, Col. Henry (Greenbrier River, W Va)
*Capron, Sgt. Horace, Jr. (Chickahominy & Ashland, Va)
Carey, Sgt. Hugh (Gettysburg, Pa)
Carey, Sgt. James L. (Appomattox Courthouse, Va)
Carlisle, Pvt. Casper R. (Gettysburg, Pa)
Carman, Pvt. Warren (Waynesboro, Va)
Carmin, Cpl. Isaac H. (Vicksburg, Miss)
Carney, Sgt. William H. (Fort Wagner, SC)
Carr, Col. Eugene A. (Pea Ridge, Ark)
Carr, Cpl. Franklin (Nashville, Tenn)
Carson, Musician William J. (Chickamauga, Ga)
Cart, Pvt. Jacob (Fredericksburg, Va)
Carter, 2d Lt. John J. (Antietam, Md)
Carter, Capt. Joseph F. (Fort Stedman, Va)
Caruana, Pvt. Orlando E. (New Bern, NC & S. Mountain, Md)
Casey, Pvt. David (Cold Harbor, Va)
Casey, Pvt. Henry (Vicksburg, Miss)
Catlin, Col. Isaac S. (Petersburg, Va)
Cayer, Sgt. Ovila (Weldon Railroad, Va)
Chamberlain, Col. Joshua L. (Gettysburg, Pa)
Chamberlain, 2d Lt. Orville T. (Chickamauga, Ga)
Chambers, Pvt. Joseph B. (Petersburg, Va)
Chandler, Sgt. Henry F. (Petersburg, Va)
Chandler, QM Sgt. Stephen E. (Amelia Springs, Va)
Chapin, Pvt. Alaric B. (Fort Fisher, NC)
Chapman, Pvt. John (Sayler's Creek, Va)
Chase, Pvt. John F. (Chancellorsville, Va)
Child, Cpl. Benjamin H. (Antietam, Md)
Chisman, Pvt. William W. (Vicksburg, Miss)
Christiancy, 1st Lt. James I. (Hawes's Shops, Pa)
Churchill, Cpl. Samuel J. (Nashville, Tenn)
Cilley, Capt. Clinton A. (Chickamauga, Ga)
Clancy, Sgt. James T. (Vaughn Road, Va)
Clapp, 1st Sgt. Albert A. (Sayler's Creek, Va)
Clark, Lt. & Adj. Charles A. (Brook's Ford, Va)
Clark, Cpl. Harrison (Gettysburg, Pa)
Clark, Pvt. James G. (Petersburg, Va)
Clark, 1st Lt. & Reg'tal QM John W. (Warrenton, Va)
Clark, Cpl. William A. (Nolensville, Tenn)
Clarke, Capt. Dayton P. (Spotsylvania, Va)
Clausen, 1st Lt. Charles H. (Spotsylvania, Va)
Clay, Capt. Cecil (Fort Harrison, Va)
Cleveland, Pvt. Charles F. (Antietam, Md)
Clopp, Pvt. John E. (Gettysburg, Pa)
Clute, Cpl. George W. (Bentonville, NC)
Coates. Sgt. Jefferson (Gettysburg, Pa)
Cockley, 1st Lt. David L. (Waynesboro, Ga)
Coey, Maj. James (Hatcher's Run, Va)
Coffey, Sgt. Robert J. (Bank's Ford, Va)
Cohn, Sgt. Maj. Abraham (Wilderness, Va)
Colby, Sgt. Carlos W. (Vicksburg, Miss)
Cole, Cpl. Gabriel (Winchester, Va)
Collins, Cpl. Harrison (Richland Creek, Tenn)
Collins, Sgt. Thomas D. (Resaca, Ga)
Collis, Col. Charles H. T. (Fredericksburg, Va)
Colwell, 1st Lt. Oliver (Nashville, Tenn)
Compson, Maj. Hartwell B. (Waynesboro, Va)
Conaway, Pvt. John W. (Vicksburg, Miss)
Conboy, Sgt. Martin (Williamsburg, Va)
Connell, Cpl. Trustrim (Sayler's Creek, Va)
Conner, Pvt. Richard (Bull Run, Va)
Connors, Pvt. James (Fisher's Hill, Va)
Cook, Bugler John (Antietam, Md)
Cook, Sgt. John H. (Pleasant Hill, La)
Cooke, Capt. Walter H. (Bull Run, Va)
Copp, 2d Lt. Charles D. (Fredericksburg, Va)
Corcoran, Pvt. John (Petersburg, Va)
Corliss, Capt. George W. (Cedar Mountain, Va)
Corliss, 1st Lt. Stephen P. (South Side Railroad, Va)
Corson, Asst. Surgeon Joseph K. (Bristoe Station, Va)
Cosgriff, Pvt. Richard H. (Columbus, Ga)
Cosgrove, Pvt. Thomas (Drewry's Bluff, Va)
Coughlin, Lt. Col. John (Swift's Creek, Va)
Cox, Cpl. Robert M. (Vicksburg, Miss)
Coyne, Sgt. John H. (Williamsburg, Va)
Cranston, Pvt. William W. (Chancellorsville, Va)
Creed, Pvt. John (Fisher's Hill, Va)
Crocker, Capt. Henry H. (Cedar Creek, Va)
Crocker, Pvt. Ulric L. (Cedar Creek, Va)
Croft, Pvt. James E. (Allatoona, Ga)
Crosier, Sgt. William H. H. (Peach Tree Creek, Ga)
Cross, Cpl. James E. (Blackburn's Ford, Va)
Crowley, Pvt. Michael (Waynesboro, Va)
Cullen, Cpl. Thomas (Bristoe Station, Va)
Cummings, Sgt. Maj. Amos J. (Salem Heights, Va)
Cumpston, Pvt. James M. (Shenandoah Valley, Va)
Cunningham, 1st Sgt. Francis M. (Sayler's Creek, Va)
Cunningham, Pvt. James S. (Vicksburg, Miss)
Curran, Asst. Surgeon Richard (Antietam, Md)
Curtis, Sgt. Maj. John C. (Baton Rouge, La)
Curtis, 2d Lt. Josiah M. (Petersburg, Va)
Curtis, Brig. Gen. Newton M. (Fort Fisher, NC)
Custer, 2d Lt. Thomas W. (Namozine Church, Va)
Second award (Sayler's Creek, Va)
Cutcheon, Maj. Byron M. (Horseshoe Bend, Ky)
Cutts, Capt. James M. (Wilderness, Spotsylvania, & Petersburg, Va)
Darrough, Sgt. John S. (Eastport, Miss)
Davidsizer, Sgt. John A. (Paine's Crossroads, Va)
Davidson, Asst. Surgeon Andrew (Vicksburg, Miss)
Davidson, 1st Lt. Andrew (Petersburg, Va)
Davis, Maj. Charles C. (Shelbyville, Tenn)
Davis, Sgt. Freeman (Missionary Ridge, Tenn)
Davis, 1st Lt. George E. (Monocacy, Md)
Davis, Pvt. Harry (Atlanta, Ga)
Davis, Pvt. John (Culloden, Ga)
Davis, Cpl. Joseph (Franklin, Tenn)
Davis, Sgt. Martin K. (Vicksburg, Miss)
Davis, Pvt. Thomas (Sayler's Creek, Va)
Day, Pvt. Charles (Hatcher's Run, Va)
Day, Pvt. David F. (Vicksburg, Miss)
De Castro, Cpl. Joseph H. (Gettysburg, Pa)
De Lacey, 1st Sgt. Patrick (Wilderness, Va)
De Lavie, Sgt. Hiram H. (Five Forks, Va)
De Puy, 1st Sgt. Charles H. (Petersburg, Va)
De Witt, Cpl. Richard W. (Vicksburg, Miss)
Deane, Maj. John M. (Fort Stedman, Va)
Deland, Pvt. Frederick N. (Port Hudson, La)
Delaney, Sgt. John C. (Dabney's Mills, Va)
Di Cesnola, Col. Louis P. (Aldie, Va)
Dickey, Capt. William D. (Petersburg, Va)
Dickie, Sgt. David (Vicksburg, Miss)
Dilger, Capt. Hubert (Chancellorsville, Va)
Dillon, Pvt. Michael A. (Williamsburg, Va)
Dockum, Pvt. Warren C. (Sayler's Creek, Va)
Dodd, Pvt. Robert F. (Petersburg, Va)
Dodds, Sgt. Edward E. (Ashby's Gap, Va)
Dolloff, Cpl. Charles W. (Petersburg, Va)
Donaldson, Sgt. John (Appomattox Courthouse, Va)
Donoghue, Pvt. Timothy (Fredericksburg, Va)
Doody, Cpl. Patrick (Cold Harbor, Va)
Dore, Sgt. George H. (Gettysburg, Pa)
Dorley, Pvt. August (Mount Pleasant, Ala)
Dorsey, Cpl. Daniel A. (Georgia)
Dorsey, Sgt. Decatur (Petersburg, Va)
Dougall, 1st Lt. & Adj. Allen H. (Bentonville, NC)
Dougherty, Pvt. Michael (Jefferson, Va)
Dow, Sgt. George P. (Richmond, Va)
Downey, Pvt. William (Ashepoo River, SC)
Downs, Sgt. Henry W. (Winchester, Va)
Drake, 2d Lt. James M. (Bermuda Hundred, Va)
Drury, Sgt. James (Weldon Railroad, Va)
Du Pont, Capt. Henry A. (Cedar Creek, Va)
Duffey, Pvt. John (Ashepoo River, SC)
Dunlavy. Pvt. James (Osage, Kans)
Dunne, Cpl. James (Vicksburg, Miss)
Durham, 2d Lt. James R. (Winchester, Va)
Durham, Sgt. John S. (Perryville, Ky)
Eckes, Pvt. John N. (Vicksburg, Miss)
Eddy, Pvt. Samuel E. (Sayler's Creek, Va)
Edgerton, Lt. & Adj. Nathan H. (Chapin's Farm, Va)
Edwards, Pvt. David (Five Forks, Va)
Elliott, Sgt. Alexander (Paine's Crossroads, Va)
Elliott, Sgt. Russell C. (Natchitoches, La)
Ellis, Pvt. Horace (Weldon Railroad, Va)
Ellis, 1st Sgt. William (Dardanelles, Ark)
Ellsworth, Capt. Thomas F. (Honey Hill, SC)
Elson, Sgt. James M. (Vicksburg, Miss)
Embler, Capt. Andrew H. (Boydton Plank Road, Va)
Enderlin, Musician Richard (Gettysburg, Pa)
Engle, Sgt. James E. (Bermuda Hundred, Va)
English, 1st Sgt. Edmund (Wilderness, Va)
Ennis, Pvt. Charles D. (Petersburg, Va)
Estes, Capt. & Asst. Adj. Gen. Lewellyn G. (Flint River, Ga)
Evans, Pvt. Coron D. (Sayler's Creek, Va)
Evans, Capt. Ira H. (Hatcher's Run, Va)
Evans, Pvt. James R. (Wilderness, Va)
Evans. Pvt. Thomas (Piedmont, Va)

Everson, Pvt. Adelbert (Five Forks, Va)
Ewing, Pvt. John C. (Petersburg, Va)
Falconer, Cpl. John A. (Fort Sanders, Tenn)
Fall, Sgt. Charles S. (Spotsylvania Courthouse, Va)
Fallon, Pvt. Thomas T. (Williamsburg, Va)
*Falls, Color Sgt. Benjamin F. (Geggysburg, Pa)
Fanning, Pvt. Nicholas (Selma, Ala)
Farnsworth, Sgt. Maj. Herbert E. (Trevilian Station, Va)
Farquhar, Sgt. Maj. John M. (Stone River, Tenn)
Fasnacht, Sgt. Charles H. (Spotsylvania, Va)
Fassett, Capt. John B. (Gettysburg, Pa)
Fernald, 1st Lt. Albert E. (Five Forks, Va)
Ferrier, Sgt. Daniel T. (Varnell's Station, Ga)
Ferris, 1st Lt. & Adj. Eugene W. (Berryville, Va)
Fesq, Pvt. Frank (Petersburg, Va)
Finkenbiner, Pvt. Henry S. (Dingle's Mill, SC)
Fisher, 1st Lt. John H. (Vicksburg, Miss)
Fisher, Cpl. Joseph (Petersburg, Va)
Flanagan, Sgt. Augustin (Chapin's Farm, Va)
Flannigan, Pvt. James (Nolensville, Tenn)
Fleetwood, Sgt. Maj. Christian A. (Chapin's Farm, Va)
Flynn, Cpl. Christopher (Gettysburg, Pa)
Flynn, Sgt. James E. (Vicksburg, Miss)
Follett, Sgt. Joseph L. (New Madrid, Mo & Stone River, Tenn)
Force, Brig. Gen. Manning F. (Atlanta, Ga)
Ford, 1st Lt. George W. (Sayler's Creek, Va)
Forman, Cpl. Alexander A. (Fair Oaks, Va)
Fout, 2d Lt. Frederick W. (Harper's Ferry, W Va)
Fox, Sgt. Henry (Jackson, Tenn)
Fox, Sgt. Henry M. (Winchester, Va)
Fox, Pvt. Nicholas (Port Hudson, La)
Fox, Pvt. William R. (Petersburg, Va)
Frantz, Pvt. Joseph (Vicksburg, Miss)
Fraser, Pvt. William W. (Vicksburg, Miss)
Freeman, Pvt. Archibald (Spotsylvania, Va)
Freeman, 1st Lt. Henry B. (Stone River, Tenn)
Freeman, Pvt. William H. (Fort Fisher, NC)
French, Pvt. Samuel S. (Fair Oaks, Va)
Frey, Cpl. Franz (Vicksburg, Miss)
Frick, Col. Jacob G. (Fredericksburg, Va)
Frizzell, Pvt. Henry F. (Vicksburg, Miss)
Fuger, Sgt. Frederick (Gettysburg, Pa)
Funk, Maj. West (Appomattox Courthouse, Va)
Furman, Cpl. Chester S. (Gettysburg, Pa)
Furness, Capt. Frank (Trevilian Station, Va)
Gage, Pvt. Richard J. (Elk River, Tenn)
Galloway, Pvt. George N. (Alsop's Farm, Va)
Galloway, Commissary Sgt. John (Farmville, Va)
Gardiner, Pvt. James (Chapin's Farm, Va)
Gardner, Pvt. Charles N. (Five Forks, Va)
Gardner, Sgt. Robert J. (Petersburg, Va)
Garrett, Sgt. William (Nashville, Tenn)
*Gasson, Sgt. Richard (Chapin's Farm, Va)
Gaunt, Pvt. John C. (Franklin, Tenn)
Gause, Cpl. Isaac (Berryville, Va)
Gaylord, Sgt. Levi B. (Fort Stedman, Va)
Gere, 1st Lt. & Adj. Thomas P. (Nashville, Tenn)
Geschwind, Capt. Nicholas (Vicksburg, Miss)
Gibbs, Sgt. Wesley (Petersburg, Va)
Gifford, Pvt. Benjamin (Sayler's Creek, Va)
Gifford, Pvt. David L. (Ashepoo River, SC)
Gillespie, 1st Lt. George L. (Bethesda Church, Va)
Gilligan, 1st Sgt. Edward L. (Gettysburg, Pa)
Gilmore, Maj. John C. (Salem Heights, Va)
Ginley, Pvt. Patrick J. (Reams's Station, Va)
Gion, Pvt. Joseph (Chancellorsville, Va)
Godley, 1st Sgt. Leonidas M. (Vicksburg, Miss)
Goettel, Pvt. Philip (Ringgold, Ga)
Goheen, 1st Sgt. Charles A. (Waynesboro, Va)
Goldsbery, Pvt. Andrew E. (Vicksburg, Miss)
Goodall, 1st Sgt. Francis H. (Fredericksburg, Va)
Goodman, 1st Lt. William E. (Chancellorsville, Va)
Goodrich, 1st Lt. Edwin (Cedar Creek, Va)
Gould, Capt. Charles G. (Petersburg, Va)
Gould, Pvt. Newton T. (Vicksburg, Miss)
Gouraud, Capt. & Aide-de-Camp George E. (Honey Hill, SC)
Grace, Sgt. Peter (Wilderness, Va)
Graham, 2d Lt. Thomas N. (Missionary Ridge, Tenn)
Grant, Surgeon Gabriel (Fair Oaks, Va)
Grant, Col. Lewis A. (Salem Heights, Va)
Graul, Cpl. William (Fort Harrison, Va)
Gray, Pvt. John (Port Republic, Va)
Gray, Sgt. Robert A. (Drewry's Bluff, Va)
Grebe, Capt. M. R. William (Jonesboro, Ga)
Green, Cpl. George (Missionary Ridge, Tenn)
Greenawalt, Pvt. Abraham (Franklin, Tenn)
Greene, Maj. & Asst. Adj. Gen. Oliver D. (Antietam, Md)
Gregg, Pvt. Joseph O. (Richmond & Petersburg Railway, Va)
Greig, 2d Lt. Theodore W. (Antietam, Md)
Gresser, Cpl. Ignatz (Antietam, Md)
Gribben, Lt. James H. (Sayler's Creek, Va)
Grimshaw, Pvt. Samuel (Atlanta, Ga)
Grindlay, Col. James G. (Five Forks, Va)
Grueb, Pvt. George (Chapin's Farm, Va)
Guerin, Pvt. Fitz W. (Grand Gulf, Miss)
Guinn, Pvt. Thomas (Vicksburg, Miss)
Gwynne, Pvt. Nathaniel (Petersburg, Va)
Hack, Pvt. John (Vicksburg, Miss)
Hack, Sgt. Lester G. (Petersburg, Va)
Hadley, Sgt. Cornelius M. (Knoxville, Tenn)
Hadley, Cpl. Osgood T. (Pegram House, Va)
Hagerty, Pvt. Asel (Sayler's Creek, Va)
Haight, Sgt. John H. (Williamsburg, Bristol Station & Manassas, Va)
Haight, Cpl. Sidney (Petersburg, Va)
Hall, Chaplain Francis B. (Salem Heights, Va)
Hall, 2d Lt. & Capt. Henry S. (Gaines's Mill & Rappahannock Station, Va)
Hall, Cpl. Newton H. (Franklin, Tenn)
Hallock, Pvt. Nathan M. (Bristoe Station, Va)
Hammel, Sgt. Henry A. (Grand Gulf, Miss)
Haney, Chaplain Milton L. (Atlanta, Ga)
Hanford, Pvt. Edward R. (Woodstock, Va)
Hanks, Pvt. Joseph (Vicksburg, Miss)
Hanna, Sgt. Marcus A. (Port Hudson, La)
Hanna, Cpl. Milton (Nolensville, Tenn)
Hanscom, Cpl. Moses C. (Bristoe Station, Va)
Hapeman, Lt. Col. Douglas (Peach Tree Creek, Ga)
Harbourne, Pvt. John H. (Petersburg, Va)
*Hardenbergh, Pvt. Henry M. (Deep Run, Va)
Haring, 1st Lt. Abram P. (Bachelor's Creek, NC)
Harmon, Cpl. Amzi D. (Petersburg, Va)
Harrington, Sgt Ephraim W. (Fredericksburg, Va)
Harris, Pvt. George W. (Spotsylvania, Va)
Harris, Sgt. James H. (New Market Heights, Va)
Harris, 1st Lt. Moses (Smithfield, Va)
Harris, Pvt. Sampson (Vicksburg, Miss)
Hart, Sgt. John W. (Gettysburg, Pa)
Hart, Pvt. William E. (Shenandoah Valley, Va)
Hartranft, Col. John F. (Bull Run, Va)
Harvey, Cpl. Harry (Waynesboro, Va)
Haskell, Sgt Maj. Frank W. (Fair Oaks, Va)
Haskell, Sgt. Marcus M. (Antietam, Md)
Hastings, Capt. Smith H. (Newby's Crossroads, Va)
Hatch, Brig. Gen. John P. (South Mountain, Md)
Havron, Sgt. John H. (Petersburg, Va)
Hawkins, 1st Lt. Gardner C. (Petersburg, Va)
Hawkins, Cpl. Martin J. (Georgia)
Hawkins, Sgt. Maj. Thomas R. (Chapin's Farm, Va)
Hawthorne, Cpl. Harris S. (Sayler's Creek, Va)
Haynes, Cpl. Asbury F. (Sayler's Creek, Va)
Hays, Pvt. John H. (Columbus, Ga)
Healey, Pvt. George W. (Newnan, Ga)
Hedges, 1st Lt. Joseph (Harpeth River, Tenn)
Heermance, Capt. William L. (Chancellorsville, Va)
Heller, Sgt. Henry (Chancellorsville, Va)
Helms, Pvt. David H. (Vicksburg, Miss)
Henry, Col. Guy V. (Cold Harbor, Va)
Henry, Sgt. James (Vicksburg, Miss)
Henry, Col. William W. (Cedar Creek, Va)
Herington, Pvt. Pitt B. (Kenesaw Mountain, Ga)
Herron, Lt. Col. Francis J. (Pea Ridge, Ark)
Hesseltine, Col. Francis S. (Matagorda Bay, Tex)
Hibson, Pvt. Joseph C. (Fort Wagner, SC)
Hickey, Sgt. Dennis W. (Stony Creek Bridge, Va)
Hickok, Cpl. Nathan E. (Chapin's Farm, Va)
Higby, Pvt. Charles (Appomattox, Va)
Higgins, Pvt. Thomas J. (Vicksburg, Miss)
Highland, Cpl. Patrick (Petersburg, Va)
Hill, Capt. Edward (Cold Harbor, Va)
Hill, Cpl. Henry (Wilderness, Va)
Hill, 1st Lt. James (Champion Hill, Miss)
*Hill, Sgt. James (Petersburg, Va)
Hilliker, Musician Benjamin F. (Mechanicsburg, Miss)
Hills, Pvt. William G. (North Fork, Va)
*Hilton, Sgt. Alfred B. (Chapin's Farm, Va)
Hincks, Sgt. Maj. William B. (Gettysburg, Pa)
Hodges, Pvt. Addison J. (Vicksburg, Miss)
Hoffman, Cpl. Henry (Sayler's Creek, Va)
Hoffman, Capt. Thomas W. (Petersburg, Va)
Hogan, Cpl. Franklin (Petersburg, Va)
Hogarty, Pvt. William P. (Antietam, Md)
Holcomb, Pvt. Daniel I. (Brentwood Hills, Tenn)
Holehouse, Pvt. James (Marye's Heights, Va)
Holland, Cpl. Lemuel F. (Elk River, Tenn)
Holland, Sgt. Maj. Milton M. (Chapin's Farm, Va)
Holmes, 1st Sgt. Lovilo N. (Nolensville, Tenn)
Holmes, Pvt. William T. (Sayler's Creek, Va)
Holton, 1st Sgt. Charles M. (Falling Waters, Va)
Holton, 1st Sgt. Edward A. (Lee's Mills, Va)
Homan, Color Sgt. Conrad (Petersburg, Va)
Hooker, 1st Lt. George W. (South Mountain, Md)
Hooper, Cpl. William B. (Chamberlain's Creek, Va)
Hopkins, Cpl. Charles F. (Gaines's Mill, Va)
Horan, Sgt. Thomas (Gettysburg, Pa)
Horne, Capt. Samuel B. (Fort Harrison, Va)
Horsfall, Drummer William H. (Corinth, Miss)
Hottenstine, Pvt. Solomon J. (Peterburg & Norfolk Railroad, Va)
Hough, Pvt. Ira (Cedar Creek, Va)
Houghton, Capt. Charles H. (Petersburg, Va)
Houghton, Pvt. George L. (Elk River, Tenn)
Houlton, Comm. Sgt. William (Sayler's Creek, Va)
Howard, Cpl. Henderson C. (Glendale, Va)
Howard, Pvt. Hiram R. (Missionary Ridge, Tenn)
Howard, Sgt. James (Battery Gregg, Va)
Howard, Brig. Gen. Oliver O. (Fair Oaks, Va)
Howard, 1st Sgt. Squire E. (Bayou Teche, La)
Howe, Musician Orion P. (Vicksburg, Miss)
Howe, Sgt. William H. (Fort Stedman, Va)
Hubbell, Capt. William S. (Fort Harrison, Va)
Hudson, Pvt. Aaron R. (Culloden, Ga)
Hughes, Cpl. Oliver (Weldon Railroad, Va)
Hughey, Cpl. John (Sayler's Creek, Va)
Huidekoper, Lt. Co. Henry S. (Gettysburg, Pa)
Hunt, Pvt. Louis T. (Vicksburg, Miss)
Hunter, Sgt. Charles A. (Petersburg, Va)
Hunterson, Pvt. John C. (Peninsula, Va)
Hyatt, 1st Sgt. Theodore (Vicksburg, Miss)
Hyde, Maj. Thomas W. (Antietam, Md)
Hymer, Capt. Samuel (Buzzard's Roost Gap, Ga)
Ilgenfritz, Sgt. Charles H. (Fort Sedgwick, Va)
Immell, Cpl. Lorenzo D. (Wilson's Creek, Mo)
Ingalls, Pvt. Lewis J. (Boutte Station, La)
Inscho, Cpl. Leonidas H. (South Mountain, Md)
Irsch, Capt. Francis (Gettysburg, Pa)
Irwin, 1st Sgt. Patrick (Jonesboro, Ga)
Jackson, 1st Sgt. Frederick R. (James Island, SC)
Jacobson, Sgt. Maj. Abram P. (Chancellorsville, Va)
James, Pvt. Isaac (Petersburg, Va)
James, Cpl. Miles (Chapin's Farm, Va)
Jamieson, 1st Sgt. Walter (Petersburg, Va)
Jardine, Sgt. James (Vicksburg, Miss)
Jellison, Sgt. Benjamin H. (Gettysburg, Pa)
Jennings, Pvt. James T. (Weldon Railroad, Va)
Jewett, 1st Lt. Erastus W. (Newport Barracks, NC)
John, Pvt. William (Vicksburg, Miss)
Johndro, Pvt. Franklin (Chapin's Farm, Va)
Johns, Cpl. Elisha (Vicksburg, Miss)
Johns, Pvt. Henry T. (Port Hudson, La)
Johnson, Pvt. Andrew (Vicksburg, Miss)
Johnson, Cpl. Follett (New Hope Church, Ga)
Johnson, Pvt. John (Fredericksburg, Va)
Johnson, 1st Lt. Joseph E. (Fort Harrison, Va)
Johnson, Maj. Ruel M. (Chattanooga, Tenn)
Johnson, Pvt. Samuel (Antietam, Md)
Johnson, Sgt. Wallace W. (Gettysburg, Pa)
Johnston, Pvt. David (Vicksburg, Miss)
Johnston, Musician Willie (NOR)
Jones, Pvt. David (Vicksburg, Miss)
Jones, 1st Sgt. William (Spotsylvania, Va)
Jordan, Cpl. Absalom (Sayler's Creek, Va)
Josselyn, 1st Lt. Simeon T. (Missionary Ridge, Tenn)
Judge, 1st Sgt. Francis W. (Fort Sanders, Tenn)
Kaiser, Sgt. John (Richmond, Va)
Kaltenbach, Cpl. Luther (Nashville, Tenn)
Kane, Cpl. John (Petersburg, Va)
Kappesser, Pvt. Peter (Lookout Mountain, Tenn)
Karpeles, Sgt. Leopold (Wilderness, Va)
Kauss, Cpl. August (Five Forks, Va)
Keele, Sgt. Maj. Joseph (North Anna River, Va)
Keen, Sgt. Joseph S. (Chattahoochee River, Ga)
Keene, Pvt. Joseph (Fredericksburg, Va)
Kelley, Pvt. Andrew J. (Knoxville, Tenn)
Kelley, Capt. George V. (Franklin, Tenn)
Kelley, Sgt. Leverett M. (Missionary Ridge, Tenn)
Kelly, 1st Sgt. Alexander (Chapin's Farm, Va)
Kelly, Sgt. Daniel A. (Waynesboro, Va)
Kelly, Pvt. Thomas (Front Royal, Va)
Kemp, 1st Sgt. Joseph (Wilderness, Va)
Kendall, 1st Sgt. William W. (Black River Bridge, Miss)
Kennedy, Pvt. John (Trevilian Station, Va)
Kenyon, Sgt. John S. (Trenton, NC)
Kenyon, Pvt. Samuel P. (Sayler's Creek, Va)
Keough, Cpl. John (Sayler's Creek, Va)
Kephart, Pvt. James (Vicksburg, Miss)
Kerr, Capt. Thomas R. (Moorfield, W Va)
Kiggins, Sgt. John (Lookout Mountain, Tenn)
Kimball, Pvt. Joseph (Sayler's Creek, Va)
Kindig, Cpl. John M. (Spotsylvania, Va)
King, Maj. & QM Horatio C. (Dinwiddie Courthouse, Va)
King, 1st Lt. Rufus, Jr (White Oak Swamp Bridge, Va)
Kinsey, Cpl. John (Spotsylvania, Va)
Kirby, Maj. Dennis T. (Vicksburg, Miss)
Kirk, Capt. Jonathan C. (North Anna River, Va)
Kline, Pvt. Harry (Sayler's Creek, Va)
Kloth, Pvt. Charles H. (Vicksburg, Miss)
Knight, Cpl. Charles H. (Petersburg, Va)
Knight, Pvt. William J. (Georgia)
Knowles, Pvt. Abiather J. (Bull Run, Va)
Knox, 2d Lt. Edward M. (Gettysburg, Pa)
Koogle, 1st Lt. Jacob (Five Forks, Va)
Kountz, Musician John S. (Missionary Ridge, Tenn)
Kramer, Pvt. Theodore L. (Chapin's Farm, Va)
Kretsinger, Pvt. George (Vicksburg, Miss)
Kuder, 2d Lt. Andrew (Waynesboro, Va)
Kuder, Lt. Jeremiah (Jonesboro, Ga)
Labille, Pvt. Joseph S. (Vicksburg, Miss)
Ladd, Pvt. George (Waynesboro, Va)
*Laing, Sgt. William (Chapin's Farm, Va)
Landis, Chief Bugler James P. (Paine's Crossroads, Va)
Lane, Pvt. Morgan D. (Jetersville, Va)
Lanfare, 1st Lt. Aaron S. (Sayler's Creek, Va)
Langbein, Musician J. C. Julius (Camden, NC)
Larimer, Cpl. Smith (Sayler's Creek, Va)
Larrabee, Cpl. James W. (Vicksburg, Miss)
Lawson, 1st Sgt. Gaines (Minville, Tenn)
Lawton, Capt. Henry W. (Atlanta, Ga)
Leonard, Sgt. Edwin (Petersburg, Va)
Leonard, Pvt. William E. (Deep Bottom, Va)
Leslie, Pvt. Frank (Front Royal, Va)
Levy, Pvt. Benjamin (Glendale, Va)
Lewis, Capt. DeWitt C. (Secessionville, SC)
Lewis, Cpl. Henry (Vicksburg, Miss)
Lewis, Cpl. Samuel E. (Petersburg, Va)
Libaire, Capt. Adolphe (Antietam, Md)
Lilley, Pvt. John (Petersburg, Va)
Little, Sgt. Henry F. W. (Richmond, Va)
Littlefield, Cpl. George H. (Fort Fisher, NC)
Livingston, 1st Lt. & Adj. Josiah O. (Newport Barracks, NC)
Locke, Pvt. Lewis (Paine's Crossroads, Va)
Lonergan, Capt. John (Gettysburg, Pa)
Longshore, Pvt. William H. (Vicksburg, Miss)
Lonsway, Pvt. Joseph (Murfree's Station, Va)
Lord, Musician William (Drewry's Bluff, Va)
Lorish, Comm. Sgt. Andrew J. (Winchester, Va)
Love, Col. George M. (Cedar Creek, Va)
Lovering, 1st Sgt. George M. (Port Hudson, La)
Lower, Pvt. Cyrus B. (Wilderness, Va)
Lower, Pvt. Robert A. (Vicksburg, Miss)
Loyd, Pvt. George (Petersburg, Va)
Lucas, Pvt. George W. (Benton, Ark)
Luce, Sgt. Moses A. (Laurel Hill, Va)
Ludgate, Capt. William (Farmville, Va)
Ludwig, Pvt. Carl (Petersburg, Va)
Lunt, Sgt. Alphonso M. (Opequan Creek, Va)
Lutes, Cpl. Franklin W. (Petersburg, Va)
Luther, Pvt. James H. (Fredericksburg, Va)
Luty, Cpl. Gotlieb (Chancellorsville, Va)
Lyman, QM Sgt. Joel H. (Winchester, Va)
Lyon, Cpl. Frederick A. (Cedar Creek, Va)
McAdams, Cpl. Peter (Salem Heights, Va)
McAlwee, Sgt. Benjamin F. (Petersburg, Va)
McAnally, Lt. Charles (Spotsylvania, Va)
MacArthur, 1st Lt. & Adj. Arthur, Jr. (Missionary Ridge, Tenn)
McCammon, 1st Lt. William W. (Corinth, Miss)
McCarren, Pvt. Bernard (Gettysburg, Pa)
McCauslin, Pvt. Joseph (Petersburg, Va)
McCleary, 1st Lt. Charles H. (Nashville, Tenn)
McClelland, Pvt. James M. (Vicksburg, Miss)
McConnell, Capt. Samuel (Fort Blakely, Ala)
McCornack, Pvt. Andrew (Vicksburg, Miss)
McDonald, Pvt. George E. (Fort Stedman, Va)
McDonald, Pvt. John W. (Pittsburg Landing, Tenn)
McElhinny, Pvt. Samuel O. (Sayler's Creek, Va)
McEnroe, Sgt. Patrick H. (Winchester, Va)
McFall, Sgt. Daniel (Spotsylvania, Va)
McGinn, Pvt. Edward (Vicksburg, Miss)
McGonagle, Pvt. Wilson (Vicksburg, Miss)
McGonnigle, Capt. & Asst. QM Andrew J. (Cedar Creek, Va)
McGough, Cpl. Owen (Bull Run, Va)
McGraw, Sgt. Thomas (Petersburg, Va)
McGuire, Pvt. Patrick (Vicksburg, Miss)
McHale, Cpl. Alexander U. (Spotsylvania Courthouse, Va)
McKay, Sgt. Charles W. (Dug Gap, Ga)
McKee, Color Sgt. George (Petersburg, Va)
McKeen, 1st Lt. Nineveh S. (Stone River & Liberty Gap, Tenn)
McKeever, Pvt. Michael (Burnt Ordinary, Va)
McKown, Sgt. Nathaniel A. (Chapin's Farm, Va)
McMahon, Capt. & Aide-de-Camp Martin T. (White Oak Swamp, Va)
McMillen, Sgt. Francis M. (Petersburg, Va)
*McVeane, Cpl. John P. (Fredericksburg Heights, Va)
McWhorter, Comm. Sgt. Walter F. (Sayler's Creek, Va)
Madden, Pvt. Michael (Mason's Island, Md)
Madison, Sgt. James (Waynesboro, Va)
Magee, Drummer William (Murfreesboro, Tenn)
Mahoney, Sgt. Jeremiah (Fort Sanders, Tenn)
Mandy, 1st Sgt. Harry J. (Front Royal, Va)
Mangam, Pvt. Richard C. (Hatcher's Run, Va)
Manning, Pvt. Joseph S. (Fort Sanders, Tenn)
Marland, 1st Lt. William (Grand Coteau, La)
Marquette, Sgt. Charles (Petersburg, Va)
Marsh, Sgt. Albert (Spotsylvania, Va)
Marsh, Pvt. Charles H. (Back Creek Valley, Va)
Marsh, Sgt. George (Elk River, Tenn)
Martin, Lt. Sylvester H. (Weldon Railroad, Va)
Mason, Sgt. Elihu H. (Georgia)
Mathews, 1st Sgt. William H. (Petersburg, Va)
Matthews, Cpl. John C. (Petersburg, Va)
Matthews, Pvt. Milton (Petersburg, Va)
Mattingly, Pvt. Henry B. (Jonesboro, Ga)
Mattocks, Maj. Charles P. (Sayler's Creek, Va)
Maxham, Cpl. Lowell M. (Fredericksburg, Va)
May, Pvt. William (Nashville, Tenn)
Mayberry, Pvt. John B. (Gettysburg, Pa)

Mayes, Pvt. William B. (Kenesaw Mountain, Ga)
Maynard, Pvt. George H. (Fredericksburg, Va)
Meach, Farrier George E. (Winchester, Va)
Meagher, 1st Sgt. Thomas (Chapin's Farm, Va)
Mears, Sgt. George W. (Gettysburg, Pa)
Menter, Sgt. John W. (Sayler's Creek, Va)
Merriam, Lt. Col. Henry C. (Fort Blakely, Ala)
Merrifield, Cpl. James K. (Franklin, Tenn)
Merrill, Capt. Augustus (Petersburg, Va)
Merrill, Pvt. George (Fort Fisher, NC)
Merritt, Sgt. John G. (Bull Run, Va)
Meyer, Capt. Henry C. (Petersburg, Va)
Miles, Col. Nelson A. (Chancellorsville, Va)
Miller, Pvt. Frank (Sayler's Creek, Va)
Miller, Capt. Henry A. (Fort Blakely, Ala)
Miller, Pvt. Jacob C. (Vicksburg, Miss)
Miller, Pvt. James P. (Selma, Ala)
Miller, Cpl. John (Gettysburg, Pa)
Miller, Pvt. John (Waynesboro, Va)
Miller, Capt. William E. (Gettysburg, Pa)
Mills, Sgt. Frank W. (Sandy Cross Roads, NC)
Mindil, Capt. George W. (Williamsburg, Va)
Mitchell, 1st Lt. Alexander H. (Spotsylvania, Va)
Mitchell, Pvt. Theodore (Petersburg, Va)
Moffitt, Cpl. John H. (Gaines's Mill, Va)
Molbone, Sgt. Archibald (Petersburg, Va)
Monaghan, Cpl. Patrick (Petersburg, Va)
Moore, Cpl. Daniel B. (Fort Blakely, Ala)
Moore, Pvt. George G. (Fisher's Hill, Va)
Moore, Pvt. Wilbur F. (Nashville, Tenn)
Morey, Pvt. Delano (McDowell, Va)
Morford, Pvt. Jerome (Vicksburg, Miss)
*Morgan, Pvt. Lewis (Spotsylvania, Va)
Morgan, Cpl. Richard H. (Columbus, Ga)
Morrill, Capt. Walter G. (Rappahannock Station, Va)
Morris, Sgt. William (Sayler's Creek, Va)
Morrison, Pvt. Francis (Bermuda Hundred, Va)
Morse, Pvt. Benjamin (Spotsylvania, Va)
Morse, Sgt. Charles E. (Wilderness, Va)
Mostoller, Pvt. John W. (Lynchburg, Va)
Mulholland, Maj. St. Clair A. (Chancellorsville, Va)
Mundell, Cpl. Walter L. (Sayler's Creek, Va)
Munsell, Sgt. Harvey M. (Gettysburg, Pa)
Murphy, 1st Lt. & QM Charles J. (Bull Run, Va)
Murphy, Sgt. Daniel J. (Hatcher's Run, Va)
Murphy, Sgt. Dennis J. F. (Corinth, Miss)
Murphy, Pvt. James T. (Petersburg, Va)
Murphy, Pvt. John P. (Antietam, Md)
Murphy, Lt. Col. Michael C. (North Anna River, Va)
Murphy, Musician Robinson B. (Atlanta, Ga)
Murphy, Cpl. Thomas (Chapin's Farm, Va)
Murphy, Cpl. Thomas C. (Vicksburg, Miss)
Murphy, 1st Sgt. Thomas J. (Five Forks, Va)
Myers, Pvt. George S. (Chickamauga, Ga)
Myers, Pvt. William H. (Appomattox Courthouse, Va)
Nash, Cpl. Henry H. (Vicksburg, Miss)
Neahr, Pvt. Zachariah C. (Fort Fisher, NC)
Neville, Capt. Edwin M. (Sayler's Creek, Va)
Newman, Pvt. Marcellus J. (Resaca, Ga)
Newman, Lt. William H. (Amelia Springs, Va)
Nichols, Capt. Henry C. (Fort Blakely, Ala)
Niven, 2d Lt. Robert (Waynesboro, Va)
Nolan, Sgt. John J. (Georgia Landing, La)
Noll, Sgt. Conrad (Spotsylvania, Va)
North, Pvt. Jasper N. (Vicksburg, Miss)
Norton, 2d Lt. Elliott M. (Sayler's Creek, Va)
Norton, Lt. John R. (Sayler's Creek, Va)
Norton, Sgt. Llewellyn P. (Sayler's Creek, Va)
Noyes, Pvt. William W. (Spotsylvania, Va)
Nutting, Capt. Lee (Todd's Tavern, Va)
O'Beirne, Capt. James R. (Fair Oaks, Va)
O'Brien, Cpl. Henry D. (Gettysburg, Pa)
O'Brien, Pvt. Peter (Waynesboro, Va)
O'Connor, Sgt. Albert (Gravelly Run, Va)
O'Connor, Pvt. Timothy (NOR)
O'Dea, Pvt. John (Vicksburg, Miss)
O'Donnell, 1st Lt. Menomen (Vicksburg, Miss)
Oliver, Sgt. Charles (Petersburg, Va)
Oliver, Capt. Paul A. (Resaca, Ga)
O'Neill, Cpl. Stephen (Chancellorsville, Va)
Opel, Pvt. John N. (Wilderness, Va)
Orbansky, Pvt. David (Shiloh, Tenn, & Vicksburg, Miss, etc)
Orr, Pvt. Charles A. (Hatcher's Run, Va)
Orr, Maj. Robert I. (Petersburg, Va)
Orth, Cpl. Jacob G. (Antietam, Md)
Osborne, Pvt. William H. (Malvern Hill, Va)
Oss, Pvt. Albert (Chancellorsville, Va)
Overturf, Pvt. Jacob H. (Vicksburg, Miss)
Packard, Pvt. Loron F. (Raccoon Ford, Va)
Palmer, Musician George H. (Lexington, Mo)
Palmer, Cpl. John G. (Fredericksburg, Va)
Palmer, Col. William J. (Red Hill, Ala)
Parker, Cpl. Thomas (Petersburg & Sayler's Creek, Va)
Parks, Pvt. Henry J. (Cedar Creek, Va)
Parks, Cpl. James W. (Nashville, Tenn)
Parrott Pvt. Jacob (Georgia)
Parsons, Pvt. Joel (Vicksburg, Miss)
Patterson, 1st Lt. John H. (Wilderness, Va)
Patterson, Principal Musician John T. (Winchester, Va)
Paul, Pvt. William H. (Antietam, Md)
Pay, Pvt. Byron E. (Nolensville, Tenn)
Payne, Cpl. Irvin C. (Sayler's Creek, Va)
Payne, 1st Lt. Thomas H. L. (Fort Blakely, Ala)
Pearsall, Cpl. Platt (Vicksburg, Miss)
Pearson, Col. Alfred L. (Lewis's Farm, Va)
Peck, Pvt. Cassius (Blackburn's Ford, Va)
Peck, 1st Lt. Theodore S. (Newport Barracks, NC)
Peirsol, Sgt. James K. (Paine's Crossroads, Va)
Pennypacker, Col. Galusha (Fort Fisher, NC)
Pentzer, Capt. Patrick H. (Blakely, Ala)
Pesch, Pvt. Joseph (Grand Gulf, Miss)
Peters, Pvt. Henry C. (Vicksburg, Miss)
Petty, Sgt. Philip (Fredericksburg, Va)
Phelps, Col. Charles E. (Laurel Hill, Va)
Phillips, Pvt. Josiah (Sutherland Station, Va)
Phisterer, 1st Lt. Frederick (Stone River, Tenn)
Pickle, Sgt. Alonzo H. (Deep Bottom, Va)
Pike, 1st Sgt. Edward M. (Cache River, Ark)
Pingree, Capt. Samuel E. (Lee's Mills, Va)
Pinkham, Sgt. Maj. Charles H. (Fort Stedman, Va)
Pinn, 1st Sgt. Robert (Chapin's Farm, Va)
Pipes, Capt. James (Gettysburg, Pa)
Pitman, Sgt. George J. (Sayler's Creek, Va)
Pittinger, Sgt. William (Georgia)
Plant, Cpl. Henry E. (Bentonville, NC)
Platt, Pvt. George C. (Fairfield, Pa)
Plimley, 1st Lt. William (Hatcher's Run, Va)
Plowman, Sgt. Maj. George H. (Petersburg, Va)
Plunkett, Sgt. Thomas (Fredericksburg, Va)
Pond, Pvt. George F. (Drywood, Kans)
Pond, 1st Lt. James B. (Baxter Springs, Kans)
Porter, Comm. Sgt. Ambrose (Tallahatchie River, Miss)
Porter, Capt. Horace (Chickamauga, Ga)
Porter, Pvt. John R. (Georgia)
Porter, Sgt. William (Sayler's Creek, Va)
Post, Col. Philip S. (Nashville, Tenn)
Postles, Capt. James P. (Gettysburg, Pa)
Potter, Pvt. George W. (Petersburg, Va)
Potter, 1st Sgt. Norman F. (Lookout Mountain, Tenn)
Powell, Maj. William H. (Sinking Creek Valley, Va)
Power, Pvt. Albert (Pea Ridge, Ark)
Powers, Cpl. Wesley J. (Oostanaula, Ga)
Prentice, Pvt. Joseph R. (Stone River, Tenn)
Preston, 1st Lt. & Comm. Noble D. (Trevilian Station, Va)
Purcell, Sgt. Hiram W. (Fair Oaks, Va)
Purman, Lt. James J. (Gettysburg, Pa)
Putnam, Sgt. Edgar P. (Crump's Creek, Va)
Putnam, Cpl. Winthrop D. (Vicksburg, Miss)
Quay, Col. Matthew S. (Fredericksburg, Va)
Quinlan, Maj. James (Savage Station, Va)
Rafferty, Pvt. Peter (Malvern Hill, Va)
Ramsbottom, 1st Sgt. Alfred (Franklin, Tenn)
Rand, Pvt. Charles F. (Blackburn's Ford, Va)
Ranney, Asst. Surgeon George E. (Resaca, Ga)
Ranney, Pvt. Myron H. (Bull Run, Va)
Ratcliff, 1st Sgt. Edward (Chapin's Farm, Va)
Raub, Asst. Surgeon Jacob F. (Hatcher's Run, Va)
Raymond, Cpl. William H. (Gettysburg, Pa)
Read, Lt. Morton A. (Appomattox Station, Va)
Rebmann, Sgt. George F. (Fort Blakely, Ala)
Reddick, Cpl. William H. (Georgia)
Reed, Sgt. Axel H. (Chickamauga, Ga & Missionary Ridge, Tenn)
Reed, Bugler Charles W. (Gettysburg, Pa)
Reed, Pvt. George W. (Weldon Railroad, Va)
Reed, Pvt. William (Vicksburg, Miss)
Reeder, Pvt. Charles A. (Battery Gregg, Va)
Reid, Pvt. Robert A. (Petersburg, Va)
Reigle, Cpl. Daniel P. (Cedar Creek, Va)
Reisinger, Cpl. J. Monroe (Gettysburg, Pa)
Renninger, Cpl. Louis (Vicksburg, Miss)
Reynolds, Pvt. George (Winchester, Va)
Rhodes, Pvt. Julius D. (Thoroughfare Gap & Bull Run, Va)
Rhodes, Sgt. Sylvester D. (Fisher's Hill, Va)
Rice, Maj. Edmund (Gettysburg, Pa)
Rich, 1st Sgt. Carlos H. (Wilderness, Va)
Richardson, Pvt. William R. (Sayler's Creek, Va)
Richey, Cpl. William E. (Chickamauga, Ga)
*Richmond, Pvt. James (Gettysburg, Pa)
Ricksecker, Pvt. John H. (Franklin, Tenn)
Riddell, Lt. Rudolph (Sayler's Creek, Va)
Riley, Pvt. Thomas (Fort Blakely, Ala)
Ripley, Lt. Col. William Y. W. (Malvern Hill, Va)
Robbins, 2d Lt. Augustus J. (Spotsylvania, Va)
Roberts, Sgt. Otis O. (Rappahannock Station, Va)
Robertson, 1st Lt. Robert S. (Corbin's Bridge, Va)
*Robertson, Pvt. Samuel (Georgia)
Robie, Sgt. George F. (Richmond, Va)
Robinson, Pvt. Elbridge (Winchester, Va)
*Robinson, Pvt. James H. (Brownsville, Ark)
Robinson, Brig, Gen. John C. (Laurel Hill, Va)
Robinson, Pvt. John H. (Gettysburg, Pa)
Robinson, Pvt. Thomas (Spotsylvania, Va)
Rock, Pvt. Frederick (Vicksburg, Miss)
Rockefeller, Lt. Charles M. (Fort Blakely, Ala)
Rodenbough, Capt. Theophilus F. (Trevilian Station, Va)
Rohm, Chief Bugler Ferdinand F. (Reams's Station, Va)
Rood, Pvt. Oliver P. (Gettysburg, Pa)
Roosevelt, 1st Sgt. George W. (Bull Run, Va & Gettysburg, Pa)
*Ross, Sgt. Maj. Marion A. (Georgia)
Rossbach, Sgt. Valentine (Spotsylvania, Va)
Rought, Sgt. Stephen (Wilderness, Va)
Rounds, Pvt. Lewis A. (Spotsylvania, Va)
Roush, Cpl. J. Levi (Gettysburg, Pa)
Rowand, Pvt. Archibald H., Jr. (Virginia)
Rowe, Pvt. Henry W. (Petersburg, Va)
Rundle, Pvt. Charles W. (Vicksburg, Miss)
Russell, Cpl. Charles L. (Spotsylvania, Va)
Russell, Capt. Milton (Stone River, Tenn)
Rutherford, 1st Lt. John T. (Yellow Tavern & Hanovertown, Va)
Rutter, Sgt. James M. (Gettysburg, Pa)
Ryan, Pvt. Peter J. (Winchester, Va)
Sacriste, 1st Lt. Louis J. (Chancellorsville & Auburn, Va)
Sagelhurst, Sgt. John C. (Hatcher's Run, Va)
Sancrainte, Pvt. Charles F. (Atlanta, Ga)
Sands, 1st Sgt. William (Dabney's Mills, Va)
Sanford, Pvt. Jacob (Vicksburg, Miss)
Sargent Sgt. Jackson (Petersburg, Va)
Sartwell, Sgt. Henry (Chancellorsville, Va)
*Savacool, Capt. Edwin F. (Sayler's Creek, Va)
Saxton, Brig. Gen. Rufus (Harper's Ferry, W Va)
Scanlan, Pvt. Patrick (Ashepoo River, SC)
Scheibner, Pvt. Martin E. (Mine Run, Va)
Schenck, Pvt. Benjamin W. (Vicksburg, Miss)
Schiller, Pvt. John (Chapin's Farm, Va)
Schlachter, Pvt. Philipp (Spotsylvania, Va)
Schmal, Blacksmith George W. (Paine's Crossroads, Va)
Schmauch, Pvt. Andrew (Vicksburg, Miss)
Schmidt, 1st Sgt. Conrad (Winchester, Va)
Schmidt, Pvt. William (Missionary Ridge, Tenn)
Schneider, Sgt. George (Petersburg, Va)
Schnell, Cpl. Christian (Vicksburg, Miss)
Schofield, Maj. John M. (Wilson's Creek, Mo)
Schoonmaker, Col. James M. (Winchester, Va)
Schorn, Chief Bugler Charles (Appomattox, Va)
Schubert, Pvt. Martin (Fredericksburg, Va)
Schwan, 1st Lt. Theodore (Peebles's Farm, Va)
Schwenk, Sgt. Martin (Millerstown, Pa)
Scofield, QM Sgt. David H. (Cedar Creek, Va)
Scott, Cpl. Alexander (Monocacy, Md)
*Scott, Sgt. John M. (Georgia)
Scott, Capt. John W. (Five Forks, Va)
Scott, Drummer Julian A. (Lee's Mills, Va)
Seaman, Pvt. Elisha B. (Chancellorsville, Va)
Sears, 1st Lt. Cyrus (Iuka, Miss)
Seaver, Col. Thomas O. (Spotsylvania Courthouse, Va)
Seitzinger, Pvt. James M. (Cold Harbor, Va)
Sellers, Maj. Alfred J. (Gettysburg, Pa)
*Seston, Sgt. Charles H. (Winchester, Va)
Sewell, Col. William J. (Chancellorsville, Va)
Shafter, 1st Lt. William R. (Fair Oaks, Va)
Shahan, Cpl. Emisire (Sayler's Creek, Va)
Shaler, Col. Alexander (Marye's Heights, Va)
Shambaugh, Cpl. Charles (Charles City Crossroads, Va)
Shanes, Pvt. John (Carter's Farm, Va)
Shapland, Pvt. John (Elk River, Tenn)
Shea, Pvt. Joseph H. (Chapin's Farm, Va)
Shellenberger, Cpl. John S. (Deep Run, Va)
Shepard, Cpl. Irwin (Knoxville, Tenn)
Shepherd, Pvt. William (Sayler's Creek, Va)
Sherman, Pvt. Marshall (Gettysburg, Pa)
Shiel, Cpl. John (Fredericksburg, Va)
Shields, Pvt. Bernard (Appomattox, Va)
Shilling, 1st Sgt. John (Weldon Railroad, Va)
Shipley, Sgt. Robert F. (Five Forks, Va)
Shoemaker, Sgt. Levi (Nineveh, Va)
Shopp, Pvt. George J. (Five Forks, Va)
Shubert, Sgt. Frank (Petersburg, Va)
Sickles, Maj. Gen. Daniel E. (Gettysburg, Pa)
Sickles, Sgt. William H. (Gravelly Run, Va)
Sidman, Pvt. George E. (Gaines's Mill, Va)
Simmons, Pvt. John (Sayler's Creek, Va)
Simmons, Lt. William T. (Nashville, Tenn)
Simonds, Sgt. Maj. William E. (Irish Bend, La)
Simons, Sgt. Charles J. (Petersburg, Va)
Skellie, Cpl. Ebenezer (Chapin's Farm, Va)
Sladen, Pvt. Joseph A. (Resaca, Ga)
Slagle, Pvt. Oscar (Elk River, Tenn)
*Slavens, Pvt. Samuel (Georgia)
Sloan, Pvt. Andrew J. (Nashville, Tenn)
Slusher, Pvt. Henry C. (Moorefield, W Va)
Smalley, Pvt. Reuben (Vicksburg, Miss)
Smalley, Pvt. Reuben S. (Elk River, Tenn)
Smith, Sgt. Alonzo (Hatcher's Run, Va)
Smith, Col. Charles H. (St. Mary's Church, Va)
Smith, Sgt. David L. (Warwick Courthouse, Va)
Smith, 1st Lt. & Adj. Francis M. (Dabney Mills, Va)
Smith, 1st Lt. Henry I. (Black River, NC)
Smith, Pvt. James (Georgia)
Smith, Lt. Col. Joseph S. (Hatcher's Run, Va)
Smith, Pvt. Otis W. (Nashville, Tenn)
Smith, Pvt. Richard (Weldon Railroad, Va)
Smith, Capt. S. Rodmond (Rowanty Creek, Va)
Smith, Cpl. Thaddeus S. (Gettysburg, Pa)
Smith, Cpl. Wilson (Washington, NC)
Snedden, Musician James (Piedmont, Va)
Southard, Sgt. David (Sayler's Creek, Va)
Sova, Saddler Joseph E. (Appomattox, Va)
Sowers, Pvt. Michael (Stony Creek Station, Va)
Spalding, Sgt. Edward B. (Pittsburg Landing, Tenn)
Sperry, Maj. William J. (Petersburg, Va)
Spillane, Pvt. Timothy (Hatcher's Run, Va)
Sprague, Cpl. Benona (Vicksburg, Miss)
Sprague, Col. John W. (Decatur, Ga)
Spurling, Lt. Col. Andrew B. (Evergreen, Ala)
Stacey, Pvt. Charles (Gettysburg, Pa)
Stahel, Maj. Gen. Julius (Piedmont, Va)
Stanley, Maj. Gen. David S. (Franklin, Tenn)
Starkins, Sgt. John H. (Campbell Station, Tenn)
Steele, Maj. & Aide-de-Camp John W. (Spring Hill, Tenn)
Steinmetz, Pvt. William (Vicksburg, Miss)
Stephens, Pvt. William G. (Vicksburg, Miss)
Sterling, Pvt. John T. (Winchester, Va)
Stevens, Capt. & Asst. Adj. Gen. Hazard (Fort Huger, Va)
Stewart, 1st Sgt. George W. (Paine's Crossroads, Va)
Stewart, Pvt. Joseph (Five Forks, Va)
Stickels, Sgt. Joseph (Fort Blakely, Ala)
Stockman, 1st Lt. George H. (Vicksburg, Miss)
Stokes, Pvt. George (Nashville, Tenn)
Stolz, Pvt. Frank (Vicksburg, Miss)
Storey, Sgt. John H. R. (Dallas, Ga)
*Strausbaugh, 1st Sgt. Bernard A. (Petersburg, Va)
Streile, Pvt. Christian (Paine's Crossroads, Va)
Strong, Sgt. James N. (Port Hudson, La)
Sturgeon, Pvt. James K. (Kenesaw Mountain, Ga)
Summers, Pvt. James C. (Vicksburg, Miss)
Surles, Pvt. William H. (Perryville, Ky)
Swan, Pvt. Charles A. (Selma, Ala)
Swap, Pvt. Jacob E. (Wilderness, Va)
Swayne, Lt. Col. Wager (Corinth, Miss)
Sweatt, Pvt. Joseph S. G. (Carrsville, Va)
Sweeney, Pvt. James (Cedar Creek, Va)
Swegheimer, Pvt. Jacob (Vicksburg, Miss)
Swift, Lt. Col. Frederic W. (Lenoire Station, Tenn)
Swift, 2d Lt. Harlan J. (Petersburg, Va)
Sype, Pvt. Peter (Vicksburg, Miss)
Tabor, Pvt. William L. S. (Port Hudson, La)
Taggart, Pvt. Charles A. (Sayler's Creek, Va)
Tanner, 2d Lt. Charles B. (Antietam, Md)
Taylor, 1st Lt. Anthony (Chickamauga, Ga)
Taylor, Capt. Forrester L. (Chancellorsville, Va)
Taylor, Sgt. Henry H. (Vicksburg, Miss)
Taylor, Pvt. Joseph (Weldon Railroad, Va)
Taylor, Pvt. Richard (Cedar Creek, Va)
Taylor, Sgt. William (Front Royal & Weldon Railroad, Va)
Terry, Sgt. John D. (New Bern, NC)
Thackrah, Pvt. Benjamin (Fort Gates, Fla)
Thatcher, Pvt. Charles M. (Petersburg, Va)
Thaxter, Maj. Sidney W. (Hatcher's Run, Va)
Thomas, Maj. Hampton S. (Amelia Springs, Va)
Thomas, Col. Stephen (Cedar Creek, Va)
Thompkins, Cpl. George W. (Petersburg, Va)
Thompson, Pvt. Allen (White Oak Road, Va)
Thompson, Sgt. Charles A. (Spotsylvania, Va)
Thompson, Cpl. Freeman C. (Petersburg, Va)
Thompson, Pvt. James (White Oak Road, Va)
Thompson, Surgeon J. Harry (New Bern, NC)
Thompson, Sgt. James B. (Gettysburg, Pa)
Thompson, Cpl. John (Hatcher's Run, Va)
Thompson, Sgt. Thomas (Chancellorsville, Va)
*Thompson, Sgt. William P. (Wilderness, Va)
Thompson, 1st Lt. Clifford (Chancellorsville, Va)
Thorn, 2d Lt. Walter (Dutch Gap Canal, Va)
Tibbets, Pvt. Andrew W. (Columbus, Ga)
Tilton, Sgt. William (Richmond, Va)
Tinkham, Cpl. Eugene M. (Cold Harbor, Va)
Titus, Sgt. Charles (Sayler's Creek, Va)
Toban, Sgt. James W. (Aiken, SC)
Tobie, Sgt. Maj. Edward P. (Appomattox, Va)
Tobin, 1st Lt. & Adj. John M. (Malvern Hill, Va)
Toffey, 1st Lt. John J. (Chattanooga, Tenn)
Tompkins, Sgt. Aaron B. (Sayler's Creek, Va)
Tompkins, 1st Lt. Charles H. (Fairfax, Va)
Toohey, Sgt. Thomas (Franklin, Tenn)
Toomer, Sgt. William (Vicksburg, Miss)
Torgler, Sgt. Ernst (Ezra Chapel, Ga)
Tozier, Sgt. Andrew J. (Gettysburg, Pa)
Tracy, Lt. Col. Amasa A. (Cedar Creek, Va)
Tracy, Col. Benjamin F. (Wilderness, Va)
Tracy, Sgt. Charles H. (Spotsylvania & Petersburg, Va)
Tracy, 2d Lt. William G. (Chancellorsville, Va)
Traynor, Cpl. Andrew (Mason's Hill, Va)
Treat, Sgt. Howell B. (Buzzard's Roost, Ga)
Tremain, Maj. & Aide-de-Camp Henry E. (Resaca, Ga)
Tribe, Pvt. John (Waterloo Bridge, Va)
Trogden, Pvt. Howell G. (Vicksburg, Miss)
Truell, Pvt. Edwin M. (Atlanta, Ga)
Tucker, Sgt. Allen (Petersburg, Va)
Tucker, Cpl. Jacob R. (Petersburg, Va)
Tweedale, Pvt. John (Stone River, Tenn)

Register Of Recipients

Twombly, Cpl. Voltaire P. (Fort Donelson, Tenn)
Tyrrell, Cpl. George W. (Resaca, Ga)
Uhrl, Sgt. George (White Oak Swamp Bridge, Va)
Urell, Pvt. M. Emmet (Bristoe Station, Va)
Vale, Pvt. John (Nolensville, Tenn)
Vance, Pvt. Wilson (Stone River, Tenn)
Vanderslice, Pvt. John M. (Hatcher's Run, Va)
Van Matre, Pvt. Joseph (Petersburg, Va)
Van Winkle, Cpl. Edward (Chapin's Farm, Va)
Veal, Pvt. Charles (Chapin's Farm, Va)
Veale, Capt. Moses (Wauhatchie, Tenn)
Veazey, Col. Wheelock G. (Gettysburg, Pa)
Vernay, 2d Lt. James D. (Vicksburg, Miss)
Vifquain, Lt. Col. Victor (Fort Blakely, Ala)
Von Vegesack, Maj. & Aide-de-Camp Ernest (Gaines's Mill, Va)
Wageman, Pvt. John H. (Petersburg, Va)
Wagner, Cpl. John W. (Vicksburg, Miss)
Wainwright, 1st Lt. John (Fort Fisher, NC)
Walker, Pvt. James C. (Missionary Ridge, Tenn)
Walker, Contract Surgeon (Civilian) Mary (Bull Run, Va & Chattanooga, Tenn, etc.)
Wall, Pvt. Jerry (Gettysburg, Pa)
Waller, Cpl. Francis A. (Gettysburg, Pa)
Walling, Capt. William H. (Fort Fisher, NC)
Walsh, Cpl. John (Cedar Creek, Va)
Walton, Pvt. George W. (Petersburg, Va)
Wambsgan, Pvt. Martin (Cedar Creek, Va)
Ward, Pvt. Nelson W. (Staunton River Bridge, Va)
Ward, Pvt. Thomas J. (Vicksburg, Miss)
Ward, Capt. William H. (Vicksburg, Miss)
Warden, Cpl. John (Vicksburg, Miss)
Warfel, Pvt. Henry C. (Paine's Crossroads, Va)
Warren, Cpl. Francis E. (Port Hudson, La)
Webb, Brig. Gen. Alexander S. (Gettysburg, Pa)
Webb, Pvt. James (Bull Run, Va)
Webber, Musician Alason P. (Kenesaw Mountian, Ga)
Weeks, Pvt. John H. (Spotsylvania, Va)
Weir, Capt. & Asst. Adj. Gen. Henry C. (St. Mary's Chruch, Va)
Welch, Pvt. George W. (Nashville, Tenn)
Welch, Cpl. Richard (Petersburg, Va)
Welch, Sgt. Stephen (Dug Gap, Ga)
*Wells, Pvt. Henry S. (Chapin's Farm, Va)
Wells, Chief Bugler Thomas M. (Cedar Creek, Va)
Wells, Maj. William (Gettysburg, Pa)
Welsh, Pvt. Edward (Vicksburg, Miss)
Welsh, Pvt. James (Petersburg, Va)
Westerhold, Sgt. William (Spotsylvania, Va)
Weston, Maj. John F. (Wetumpka, Ala)
Wheaton, Lt. Col. Loyd (Fort Blakely, Ala)
Wheeler, 1st Lt. Daniel D. (Salem Heights, Va)
Wheeler, Pvt. Henry W. (Bull Run, Va)
Wherry, 1st Lt. William M. (Wilson's Creek, Mo)
Whitaker, Capt. Edward W. (Reams's Station, Va)
White, Cpl. Adam (Hatcher's Run, Va)
White, Pvt. J. Henry (Rappahannock Station, Va)
White, Capt. Patrick H. (Vicksburg, Miss)
Whitehead, Chaplain John M. (Stone River, Tenn)
Whitman, Pvt. Frank M. (Antietam, Md & Spotsylvania, Va)
Whitmore, Pvt. John (Fort Blakely, Ala)
Whitney, Sgt. William G. (Chickamauga, Ga)
Whittier, 1st Lt. Edward N. (Fisher's Hill, Va)
Widick, Pvt. Andrew J. (Vicksburg, Miss)
Wilcox, Sgt. William H. (Spotsylvania, Va)
Wiley, Sgt. James (Gettysburg, Pa)
Wilhelm, Capt. George (Champion Hill, Miss)
Wilkins, Sgt. Leander A. (Petersburg, Va)
Willcox, Col. Orlando B. (Bull Run, Va)
Williams, Pvt. Elwood N. (Shiloh, Tenn)
Williams, QM Sgt. George C. (Gaines's Mill, Va)
Williams, Sgt. Le Roy (Cold Harbor, Va)
Williams, Pvt. William H. (Peach Tree Creek, Ga)
Williamson, Col. James A. (Chickasaw Bayou, Miss)
Williston, 1st Lt. Edward B. (Trevilian Station, Va)
Wilson, Sgt. Charles E. (Sayler's Creek, Va)
Wilson, Pvt. Christopher W. (Spotsylvania, Va)
Wilson, Cpl. Francis A. (Petersburg, Va)
Wilson, Sgt. John (Chamberlain's Creek, Va)
Wilson, Pvt. John A. (Georgia)
Wilson, 1st Lt. John M. (Malvern Hill, Va)
Winegar, Lt. William W. (Five Forks, Va)
Wisner, 1st Lt. Lewis S. (Spotsylvania, Va)
Withington, Capt. William H. (Bull Run, Va)
Wollam, Pvt. John (Georgia)
Wood, 1st Lt. H. Clay (Wilson's Creek, Mo)
Wood, Pvt. Mark (Georgia)
Wood, Capt. Richard H. (Vicksburg, Miss)
Woodbury, Sgt. Eri D. (Cedar Creek, Va)
Woodruff, Sgt. Alonzo (Hatcher's Run, Va)
Woodruff, 1st Lt. Carle A. (Newby's Crossroads, Va)
Woods, Pvt. Daniel A. (Sayler's Creek, Va)
Woodward, 1st Lt. & Adj. Evan M. (Fredericksburg, Va)
Wortick, Pvt. Joseph (Vicksburg, Miss)
Wray, Sgt. William J. (Fort Stevens, DC)
Wright, Capt. Albert D. (Petersburg, Va)
Wright, Pvt. Robert (Chapel House Farm, Va)
Wright, Cpl. Samuel (Nolensville, Tenn)
Wright, Pvt. Samuel C. (Antietam, Md)
Yeager, Pvt. Jacob F. (Buzzard's Roost, Ga)
Young, Sgt. Andrew J. (Paine's Crossroads, Va)
Young Cpl. Benjamin F. (Petersburg, Va)
Young, Sgt. Calvary M. (Osage, Kans)
Young, Pvt. James M. (Wilderness, Va)
Younker, Pvt. John L. (Cedar Mountain, Va)

MARINES

Binder, Sgt. Richard (Fort Fisher, NC)
Denig, Sgt. J. Henry (Mobile Bay, Ala)
Fry, Orderly Sgt. Isaac N. (Fort Fisher, NC)
Hudson, Sgt. Michael (Mobile Bay, Ala)
Mackie, Cpl. John F. (Drewry's Bluff, Va)
Martin, Sgt. James (Mobile Bay, Ala)
Miller, Sgt. Andrew (Mobile Bay, Ala)
Nugent, Orderly Sgt. Christopher (Crystal River, Fla)
Oviatt, Cpl. Miles M. (Mobile Bay, Ala)
Rannahan, Cpl. John (Fort Fisher, NC)
Roantree, Sgt. James S. (Mobile Bay, Ala)
Shivers, Pvt. John (Fort Fisher, NC)
Smith, Cpl. Willard M. (Mobile Bay, Ala)
Sprowle, Orderly Sgt. David (Mobile Bay, Ala)
Thompson, Pvt. Henry A. (Fort Fisher, NC)
Tomlin, Cpl. Andrew J. (Fort Fisher, NC)
Vaughn, Sgt. Pinkerton R. (Port Hudson, La)

NAVY

Aheam, Paymaster's Steward Michael (Cherbourg, France)
Anderson, QM Robert (Various)
Angling, Cabin Boy John (Fort Fisher, NC)
Arther, SQM Matthew (Forts Henry & Donelson, Ten.)
Asten, QG Charles (Red River, Va)
Atkinson, Yeoman Thomas E. (Mobile Bay, Ala)
Avery, Sman James (Mobile Bay, Ala)
Baker, QC Charles (Mobile Bay, Ala)
Baldwin, Coal Heaver Charles (Roanoke River, NC)
Barnum, BM James (Fort Fisher, NC)
Barter, Lman Gurdon H. (Fort Fisher, NC)
Barton, Sman Thomas (Franklin, Va)
Bass, Sman David L. (Fort Fisher, NC)
Bazaar, Ord. Sman Philip (Fort Fisher, NC)
Bell, Capt. of the Afterguard George (Galveston Bay, Tex)
Betham, Coxswain Asa (Fort Fisher, NC)
Bibber, GM Charles J. (Fort Fisher, NC)
Bickford, Capt. of the Top John F. (Cherbourg, France)
Blagheen, Ship's Cook William (Mobile Bay, Ala)
Blair, BM Robert M. (Fort Fisher, NC)
Blake, Robert (Legareville, SC)
Bois, QM Frank (Vicksburg, Miss)
Bond, BM William (Cherbourg, France)
Bourne, Sman & Gun Capt. Thomas (Forts Jackson & St. Philip, La)
Bowman, QM Edward R. (Fort Fisher, NC)
Bradley, Lman Amos (Forts Jackson & St. Philip, La)
Bradley, BM Charles (NOR)
Brazell, QM John (Mobile Bay, Ala)
Breen, BM John (Franklin, Va)
Brennan, Sman Christopher (Forts Jackson & St. Philip, La)
Brinn, Sman Andrew (Port Hudson, La)
Brown, QM James (Red River, Tex)
Brown, Capt. of the Forecastle John (Mobile Bay, Ala)
Brown, Capt. of the Top Robert (Mobile Bay, Ala)
Brown, Lman William H. (Mobile Bay, Ala)
Brown, Lman Wilson (Mobile Bay, Ala)
Brownell, Coxswain William P. (Great Gulf Bay & Vicksburg, Miss)
Brutsche, Lman Henry (Plymouth, NC)
Buck, QM James (Forts Jackson & St. Philip, La)
Burns, Sman John M. (Mobile Bay, Ala)
Burton, Sman Albert (Fort Fisher, NC)
Butts, GM George (Red River, Tex)
Byrnes, BM James (NOR)
Campbell, BM William (Fort Fisher, NC)
Carr, Master-at-Arms William M. (Mobile Bay, Ala)
Cassidy, Lman Michael (Mobile Bay, Ala)
Chandler, Coxswain James B. (Mobile Bay, Ala)
Chaput, Lman Louis G. (Mobile Bay, Ala)
Clifford, Master-at-Arms Robert T. (Wilmington, NC)
Colbert, Coxswain Patrick (Plymouth, NC)
Conlan, Sman Dennis (Fort Fisher, NC)
Connor, Ord. Sman Thomas (Fort Fisher, NC)
Connor, BM William C. (Wilmington, NC)
Cooper, Coxswain John (Mobile Bay, Ala)
Corcoran, Lman Thomas E. (Vicksburg, Miss)
Cotton, Ord. Sman Peter (Yazoo River, Miss)
Crawford, Fireman Alexander (Roanoke River, NC)
Cripps, QM Thomas (Mobile Bay, Ala)
Davis, QG John (Elizabeth City, NC)
Davis, Ord. Sman Samuel W. (Mobile Bay, Ala)
Deakin, BM Charles (Mobile Bay, Ala)
Dempster, Coxswain John (Fort Fisher, NC)
Denning, Lman Lorenzo (NOR)
Dennis, BM Richard (Mobile Bay, Ala)
Densmore, Chief BM William (Mobile Bay, Ala)
Diggins, Ord. Sman Bartholomew (Mobile Bay, Ala)
Ditzenback, QM John (Bell's Mills, Tenn)
Donnelly, Ord. Sman John (Mobile Bay, Ala)
Doolen, Coal Heaver William (Mobile Bay, Ala)
Dorman, Sman John (Various)
Dougherty, Lman Patrick (NOR)
Dow, BM Henry (Vicksburg, Miss)
Duncan, BM Adam (Mobile Bay, Ala)
Duncan, Ord. Sman James K. L. (Harrisonburg, La)
Dunn, QM William (Fort Fisher, NC)
Dunphy, Coal Heaver Richard D. (Mobile Bay, Ala)
Edwards, Capt. of the Top John (Mobile Bay, Ala)
English, Signal QM Thomas (Fort Fisher, NC)
Erickson, Capt. of the Forecastle John P. (Fort Fisher, NC)
Farley, BM William (Stono River, SC)
Farrell, QM Edward (Forts Jackson & St. Philip, La)
Ferrell, Pilot John H. (Bell's Mills, Tenn)
Fitzpatrick, Coxswain Thomas (Mobile Bay, Ala)
Flood, Boy Thomas (Forts Jackson & St. Philip, La)
Foy, Signal QM Charles H. (Fort Fisher, NC)
Franks, Sman William J. (Yazoo City, Miss)
Freeman, Pilot Martin (Mobile Bay, Ala)
Frisbee, GM John B. (Forts Jackson & St. Philip, La)
Gardner, Sman William (Mobile Bay, Ala)
Garrison, Coal Heaver James R. (Mobile Bay, Ala)
Garvin, Capt. of the Forecastle William (Fort Fisher, NC)
George, Ord. Sman Daniel G. (NOR)
Gile, Lman Frank. S. (Charleston Harbor, SG)
Graham, Lman Robert (Plymouth, NC)
Greene, Capt. of the Forecastle John (Forts Jackson & St. Philip, La)
Griffiths, Capt. of the Forecastle John (Fort Fisher, NC)
Griswold, Ord. Sman Luke M. (Cape Hatteras, NC)
Haffee, QG Edmund (Fort Fisher, NC)
Haley, Capt. of the Forecastle James (Cherbourg, France)
Halstead, Coxswain William (Mobile Bay, Ala)
Ham, Carpenter's Mate Mark G. (Cherbourg, France)
Hamilton, Coxswain Hugh (Mobile Bay, Ala)
Hamilton, Coal Heaver Richard (NOR)
Hamilton, QM Thomas W. (Vicksburg, Miss)
Hand, QM Allexander (Roanoke River, NC)
Harcourt, Ord. Sman Thomas (Fort Fisher, NC)
Harding, Capt. of the Forecastle Thomas (Beauford, NC)
Harley, Ord. Sman Bernard (NOR)
Harrington, Lman Daniel (NOR)
Harris, Capt. of the Forecastle John (Mobile Bay, Ala)
Harrison, Sman George H. (Cherbourg, France)
Hathaway, Sman Edward W. (Vicksburg, Miss)
Hawkins, Sman Charles (Fort Fisher, NC)
Hayden, QM Joseph B. (Fort Fisher, NC)
Hayes, Coxswain John (Cherbourg, France)
Hayes, Coxswain Thomas (Mobile Bay, Ala)
Hickman, 2d Class Fireman John (Port Hudson, La)
Hinnegan, 2d Class Fireman William (Fort Fisher, NC)
Hollat, 3d Class Boy George (Forts Jackson & St. Philip, La)
Horton, GM James (NOR)
Horton, Sman Lewis A. (Cape Hatteras, NC)
Houghton, Ord. Sman Edward J. (NOR)
Howard, Lman Martin (Plymouth, NC)
Howard, BM Peter (Port Hudson, La)
Huskey, Fireman Michael (Deer Creek, Miss)
Hyland, Sman John (Red River, Tex)
Irlam, Sman Joseph (Mobile Bay, Ala)
Irving, Coxswain John (Mobile Bay, Ala)
Irving, Coxswain Thomas (Charleston Harbor, SC)
Irwin, Sman Nicholas (Mobile Bay, Ala)
James, Capt. of the Top John H. (Mobile Bay, Ala)
Jenkins, Sman Thomas (Vicksburg, Miss)
Johnson, Sman Henry (Mobile Bay, Ala)
Johnston, Lman William P. (Harrisonburg, La)
Jones, Chief BM Andrew (Mobile Bay, Ala)
Jones, Lman John (Cape Hatteras, NC)
Jones, QM John E. (Mobile Bay, Ala)
Jones, Coxswain Thomas (Fort Fisher, NC)
Jones, Capt. of the Top William (Mobile Bay, Ala)
Jordan, Coxswain Robert (Nansemond River, Va)
Jordan, QM Thomas (Mobile Bay, Ala)
Kane, Capt. of the Hold Thomas (Fort Fisher, NC)
Kelley, 2d Class Fireman John (Roanoke River, NC)
Kendrick, Coxswain Thomas (Mobile Bay, Ala)
Kenna, QM Barnett (Mobile Bay, Ala)
Kenyon, Fireman Charles (Drewry's Bluff, Va)
King, Lman Robert H. (NOR)
Kinnaird, Lman Samuel W. (Mobile Bay, Ala)
Lafferty, Fireman John (Roanoke River, NC)
Laffey, Sman Bartlett (Yazoo City, Miss)
Lakin, Sman Daniel (Franklin, Va)
Lann, Lman John S. (St. Marks, Fla)
Lawson, Lman John (Mobile Bay, Ala)
Lear, QM Nicholas (Fort Fisher, NC)
Lee, Sman James H. (Cherbourg, France)
Leland, GM George W. (Charleston Harbor, SC)
Leon, Capt. of the Forecastle Pierre (Yazoo River, Miss)
Lloyd, Coal Heaver Benjamin (Roanoke River, NC)
Lloyd, Coxswain John W. (Roanoke River, NC)
*Logan, Capt. of the Afterguard Hugh (Cape Hatteras, NC)
Lyons, Sman Thomas (Forts Jackson & St. Philip, La)
McClelland, 1st Class Fireman Matthew (Port Hudson, La)
McCormick, BM Michael (Red River, Tex)
McCullock, Sman Adam (Mobile Bay, Ala)
McDonald, BM John (Yazoo River, Miss)
McFarland, Capt. of the Forecastle John (Mobile Bay, Ala)
McGowan, QM (Forts Jackson & St. Philip, La)
Machon, Boy James (Mobile Bay, Ala)
McHugh , Sman Martin (Vicksburg, Miss)
McIntosh, Capt. of the Top James (Mobile Bay, Ala)
Mack, Capt. of the Top Alexander (Mobile Bay, Ala)
Mack, Sman John (St. Marks, Fla)
McKnight, Coxswain William (Forts Jackson & St. Philip, La)
McLeod, Capt. of the Foretop James (Forts Jackson & St. Philip, La)
McWilliams, Lman George W. (Fort Fisher, NC)
Madden, Coal Heaver William (Mobile Bay, Ala)
Martin, QM Edward S. (Mobile Bay, Ala)
Martin, BM William (Yazoo River, Miss)
Martin, Sman William (Forts Jackson & St. Philip, La)
Melville, Ord. Sman Charles (Mobile Bay, Ala)
Miffin, Engineer's Cook James (Mobile Bay, Ala)
Miller, QM James (Legarevill, SC)
Milliken, QG Daniel (Fort Fisher, NC)
Mills, Sman Charles (Fort Fisher, NC)
Molloy, Ord. Sman Hugh (Harrisonburg, La)
Montgomery, Capt. of the Afterguard Robert (Fort Fisher, NC)
Moore, Lman Charles (Legareville, SC)
Moore, Sman Charles (Cherbourg, France)
Moore, Sman George (Cape Hatteras, NC)
Moore, BM William (Haines's Bluff, Miss)
Morgan, Capt. of the Top James H. (Mobile Bay, Ala)
Morrison, Coxswain John G. (Yazoo River, Miss)
Morton, BM Charles W. (Yazoo River, Miss)
Mullen, BM Patrick (Mattox Creek, Va)
Murphy, BM Patrick (Mobile Bay, Ala)
Naylor, Lman David (Mobile Bay, Ala)
Neil, QG John (Fort Fisher, NC)
Newland, Ord Sman William (Mobile Bay, Ala)
Nibbe, QM John H. (Yazzo River, Miss)
Nichols, QM William (Mobile Bay, Ala)
Noble, Lman Daniel (Mobile Bay, Ala)
O'Brien, Coxswain Oliver (Sullivan's Island Channel, SC)
O'Connell, Coal Heaver Thomas (Mobile Bay, Ala)
O'Donoghue, Sman Timothy (Red River, Tex)
Ortega, Sman John (NOR)
Parker, Capt. of the Afterguard William (Forts Jackson & St. Philip, La)
Parks, Capt. of the Forecastle George (Mobile Bay, Ala)
Pease, Sman Joachim (Cherbourg, France)
Peck, 2d Class Boy Oscar E. (Forts Jackson & St. Philip, La)
Pelham, Lman William (Mobile Bay, Ala)
Perry, BM Thomas (Cherbourg, France)
Peterson, Sman Alfred (Franklin, Va)
Phinney, BM William (Mobile Bay, Ala)
Poole, QM William B. (Cherbourg, France)
Prance, Capt. of the Main Top George (Fort Fisher, NC)
Preston, Lman John (Mobile Bay, Ala)
Price, Coxswain Edward (Mobile Bay, Ala)
Province, Ord. Sman George (Fort Fisher, NC)
Pyne, Sman George (St. Marks, Fla)
Read, Ord. Sman Charles (St. Marks, Fla)
Read, Coxswain Charles A. (Cherbourg, France)
Read, Sman George E. (Cherbourg, France)
Regan, QM Jeremiah (Drewry's Bluff, Va)
Rice, Coal Heaver Charles (Fort Fisher, NC)
Richards, QM Louis (Forts Jackson & St. Philip, La)
Ringold, Coxswain Edward (Pocataligo, SC)
Roberts, Sman James (Fort Fisher, NC)
Robinson, BM Alexander (Wilmington, NC)
Robinson, BM Charles (Yazoo River, Miss)
Rountry, 1st Class Fireman John (NOR)
Rush, 1st Class Fireman John (Port Hudson, La)
Sanderson, Lman Aaron (Mattox Creek, Va)
Saunders, QM James (Cherbourg, France)
Savage, Ord. Sman Auzella (Fort Fisher, NC)
Schutt, Coxswain George (St. Marks, Fla)
Seanor, Master-at-Arms James (Mobile Bay, Ala)
Seward, Paymaster's Steward Richard E. (Ship Island Sound, La)
Sharp, Sman Hendrick (Mobile Bay, Ala)
Shepard, Ord. Sman Louis C. (Fort Fisher, NC)
Sheridan, QM James (Mobile Bay, Ala)
Shipman, Coxswain William (Fort Fisher, NC)
Shutes, Capt. of the Forecastle Henry (New Orleans, La, & Fort McAllister, Ga)
Simkins, Coxswain Lebbeus (Mobile Bay, Ala)
*Smith, Coxswain Charles H. (Mobile Bay, Ala)
Smith, Ord. Sman Edwin (Franklin, Va)
Smith, Capt. of the Forecastle James (Mobile Bay, Ala)
Smith, 2d Capt. of the Top John (Mobile Bay, Ala)
Smith, Capt. of the Forecastle John (Mobile Bay, Ala)
Smith, Coxswain Oloff (Mobile Bay, Ala)
Smith, Sman Thomas (St. Marks, Fla)
Smith, Ord. Sman Walter B. (Mobile Bay, Ala)
Smith, QM William (Cherbourg, France)
Stanley, Shell Man William A. (Mobile Bay, Ala)
Sterling, Coal Heaver James E. (Mobile Bay, Ala)

Stevens, QM Daniel D. (Fort Fisher, NC)
Stoddard, Sman James (Yazoo River, Miss)
Stout, Lman Richard (Stono River, SC)
Strahan, Capt. of the Top Rovert (Cherbourg, France)
Sullivan, Ord. Sman James (Fort Fisher, NC)
Sullivan, Sman John (Wilmington, NC)
Sullivan, Coxswain Timothy (NOR)
Summers, Chief QM Robert (Fort Fisher, NC)
Swanson, Sman John (Fort Fisher, NC)
Swatton, Sman Edward (Fort Fisher, NC)
Swearer, Sman Benjamin (Fort Clark, Md)
Talbott, Capt. of the Forecastle William (Arkansas)
*Tallentine, QC James (Plymouth, NC)
Taylor, Armorer George (Mobile Bay, Ala)
Taylor, Coxswain Thomas (Mobile Bay, Ala)
Taylor, Capt. of the Forecastle William G. (Fort Fisher, NC)
Thielberg, Sman Henry (Nansemond River, Va)
Thompson, Signal QM William (Hilton Head, NC)
Todd, QM Samuel (Mobile Bay, Ala)
Tripp, Chief BM Othniel (Fort Fisher, NC)
Truett, Coxswain Alexander H. (Mobile Bay, Ala)
Vantine, 1st Class Fireman Joseph E. (Port Hudson, La)
Verney, Chief QM James W. (Fort Fisher, NC)
Wagg, Coxswain Maurice (Cape Hatteras, NC)
Ward, QG James (Mobile Bay, Ala)
Warren, Coxswain David (Wilmington, NC)
Webster, Lman Henry S. (Fort Fisher, NC)
Weeks, Capt. of the Foretop Charles H. (NOR)
Wells, QM William (Mobile Bay, Ala)
White, Capt. of the Gun Joseph (Fort Fisher, NC)
Whitfield, QM Daniel (Mobile Bay, Ala)
Wilcox, Ord. Sman Franklin L. (Fort Fisher, NC)
Wilkes, Lman Henry (NOR)
Wilkes, Pilot Perry (Red River, Tex)
Williams, Sailmaker's Mate Anthony (Fort Fisher, NC)
Williams, Sman Augustus (Fort Fisher, NC)
Williams, BM John (Hilton Head, NC)
Williams, Capt. of the Maintop John (Mathias Point, Va)
Williams, Sman John (Franklin, Va)
Williams, Sman Peter (Hampton Roads, Va)
Williams, Signal QM Robert (Yazoo River, Miss)
Williams, Lman William (Charleston Harbor, SC)
Willis, Coxswain Richard (Fort Fisher, NC)
Wood, Coxswain Robert B. (Nansemond River, Va)
Woods, Sman Samuel (Nansemond River, Va)
Woon, BM John (Grand Gulf, Miss River)
Woram, Sman Charles B. (Mobile Bay, Ala)
Wright, QM Edward (Forts Jackson & St. Philip, La)
Wright, Yeoman William (Wilmington, NC)
Young, Coxswain Edward B. (Mobile Bay, Ala)
Young, Sman Horatio N. (Charleston Harbor, SC)
Young, BM William (Forts Jackson & St. Philip, La)

THE INDIAN CAMPAIGNS
1861–1898

ARMY

Albee, 1st Lt. George E. (Brazos River, Tex)
Alchesay, Sgt. (Arizona)
Allen, 1st Sgt. William (Turret Mountain, Ariz)
Anderson, Pvt. James (Wichita River, Tex)
Aston, Pvt. Edgar R. (San Carlos, Ariz)
Austin, Sgt. William G. (Wounded Knee Creek, S Dak)
Ayers, Pvt. James F. (Sappa Creek, Kans)
Babcock, 1st Lt. John B. (Spring Creek, Neb)
Bailey, Sgt. James E. (Arizona)
Baird, 1st Lt. & Adj. George W. (Bear Paw Mountain, Mont)
Baker, Musician John (Cedar Creek, Mont)
†Baldwin, 1st Lt. Frank D. (McClellan's Creek, Tex)
Bancroft, Pvt. Neil (Little Big Horn, Mont)
Barnes, Pfc. Will C. (Fort Apache, Ariz)
Barrett, 1st Sgt. Richard (Sycamore Canyon, Ariz)
Beauford, 1st Sgt. Clay (Arizona)
Bell, Pvt. James (Big Horn, Mont)
Bergerndahl, Pvt. Frederick (Staked Plains, Tex)
Bertram, Cpl. Heinrich (Arizona)
Bessey, Cpl. Charles A. (Elkhorn Creek, Wyo)
Bishop, Sgt. Daniel (Turret Mountain, Ariz)
Blair, 1st Sgt. James (Arizona)
Blanquet (Arizona)
Bowden, Cpl. Samuel (Wichita River, Tex)
Bowman, Sgt. Alonzo (Cibicue Creek, Ariz)
Boyne, Sgt. Thomas (Mimbres Mountains & Ojo Caliente, N Mex)
Bradbury, 1st Sgt. Sanford (Hell Canyon, Ariz)
Branagan, Pvt. Edward (Red River, Tex)
Brant, Pvt. Abram B. (Little Big Horn, Mont)
*Bratling, Cpl. Frank (Fort Selden, N Mex)
Brett, 2d Lt. Lloyd M. (O'Fallon's Creek, Mont)
Brogan, Sgt. James (Simon Valley, Ariz)
Brophy, Pvt. James (Arizona)
Brown, Sgt. Benjamin (Arizona)
Brown, Sgt. James (Davidson Canyon, Ariz)
Brown, Pvt. Lorenzo D. (Big Hole, Mont)
Bryan, Hospital Steward William C. (Powder River, Wyo)
Burkard, Pvt. Oscar (Leech Lake, Minn)
Burke, Farrier Patrick J. (Arizona)
Burke, Pvt. Richard (Cedar Creek, Mont)
Burnet, 2d Lt. George R. (Cuchillo Negro Mountains, N Mex)
Butler, Capt. Edmond (Wolf Mountain, Mont)
Byrne, Sgt. Denis (Cedar Creek, Mont)
Cable, Pvt. Joseph A. (Cedar Creek, Mont)
Callen, Pvt. Thomas J. (Little Big Horn, Mont)
Calvert, Pvt. James S. (Cedar Creek, Mont)
Canfield, Pvt. Heth (Little Blue, Neb)
Carpenter, Capt. Louis H. (Kansas & Colorado)
Carr, Pvt. John (Chiricahua Mountains, Ariz)
Carroll, Pvt. Thomas (Arizona)
Carter, Pvt. George (Arizona)
Carter, 1st Lt. Mason (Bear Paw Mountain, Mont)
Carter, 2d Lt. Robert G. (Brazos River, Tex)
Carter, 1st Lt. William H. (Cibicue, Ariz)
Casey, Capt. James S. (Wolf Mountain, Mont)
Cheever, 1st Lt. Benhamin H., Jr (White River, S Dak)
Chiquito (Arizona)
Clancy, Musician John E. (Wounded Knee Creek, S Dak)
Clark, Pvt. Wilfred (Big Hole, Mont & Camas Meadows, Idaho)
Clarke, 2d Lt. Powhatan H. (Sonora, Mex)
Comfort, Cpl. John W. (Staked Plains, Tex)
Connor, Cpl. John (Wichita River, Tex)
Coonrod, Sgt. Aquilla (Cedar Creek, Mont)
Corcoran, Cpl. Michael (Agua Fria River, Ariz)
Co-Rux-Te-Chod-Ish (Mad Bear), Sgt. (Republican River, Kans)
Craig, Sgt. Samuel H. (Santa Cruz Mountains, Mex)
Crandall, Pvt. Charles (Arizona)
Crist, Sgt. John (Arizona)
Criswell, Sgt. Banjamin C. (Little Big Horn River, Mont)
Cruse, 2d Lt. Thomas (Big Dry Fork, Ariz)
Cubberly, Pvt. William G. (San Carlos, Ariz)
Cunningham, Cpl. Charles (Little Big Horn River, Mont)
Daily, Pvt. Charles (Arizona)
Daniels, Sgt. James T. (Arizona)
Dawson, Trumpeter Michael (Sappa Creek, Kans)
Day, 2d Lt. Matthias W. (Las Animas Canyon, N Mex)
Day, 1st Sgt. William L. (Arizona)
*De Armond, Sgt. William (Upper Washita, Tex)
Deary, Sgt. George (Apache Creek, Ariz)
Deetline, Pvt. Frederick (Little Big Horn, Mont)
Denny, Sgt. John (Las Animas Canyon, N Mex)
Dickens, Cpl. Charles H. (Chiricahua Mountains, Ariz)
Dodge, Capt. Francis S. (White River Agency, Colo)
Donahue, Pvt. John L. (Chiricahua Mountains, Ariz)
Donavan, Sgt. Cornelius (Agua Fria River, Ariz)
Donelly, Pvt. John S. (Cedar Creek, Mont)
Doughterty, Blacksmith William (Arizona)
Dowling, Cpl. James (Arizona)
Edwards, 1st Sgt. William D. (Big Hole, Mont)
Eldrige, Sgt. George H. (Wichita River, Tex)
Elsatsoosu, Cpl (Arizona)
Elwood, Pvt. Edwin L. (Chiricahua Mountains, Ariz)
Emmer, 2d Lt. Robert T. (Las Animas Canyon, N Mex)
Evans, Pvt. William (Big Horn, Mont)
Factor, Pvt. Pompey (Pecos River, Tex)
Falcott, Sgt. Henry (Arizona)
Farren, Pvt. Daniel (Arizona)
Feaster, Pvt. Mosheim (Wounded Knee Creek, S Dak)
Fegan, Sgt. James (Plum Creek, Kans)
Ferrari, Cpl. George (Red Creek, Ariz)
Fichter, Pvt. Hermann (Whetstone Mountains, Ariz)
Foley, Sgt. John H. (Platte River, Neb)
Folly, Pvt. William H. (Arizona)
Foran, Pvt. Nicholas (Arizona)
Forsyth, 1st Sgt. Thomas H. (Powder River, Wyo)
Foster, Sgt. William (Red River, Tex)
Freemeyer, Pvt. Christopher (Cedar Creek, Mont)
Gardiner, Pvt. Peter W. (Sappa Creek, Kans)
Gardner, Pvt. Charles (Arizona)
Garland, Cpl. Harry (Little Muddy Creek, Mont & Camas Meadows, Idaho)
Garlington, 1st Lt. Ernest A. (Wounded Knee Creek, S Dak)
Gates, Bugler George (Picacho Mountain, Ariz)
Gay, Pvt. Thomas H. (Arizona)
Geiger, Sgt. George (Little Big Horn River, Mont)
Georgian, Pvt. John (Chiricahua Mountains, Ariz)
Gerber, Sgt. Maj. Frederick W. (Various)
*Given, Cpl. John J. (Wichita River, Tex)
Glavinski, Blacksmith Albert (Powder River, Mont)
Glover, Sgt. T. B. (Mizpah Creek & Pumpkin Creek, Mont)
Glynn, Pvt. Michael (Wheatstone Mountains, Ariz)
Godfrey, Capt. Edward S. (Bear Paw Mountain, Mont)
Golden, Sgt. Patrick (Arizona)
Goldin, Pvt. Theodore W. (Little Big Horn, Mont)
Goodman, Pvt. David (Lyry Creek, Ariz)
Grant, Sgt. George (Fort Phil Kearny-Fort C. F. Smith, Dak Terr)
Greaves, Cpl. Clinton (Florida Mountains, N Mex)
Green, Sgt. Francis C. (Arizona)
Green, Maj. John (Lava Beds, Calif)
Gresham, 1st Lt. John C. (Wounded Knee Creek, S Dak)
Grimes, Sgt. Edward P. (Milk River, Colo)
Gunther, Cpl. Jacob (Arizona)
Haddoo, Cpl. John (Cedar Greek, Mont)
Hall, Pvt. John (Arizona)
Hall, 1st Lt. William P. (White River, Colo)
Hamilton, Pvt. Frank (Agua Fria River, Ariz)
Hamilton, Pvt. Mathew H. (Wounded Knee Creek, S Dak)
Hanley, Sgt. Richard P. (Little Big Horn River, Mont)
Harding, Blacksmith Mosher A. (Chiricahua Mountains, Ariz)
Harrington, Pvt. John (Wichita River, Tex)
Harris, Sgt. Charles D. (Red Creek, Ariz)
Harris, Pvt. David W. (Little Big Horn River, Mont)
Harris, Pvt. William M. (Little Big Horn River, Mont)
Hartzog, Pvt. Joshua B. (Wounded Knee Creek, S Dak)
Haupt, Cpl. Paul (Hell Canyon, Ariz)
Hawthorne, 2d Lt. Harry L. (Wounded Knee Creek, S Dak)
Hay, Sgt. Fred S. (Upper Wichita, Tex)
Heartery, Pvt. Richard (Cibicue, Ariz)
Heise, Pvt. Clamor (Arizona)
Herron, Cpl. Leander (Fort Dodge, Kans)
Heyl, 2d Lt. Charles H. (Fort Hartsuff, Neb)
Higgins, Pvt. Thomas P. (Arizona)
Hill, Sgt. Frank E. (Date Creek, Ariz)
Hill, 1st Sgt. James M. (Turret Mountain, Ariz)
Hillock, Pvt. Marvin C. (Wounded Knee Creek, S Dak)
Himmelsback, Pvt. Michael (Little Blue, Neb)
Hinemann, Sgt. Lehmann (Arizona)
Hobday, Pvt. George (Wounded Knee Creek, S Dak)
Hogan, 1st Sgt. Henry (Cedar Creek, Mont)
Second award (Bear Paw Mountain, Mont)
Holden, Pvt. Henry (Little Big Horn River, Mont)
Holland, Cpl. David (Cedar Creek, Mont)
*Hooker, Pvt. George (Tonto Creek, Ariz)
Hoover, Bugler Samuel (Santa Maria Mountains, Ariz)
Hornaday, Pvt. Simpson (Sappa Creek, Kans)
Howze, 2d Lt. Robert L. (White River, S Dak)
Hubbard, Pvt. Thomas (Little Blue, Neb)
Huff, Pvt. James W. (Arizona)
Huggins, Capt. Eli L. (O'Fallons Creek, Mont)
Humphrey, 1st Lt. Charles F. (Clearwater, Idaho)
Hunt, Pvt. Fred O. (Cedar Creek, Mont)
Hutchinson, Sgt. Rufus D. (Little Big Horn River, Mont)
Hyde, Sgt. Henry J. (Arizona)
Irwin, Asst. Surgeon Bernard J. D. (Apache Pass, Ariz)
Jackson, Capt. James (Camas Meadows, Idaho)
James, Cpl. John (Upper Wichita, Tex)
Jarvis, Sgt. Frederick (Chiricahua Mountains, Ariz)
Jetter, Sgt. Bernhard (South Dakota)
Jim, Sgt. (Arizona)
Johnson, Sgt. Henry (Milk River, Colo)
Johnston, Cpl. Edward (Cedar Creek, Mont)
Jones, Farrier William H. (Little Muddy Creek, Mont, & Camas Meadows, Idaho)
Jordan, Sgt. George (Fort Tularosa & Carrizo Canyon, N Mex)
Kay, Pvt. John (Arizona)
Keating, Cpl. Daniel (Wichita River, Tex)
Keenan, Trumpeter Bartholomew T. (Chiricahua Mountains, Ariz)
Keenan, Pvt. (Arizona)
Kelley, Pvt. Charles (Chiricahua Mountains, Ariz)
Kelly, Cpl. John J. H. (Upper Wichita, Tex)
Kelly, Pvt. Thomas (Upper Wichita, Tex)
Kelsay (Arizona)
Kennedy, Pvt. Philip (Cedar Creek, Mont)
Kerr, Capt. John B. (White River, S Dak)
Kerrigan, Sgt. Thomas (Wichita River, Tex)
Kilmartin, Pvt. John (Whetstone Mountains, Ariz)
Kirk, 1st Sgt. John (Wichita River, Tex)
Kirkwood, Sgt. John A. (Slim Buttes, Dak Terr)
Kitchen, Sgt. George K. (Upper Wichita, Tex)
Knaak, Pvt. Albert (Arizona)
Knight, Sgt. Joseph F. (White River, S Dak)
Knox, Sgt. John W. (Upper Wichita, Tex)
Koelpin, Sgt. William (Upper Wichita, Tex)
Kosoha (Arizona)
Kreher, 1st Sgt. Wendelin (Cedar Creek, Mont)
Kyle, Cpl. John (Republican River, Kans)
Larkin, Farrier David (Red River, Tex)
Lawrence, Pvt. James (Arizona)
Lawton, Sgt. John S. (Milk River, Colo)
Lenihan, Pvt. James (Clear Creek, Ariz)
Leonard, Sgt. Patrick (Little Blue, Neb)
Leonard, Cpl. Patrick T. (Fort Hartsuff, Neb)
Leonard, Pvt. William (Muddy Creek, Mont)
Lewis, Sgt. William B. (Bluff Station, Wyo)
Little, Bugler Thomas (Arizona)
Lohnes, Pvt. Francis W. (Gilman's Ranch, Neb)
Long, 2d Lt. Oscar F. (Bear Paw Mountain, Mont)
Lowthers, Pvt. James (Sappa Creek, Kans)
*Loyd, Sgt. George (Wounded Knee Creek, S Dak)
Lytle, Sgt. Leonidas S. (Fort Selden, N Mex)
Lytton, Cpl. Jeptha L. (Fort Hartsuff, Neb)
McBride, Pvt. Bernard (Arizona)
McBryar, Sgt. William (Arizona)
McCabe, Pvt. William (Red River, Tex)
*McCann, Pvt. Bernard (Cedar Creek, Mont)
McCarthy, 1st Sgt. Michael (White Bird Canyon, Idaho)
McClernand, 2d Lt. Edward J. (Bear Paw Mountain, Mont)
McCormick, Pvt. Michael (Cedar Creek, Mont)
McDonald, Pvt. Franklin M. (Fort Griffin, Tex)
McDonald, Cpl. James (Arizona)
McDonald, 1st Lt. Robert (Wolf Mountain, Mont)
McGann, 1st Sgt. Michael A. (Rosebud River, Mont)
McGar, Pvt. Owen (Cedar Creek, Mont)
Machol, Pvt. (Arizona)
McHugh, Pvt. John (Cedar Creek, Mont)
McKinley, Pvt. Daniel (Arizona)
McLennon, Musician John (Big Hole, Mont)
McLoughlin, Sgt. Michael (Cedar Creek, Mont)
*McMasters, Cpl. Henry A. (Red River, Tex)
McMillan, Sgt. Albert W. (Wounded Knee Creek, S Dak)
McNaly, 1st Sgt. James (Arizona)
McNamara, 1st Sgt. William (Red River, Tex)
McPhelan, Sgt. Robert (Cedar Creek, Mont)
McVeagh, Pvt. Charles H. (Arizona)
Mahers, Pvt. Herbert (Seneca Mountain, Ariz)
Mahoney, Pvt. Gregory (Red River, Tex)
Martin, Sgt. Patrick (Castle Dome & Santa Maria Mountains, Ariz)
Matthews, Cpl. David A. (Arizona)
Maus, 1st Lt. Marion P. (Sierra Madre Mountains, Mex)
May, Sgt. John (Wichita River, Tex)
Mays, Cpl. Isaiah (Arizona)
Meaher, Cpl. Nicholas (Chiricahua Mountains, Ariz)
Mechlin, Blacksmith Henry W. B. (Little Big Horn, Mont)
Merrill, Sgt. John (Milk River, Colo)
Miller, Pvt. Daniel H. (Whetstone Mountains, Ariz)
Miller, Cpl. George (Cedar Creek, Mont)
Miller, Pvt. George W. (Arizona)
Mitchell, 1st Sgt. John (Upper Washita, Tex)
Mitchell, Cpl. John J. (Hell Canyon, Ariz)
Montrose, Pvt. Charles H. (Cedar Creek, Mont)
Moquin, Cpl. George (Milk River, Colo)
Moran, Pvt. John (Seneca Mountain, Ariz)
Morgan, 2d Lt. George H. (Big Dry Fork, Ariz)
Moriarity, Sgt. John (Arizona)
Morris, 1st Sgt. James L. (Fort Selden, N Mex)
Morris, Cpl. William W. (Upper Washita, Tex)
Mott, Sgt. John (Whetstone Mountains, Ariz)
Moylan, Capt. Myles (Bear Paw Mountain, Mont)
Murphy, Pvt. Edward (Chiricahua Mountains, Ariz)
Murphy, Cpl. Edward F. (Milk River, Colo)
Murphy, Pvt. Jeremiah (Powder River, Mont)
Murphy, Cpl. Philip (Seneca Mountain, Ariz)
Murphy, Cpl. Thomas (Seneca Mountain, Ariz)
Murray, Sgt. Thomas (Little Big Horn, Mont)
Myers, Sgt. Fred (White River, S Dak)
Nannasaddie (Arizona)
Nantaje (Arizona)
Neal, Pvt. Solon D. (Wichita River, Tex)
Neder, Pvt. Adam (South Dakota)
Neilon, Sgt. Frederick S. (Upper Washita, Tex)
Newman, 1st Sgt. Henry (Whetstone Mountains, Ariz)
Nihill, Pvt. John (Whetstone Mountains, Ariz)
Nolan, Farrier Richard J. (White Clay Creek, S Dak)
O'Callaghan, Sgt. John (Arizona)
Oliver, 1st Sgt. Francis (Chiricahua Mountains, Ariz)
O'Neill, Cpl. William (Red River, Tex)
O'Regan, Pvt. Michael (Arizona)
Orr, Pvt. Moses (Arizona)
Osborne, Sgt. William (Arizona)
O'Sullivan, Pvt. John (Staked Plains, Tex)
Paine, Pvt. Adam (Red River, Tex)
Parnell, 1st Lt. William R. (White Bird Canyon, Idaho)
Payne, Trumpeter Isaac (Pecos River, Tex)
Pengally, Pvt. Edward (Chiricahua Mountains, Ariz)
Pennsyl, Sgt. Josiah (Upper Washita, Tex)
Phife, Sgt. Lewis (Arizona)
Philipsen, Blacksmith Wilhelm O. (Milk River, Colo)
Phillips, Pvt. Samuel D. (Muddy Creek, Mont)
Phoenix, Cpl. Edwin (Red River, Tex)
Platten, Sgt. Frederick (Sapa Creek, Kans)
Poppe, Sgt. John A. (Milk River, Colo)
Porter, Farrier Samuel (Wichita River, Tex)
Powers, Cpl. Thomas (Chiricahua Mountains, Ariz)
Pratt, Blacksmith James (Red River, Tex)
Pym, Pvt. James (Little Big Horn River, Mont)
Raerick, Pvt. John (Lyry Creek, Ariz)
Ragnar, 1st Sgt. Theodore (White Clay Creek, S Dak)
Rankin, Pvt. William (Red River, Tex)
Reed, Pvt. James C. (Arizona)
Richman, Pvt. Samuel (Arizona)
Roach, Cpl. Hampton M. (Milk River, Colo)
Robbins, Pvt. Marcus M. (Sappa Creek, Kans)
Robinson, 1st Sgt. Joseph (Rosebud River, Mont)
Roche, 1st Sgt. David (Cedar Creek, Mont)
Rodenburg, Pvt. Henry (Cedar Creek, Mont)
Rogan, Sgt. Patrick (Big Hole, Mont)
Romeyn, 1st Lt. Henry (Bear Paw Mountain, Mont)
Rooney, Pvt. Edward (Cedar Creek, Mont)
Roth, Pvt. Peter (Wichita River, Tex)
Rowalt, Pvt. John F. (Lyry Creek, Ariz)
Rowdy, Sgt. (Arizona)
Roy, Sgt. Stanislaus (Little Big Horn, Mont)
Russell, Pvt. James (Chiricahua Mountains, Ariz)
Ryan, Pvt. David (Cedar Creek, Mont)
Ryan, 1st Sgt. Dennis (Gageby Creek, Indian Terr)

Sale, Pvt. Albert (Santa Maria River, Ariz)
Schnitzer, Wagoner John (Horseshoe Canyon, N Mex)
Schou, Cpl. Julius (Dakota Territory)
Schroeter, Pvt. Charles (Chiricahua Mountains, Ariz)
Scott, Pvt. George D. (Little Big Horn, Mont)
Scott, Pvt. Robert B. (Chiricahua Mountains, Ariz)
Seward, Wagoner Griffin (Chiricahua Mountains, Ariz)
Shaffer, Pvt. William (Arizona)
Sharpless, Cpl. Edward C. (Upper Washita, Tex)
Shaw, Sgt. Thomas (Carrizo Canyon, N Mex)
Sheerin, Blacksmith John (Fort Selden, N Mex)
Sheppard, Pvt. Charles (Cedar Creek, Mont)
Shingle, 1st Sgt. John H. (Rosebud River, Mont)
Skinner, Contract Surgeon John O. (Lava Beds, Ore)
Smith, Sgt. Andrew J. (Chiricahua Mountains, Ariz)
Smith, Cpl. Charles E. (Wichita River, Tex)
Smith, Cpl. Cornelius C. (White River, S Dak)
*Smith, Pvt. George W. (Wichita River, Tex)
Smith, Pvt. Otto (Arizona)
Smith, Pvt. Robert (Slim Buttes, Mont)
Smith, Pvt. Theodore F. (Chiricahua Mountains, Ariz)
Smith, Pvt. Thomas (Chiricahua Mountains, Ariz)
Smith, Pvt. Thomas J. (Chiricahua Mountains, Ariz)
Smith, Pvt. William (Chiricahua Mountains, Ariz)
Smith, Pvt. William H. (Chiricahua Mountains, Ariz)
Snow, Trumpeter Elmer A. (Rosebud Creek, Mont)
Spence, Pvt. Orizoba (Chiricahua Mountains, Ariz)
Springer, Pvt. George (Chiricahua Mountains, Ariz)
Stance, Sgt. Emanuel (Kickapoo Springs, Tex)
Stanley, Pvt. Eben (Turret Mountain, Ariz)
Stanley, Cpl. Edward (Seneca Mountain, Ariz)
Stauffer, 1st Sgt. Rudolph (Camp Hualpai, Ariz)
Steiner, Saddler Christian (Chiricahua Mountains, Ariz)
Stewart, Pvt. Benjamin F. (Big Horn River, Mont)
Stickoffer, Saddler Julius H. (Cienaga Springs, Utah)
Stivers, Pvt. Thomas W. (Little Big Horn, Mont)
Stokes, 1st Sgt. Alonzo (Wichita River, Tex)
Strayer, Pvt. William H. (Platte River, Neb)
Strivson, Pvt. Benoni (Arizona)
Sullivan, Pvt. Thomas (Chiricahua Mountains, Ariz)
Sullivan, Pvt. Thomas (Wounded Knee Creek, S Dak)
Sumner, Pvt. James (Chiricahua Mountains, Ariz)
Sutherland, Cpl. John A. (Arizona)
Taylor, Sgt. Bernard (Sunset Pass, Ariz)
Taylor, 1st Sgt. Charles (Big Dry Wash, Ariz)
Taylor, Cpl. Wilbur N. (Arizona)
Tea, Sgt. Richard L. (Sappa Creek, Kans)
Thomas, Sgt. Charles L. (Dakota Territory)
Thompson, Pvt. George W. (Little Blue, Neb)
Thompson, Sgt. John (Chiricahua Mountains, Ariz)
Thompson, Pvt. Peter (Little Big Horn, Mont)
Tilton, Maj. & Surgeon Henry R. (Bear Paw Mountain, Mont)
Tolan, Pvt. Frank (Little Big Horn, Mont)
Toy, 1st Sgt. Frederick E. (Wounded Knee Creek, S Dak)
Tracy, Pvt. John (Chiricahua Mountains, Ariz)
Trautman, 1st Sgt. Jacob (Wounded Knee Creek, S Dak)
Turpin, 1st Sgt. James H. (Arizona)
Varnum, Capt. Charles A. (White Clay Creek, S Dak)
Veuve, Farrier Ernest (Staked Plains, Tex)
Voit, Saddler Otto (Little Big Horn, Mont)
Vokes, 1st Sgt. Leroy H. (Platte River, Neb)
Von Medem, Sgt. Rudolph (Arizona)
Walker, Pvt. Allen (Texas)
Walker, Pvt. John (Red Creek, Ariz)
Wallace, Sgt. William (Cedar Creek, Mont)
Walley, Pvt. Augustus (Cuchillo Negro Mountains, N Mex)
Ward, Pvt. Charles H. (Chiricahua Mountains, Ariz)
Ward, Sgt. James (Wounded Knee Creek, S Dak)
Ward, Sgt. John (Pecos River, Tex)
Warrington, 1st Lt. Lewis (Muchague Valley, Tex)
Watson, Cpl. James C. (Wichita River, Tex)
Watson, Pvt. Joseph (Picacho Mountain, Ariz)
Weaher, Pvt. Andrew J. (Arizona)
Weinert, Cpl. Paul H. (Wounded Knee Creek, S Dak)
Weiss, Pvt. Enoch R. (Chiricahua Mountains, Ariz)
Welch, Sgt. Charles H. (Little Big Horn, Mont)
Welch, Sgt. Michael (Wichita River, Tex)
West, 1st Lt. Frank (Big Dry Wash, Ariz)
Whitehead, Pvt. Patton G. (Cedar Creek, Mont)
Widmer, 1st Sgt. Jacob (Milk River, Colo)
Wilder, 1st Lt. Wilber E. (Horseshoe Canyon, N Mex)
Wilkens, 1st Sgt. Henry (Little Muddy Creek, Mont)
Williams, 1st Sgt. Moses (Cuchillo Negro Mountains, N Mex)
Wills, Pvt. Henry (Fort Selden, N Mex)
Wilson, Pvt Benjamin (Wichita River, Tex)
Wilson, Cpl. Charles (Cedar Creek, Mont)
Wilson, Sgt. Milden H. (Big Hole, Mont)
Wilson, Sgt. William (Colorado Valley, Tex) Second award (Red River, Tex)
Wilson, Cpl. William O. (South Dakota)
Windolph, Pvt. Charles (Little Big Horn, Mont)
Windus, Bugler Claron A. (Wichita River, Tex)
Winterbottom, Sgt. William (Wichita River, Tex)
Witcome, Pvt. Joseph (Arizona)
Wood, Asst. Surgeon Leonard (Arizona & Mexico)
Woodall, Sgt. Zachariah (Wichita River, Tex)

Woods, Sgt. Brent (New Mexico)
Wortman, Sgt. George G. (Arizona)
Yount, Pvt. John P. (Whetstone Mountains, Ariz)
Ziegner, Pvt. Herman (Wounded Knee Creek & White Clay Creek, S Dak)

THE WARS OF AMERICAN EXPANSION 1871-1933

KOREA 1871

MARINES

Brown, Cpl. Charles (Korea)
Coleman, Pvt. John (Korea)
Dougherty, Pvt. James (Korea)
McNamara, Pvt. Michael (Korea)
Owens, Pvt. Michael (Korea)
Purvis, Pvt. Hugh (Korea)

NAVY

Andrews, Ord. Sman John (Korea)
Franklin, QM Frederick (Korea)
Grace, Chief QM Patrick H. (Korea)
Hayden, Carpenter Cyrus (Korea)
Lukes, Lman William F. (Korea)
McKenzie, BM Alexander (Korea)
Merton, Lman James F. (Korea)
Rogers, QM Samuel F. (Korea)
Troy, Ord. Sman William (Korea)

THE SPANISH-AMERICAN WAR 1898

ARMY

Baker, Sgt. Maj. Edward L, Jr. (Santiago, Cuba)
Bell, Pvt. Dennis (Tayabacoa, Cuba)
Berg, Pvt. George (El Caney, Cuba)
Brookin, Pvt. Oscar (El Caney, Cuba)
Buzzard, Cpl. Ulysses G. (El Caney, Cuba)
Cantrell, Pvt. Charles P. (Santiago, Cuba)
Church, Asst. Surgeon James R. (Las Guasimas, Cuba)
Cummins, Sgt. Andrew J. (Santiago, Cuba)
De Swan, Pvt. John F. (Santiago, Cuba)
Doherty, Cpl. Thomas M. (Santiago, Cuba)
Fournia, Pvt. Frank O. (Santiago, Cuba)
Graves, Pvt. Thomas J. (El Caney, Cuba)
Hardaway, 1st Lt. Benjamin F. (El Caney, Cuba)
Heard, 1st Lt. John W. (Manimani River, Cuba)
Keller, Pvt. William (Santiago, Cuba)
Kelly, Pvt. Thomas (Santiago, Cuba)
Lee, Pvt. Fitz (Tayabacoa, Cuba)
Mills, Capt. & Asst. Adj. Gen. Albert L. (Santiago, Cuba)
Nash, Pvt. James J. (Santiago, Cuba)
Nee, Pvt. George H. (Santiago, Cuba)
Pfisterer, Musician Herman (Santiago, Cuba)
Polond, Pvt. Alfred (Santiago, Cuba)
Quinn, Sgt. Alexander M. (Santiago, Cuba)
Ressler, Cpl. Norman W. (El Caney, Cuba)
Roberts, 2d Lt. Charles D. (El Caney, Cuba)
Shepherd, Cpl. Warren J. (El Caney, Cuba)
Thompkins, Pvt. William H. (Tayabacoa, Cuba)
Wanton, Pvt. George H. (Tayabacoa, Cuba)
Welborn, 2d Lt. Ira C. (Santiago, Cuba)
Wende, Pvt. Bruno (El Caney, Cuba)

MARINES

Campbell, Pvt. Daniel (Cienfuegos, Cuba)
Field, Pvt. Oscar W. (Cienfuegos, Cuba)
Fitzgerald, Pvt. John (Cuzco, Cuba)
Franklin, Pvt. Joseph J. (Cienfuegos, Cuba)
Gaughan, Sgt. Philip (Cienfuegos, Cuba)
Hill, Pvt. Frank (Cienfuegos, Cuba)
Kearney, Pvt. Michael (Cienfuegos, Cuba)
Kuchneister, Pvt. Hermann W. (Cienfuegos, Cuba)
MacNeal, Pvt. Harry L. (Santiago, Cuba)
Meredith, Pvt. James (Cienfuegos, Cuba)
Parker, Pvt. Pomeroy (Cienfuegos, Cuba)
Quick, Sgt. John H. (Cuzco, Cuba)
Scott, Pvt. Joseph E. (Cienfuegos, Cuba)
Sullivan, Pvt. Edward (Cienfuegos, Cuba)
West, Pvt. Walter S. (Cienfuegos, Cuba)

NAVY

Baker, Coxswain Benjamin F. (Cienfuegos, Cuba)
Barrow, Sman David D. (Cienfuegos, Cuba)
Bennett, Chief BM James H. (Cienfuegos, Cuba)
Beyer, Coxswain Albert (Cienfuegos, Cuba)
Blume, Sman Robert (Cienfuegos, Cuba)
Brady, Chief GM George F. (Cardenas, Cuba)
Bright, Coal Passer George W. (Cienfuegos, Cuba)

Carter, Blacksmith Joseph E. (Cienfuegos, Cuba)
Chadwick, Apprentice 1st Class Leonard (Cienfuegos, Cuba)
Charette, GM 1st Class George (Santiago, Cuba)
Clausen, Coxswain Claus K. (Santiago, Cuba)
Cooney, Chief Machinist Thomas C. (Cardenas, Cuba)
Crouse, Watertender William A. (Cavite, Philippines)
Davis, GM 3d Class John (Cienfuegos, Cuba)
Deignan, Coxswain Osborn (Santiago, Cuba)
Doran, BM 2d Class John J. (Cienfuegos, Cuba)
Durney, Blacksmith Austin J. (Cienfuegos, Cuba)
Eglit, Sman John (Cienfuegos, Cuba)
Ehle, Fireman 1st Class John W. (Cavite, Philippines)
Erickson, Coxswain Nick (Cienfuegos, Cuba)
Foss, Sman Herbert L. (Cienfuegos, Cuba)
Gibbons, Oiler Michael (Cienfuegos, Cuba)
Gill, GM 1st Class Freeman (Cienfuegos, Cuba)
Hart, Machinist 1st Class William (Cienfuegos, Cuba)
Hendrickson, Sman Henry (Cienfuegos, Cuba)
Hoban, Coxswain Thomas (Cienfuegos, Cuba)
Hobson, Lt. Richmond P. (Santiago, Cuba)
Hull, Fireman 1st Class James L. (Cavite, Philippines)
Itrich, Chief Carpenter's Mate Franz A. (Manila, Philippines)
Johanson, Sman John P. (Cienfuegos, Cuba)
Johansson, Ord. Sman Johan J. (Cienfuegos, Cuba)
Johnsen, Chief Machinist Hans (Cardenas, Cuba)
Johnson, Fireman 1st Class Peter (NOR)
Keefer, Coppersmith Philip B. (Santiago, Cuba)
Kelly, Watertender Francis (Santiago, Cuba)
Kramer, Sman Franz (Cienfuegos, Cuba)
Krause, Coxswain Ernest (Cienfuegos, Cuba)
Levery, Apprentice 1st Class William (Cienfuegos, Cuba)
Mager, Apprentice 1st Class George F. (Cienfuegos, Cuba)
Mahoney, Fireman 1st Class George (NOR)
Maxwell, Fireman 2d Class John (Cienfuegos, Cuba)
Meyer, Carpenter's Mate 3d Class William (Cienfuegos, Cuba)
Miller, Sman Harry II (Cienfuegos, Cuba)
Miller, Sman Willard (Cienfuegos, Cuba)
Montague, Chief Master-at-Arms Daniel (Santiago, Cuba)
Morin, BM 2d Class William H. (Caimanera, Cuba)
Muller, Mate Frederick (Manzanillo, Cuba)
Murphy, Coxswain John E. (Santiago, Cuba)
Nelson, Sailmaker's Mate Lauritz (Cienfuegos, Cuba)
Oakley, GM 2d Class William (Cienfuegos, Cuba)
Olsen, Ord. Sman Anton (Cienfuegos, Cuba)
Penn, Fireman 1st Class Robert (Santiago, Cuba)
Phillips, Machinist 1st Class George E. (Santiago, Cuba)
Rilley, Lman John P. (Cienfuegos, Cuba)
Russell, Lman Henry P. (Cienfuegos, Cuba)
Spicer, GM 1st Class William (Caimanera, Cuba)
Sundquist, Ord. Sman Gustave A. (Cienfuegos, Cuba)
Sundquist, Chief Carpenter's Mate Axel (Caimanera, Cuba)
Triplett, Ord. Sman Samuel (Caimanera, Cuba)
Vadas, Sman Albert (Cienfuegos, Cuba)
Van Etten, Sman Hudson (Cienfuegos, Cuba)
Volz, Sman Robert (Cienfuegos, Cuba)
Wilke, BM 1st Class Julius A. R. (Cienfuegos, Cuba)
Williams, Sman Frank (Cienfuegos, Cuba)

PHILIPPINES/SAMOA 1899-1913

ARMY

Anders, Cpl. Frank L. (San Miguel de Mayumo, Luzon)
Batson, 1st Lt. Matthew A. (Calamba, Luzon)
Bell, Capt. Harry (Porac, Luzon)
Bell, Col. J. Franklin (Porac, Luzon)
Bickham, 1st Lt. Charles G. (Bayong, Mindanao)
Biegler, Capt. George W. (Loac, Luzon)
Birkhimer, Capt. William E. (San Miguel de Mayumo, Luzon)
Boechler, Pvt. Otto (San Isidro, Luzon)
Byrne, Capt. Bernard A. (Bobong, Negros)
Carson, Cpl. Anthony J. (Catubig, Samar)
Cawetzka, Pvt. Charles (Sariaya, Luzon)
Cecil, 1st Lt. Josephus S. (Bud-Dajo, Jolo)
Condon, Sgt. Clarence M. (Calulut, Luzon)
Davis, Pvt. Charles P. (San Isidro, Luzon)
Downs, Pvt. Willis H. (San Miguel de Mayumo, Luzon)
Epps, Pvt. Joseph L. (Vigan, Luzon)
Ferguson, 1st Lt. Arthur M. (Porac, Luzon)
Funston, Col. Frederick (Rio Grande de la Pampanga, Luzon)
Galt, Artificer Sterling A. (Bamban, Luzon)
Gaujot, Cpl. Antoine A. (San Mateo)
Gedeon, Pvt. Louis (Mount Amia, Cebu)
Gibson, Sgt. Edward H. (San Mateo)
Gillenwater, Cpl. James R. (Porac, Luzon)
Greer, 2d Lt. Allen J. (Majada, Laguna Province)
Grove, Lt. Col. William R. (Porac, Luzon)
Hayes, Lt. Col. Webb C. (Vigan, Luzon)
Henderson, Sgt. Joseph (Patian Island)
High, Pvt. Frank C. (San Isidro Luzon)
Huntsman, Sgt John A. (Bamban, Luzon)
Jensen, Pvt. Gotfred (San Miguel de Mayumo, Luzon)
Johnston, 1st Lt. Gordon (Mount Bud Dajo, Jolo)

Kennedy, 2d Lt. John T. (Patian Island)
Kilbourne, 1st Lt. Charles E. (Paco Bridge)
Kinne, Pvt. John B. (San Isidro, Luzon)
Leahy, Pvt. Cornelius J. (Porac, Luzon)
*Logan, Maj. John A. (San Jacinto)
Longfellow, Pvt. Richard M. (San Isidro, Luzon)
Lyon, Pvt. Edward E. (San Miguel de Mayumo, Luzon)
McConnell, Pvt. James (Vigan, Luzon)
McGrath, Capt. Hugh J. (Calamba, Luzon)
Maclay, Pvt. William P. (Hilongas, Leyte)
Mathews, Asst. Surgeon George W. (Labo, Luzon)
Miller, 1st Lt. Archie (Patian Island)
Moran, Capt. John E. (Mabitac, Luzon)
Mosher, 2d Lt. Louis C. (Gagsak Mountain, Jolo)
Nisperos, Pvt. Jose B. (Lapurap, Basilan)
Nolan, Artificer Joseph A. (Labo, Luzon)
Parker, Lt. Col. James (Vigan, Luzon)
Pierce, Pvt. Charles H. (San Isidro, Luzon)
Quinn, Pvt. Peter H. (San Miguel de Mayumo, Luzon)
Ray, Sgt. Charles W. (San Isidro, Luzon)
Robertson, Pvt. Marcus W. (San Isidro, Luzon)
Ross, Pvt. Frank F. (San Isidro, Luzon)
Sage, Capt. William H. (Zapote River, Luzon)
Schroeder, Sgt. Henry F. (Carig, Leyte)
Shaw, 1st Lt. George C. (Fort Pitacus, Mindanao)
Shelton, Pvt. George M. (La Paz, Leyte)
Shiels, Surgeon George F. (Tuliahan River)
Sletteland, Pvt. Thomas (Paete, Luzon)
Steward, 2d Lt. George E. (Passi, Panay)
Straub, Surgeon Paul F. (Alos, Luzon)
Trembley, Pvt. William B. (Calumpit, Luzon)
Van Schaick, 1st Lt. Louis J. (Nasugbu, Batangas)
Walker, Pvt. Frank O. (Taal, Luzon)
Wallace, 2d Lt. George W. (Tinuba, Luzon)
Weaver, Sgt. Amos (Calubus-Malalong, Luzon)
Weld, Cpl. Seth L. (La Paz, Leyte)
Wetherby, Pvt. John C. (Imus, Luzon)
White, Pvt. Edward (Calumpit, Luzon)
Wilson, 2d Lt. Arthur H. (Patian Island)

MARINES

Bearss, Col. Hiram I. (Cadacan & Sohoton Rivers, Samar)
Buckley, Pvt. Howard M. (NOR)
Forsterer, Sgt. Bruno A. (Samoa)
Harvey, Sgt. Harry (Benictican)
Hulbert, Pvt. Henry L. (Samoa)
Leonard, Pvt. Joseph M. (NOR)
McNally, Sgt. Michael J. (Samoa)
Porter, Col. David D. (Cadacan & Sohoton Rivers, Samar)
Prendergast, Cpl. Thomas F. (NOR)

NAVY

Catherwood, Ord. Sman John H. (Basilan)
Fisher, GM 1st Class Frederick T. (Samoa)
Fitz, Ord. Sman Joseph (Mount Dajo Jolo)
Forbeck, Sman Andrew P. (Katbalogan, Samar)
Galbraith, GM 3d Class Robert (El Pardo, Cebu)
Harrison, Sman Bolden R. (Basilan)
Henrechon, Machinist's Mate 2d Class George F. (Basilan)
McGuire, Hospital Apprentice Fred H. (Basilan)
Shanahan, Chief BM Patrick (NOR)
Stoltenberg, GM 2d Class Andrew V. (Katbalogan, Samar)
Thordsen, Coxswain William G. (Hilongas)
Volz, Carpenter's Mate 3d Class Jacob (Basilan)

THE BOXER REBELLION 1900

ARMY

Brewster, Capt. Andre W. (Tientsin)
Lawton, 1st Lt. Louis B. (Tientsin)
Titus, Musician Calvin P. (Peking)
Von Schlick, Pvt. Robert H. (Tientsin)

MARINES

Adams, Sgt. John M. (Tientsin)
Adriance, Cpl. Harry C. (Tientsin)
Appleton, Cpl. Edwin N. (Tientsin)
Boydston, Pvt. Erwin J. (Peking)
Burnes, Pvt. James (Tientsin)
Campbell, Pvt. Albert R. (Tientsin)
Carr, Pvt. William L. (Peking)
Cooney, Pvt. James (Tientsin)
Dahlgren, Cpl. John O. (Peking)
Daly, Pvt. Daniel J. (Peking)
*Fisher, Pvt. Harry (Peking)
Foley, Sgt. Alexander J. (Tientsin)
Francis, Pvt. Charles R. (Tientsin)
Gaiennie, Pvt. Louis R. (Peking)
Heisch, Pvt. Henry W. (Tientsin)
Horton, Pvt. William C. (Peking)
Hunt, Pvt. Martin (Peking)
Kates, Pvt. Thomas W. (Tientsin)

Mathias, Pvt. Clarence E. (Tientsin)
Moore, Pvt. Albert (Peking)
Murphy, Drummer John A. (Peking)
Murray, Pvt. William H. (Peking)
Orndoff, Pvt. Harry W. (NOR)
Phillips, Cpl. Reuben J. (NOR)
Preston, Pvt. Herbert I. (Peking)
Scannell, Pvt. David J. (Peking)
Silva, Pvt. France (Peking)
Stewart, Gy. Sgt. Peter (NOR)
Sutton, Sgt. Clarence E. (Tientsin)
Upham, Pvt. Oscar J. (Peking)
Walker, Sgt. Edward A. (Peking)
Young, Pvt. Frank A. (Peking)
Zion, Pvt. William (Peking)

NAVY

Allen, BM 1st Class Edward (NOR)
Chatham, GM 2d Class John P. (NOR)
Clancy, Chief BM Joseph (NOR)
Hamberger, Chief Carpenter's Mate William F. (NOR)
Hanford, Machinist 1st Class Burke (NOR)
Hansen Sman Hans A. (NOR)
Holyoke, BM 1st Class William E. (NOR)
Killackey, Lman Joseph (NOR)
McAllister, Ord. Sman Samuel (Tientsin)
McCloy, Coxswain John (China)
Mitchell, GM 1st Class Joseph (Peking)
Petersen, Chief Machinist Carl E. (Peking)
Rose, Sman George (Peking)
Ryan, Coxswain Francis T. (NOR)
Seach, Ord. Sman William (NOR)
Smith, Lman James (NOR)
Stanley, Hospital Apprentice Robert H. (Peking)
Thomas, Coxswain Karl (NOR)
Torgerson, GM 3d Class Martin T. (NOR)
Westermark, Sman Axel (Peking)
Williams, Coxswain Jay (China)

VERACRUZ 1914

MARINES

Berkeley, Maj. Randolph C. (Veracruz)
Butler, Maj. Smedley D. (Veracruz)
Catlin, Maj. Albertus W. (Veracruz)
Dyer, Capt. Jesse F. (Veracruz)
Fryer, Capt. Eli T. (Veracruz)
Hill, Capt. Walter N. (Veracruz)
Hughes, Capt. John A. (Veracruz)
Neville, Lt. Col. Wendell C. (Veracruz)
Reid, Maj. George C. (Veracruz)

NAVY

Anderson, Capt. Edwin A. (Veracruz)
Badger, Ensign Oscar C. (Veracruz)
Beasley, Sman Harry C. (Veracruz)
Bishop, QM 2d Class Charles F. (Veracruz)
Bradley, Chief GM George (Veracruz)
Buchanan, Lt. Cmdr. Allen (Veracruz)
Castle. Lt. Guy W. S. (Veracruz)
Courts, Lt. (j.g.) George M. (Veracruz)
Cregan, Coxswain George (Veracruz)
Decker, BM 2d Class Percy A. (Veracruz)
DeSomer, Lt. Abraham (Veracruz)
Drustrup, Lt. Neils (Veracruz)
Elliott, Surgeon Middleton S. (Veracruz)
Fletcher, Rear Adm. Frank F. (Veracruz)
Fletcher, Lt. Frank J. (Veracruz)
Foster, Ensign Paul F. (Veracruz)
Frazer, Ensign Hugh C. (Veracruz)
Gisburne, Electrician 3d Class Edward A. (Veracruz)
Grady, Lt. John (Veracruz)
Harner, BM 2d Class Joseph G. (Veracruz)
Harrison, Cmdr. William K. (Veracruz)
Hartigan, Lt. Charles C. (Veracruz)
Huse, Capt. Henry M. P. (Veracruz)
Ingram, Lt. (j.g.) Jonas H. (Veracruz)
Jarrett, Sman Berrie H. (Veracruz)
Johnston, Lt. Cmdr. Rufus Z. (Veracruz)
Langhorne, Surgeon Cary D. (Veracruz)
Lannon, Lt. James P. (Veracruz)
Lowry, Ensign George M. (Veracruz)
McCloy, Chief Boatswain John (Veracruz)
McDonnell, Ensign Edward O. (Veracruz)
McNair, Lt. Frederick V., Jr (Veracruz)
Moffett, Cmdr. William A. (Veracruz)
Nickerson, BM 2d Class Henry N. (Veracruz)
Nordsiek, Ord. Sman Charles I. (Veracruz)
Rush, Capt. William R. (Veracruz)
Schnepel, Ord. Sman Fred J. (Veracruz)
Semple, Chief Gunner Robert (Veracruz)
Sinnett, Sman Lawrence C. (Veracruz)
Staton, Lt. Adolphus (Veracruz)
Stickney, Cmdr. Herman O. (Veracruz)
Townsend, Lt. Julius C, (Veracruz)
Wainwright, Lt. Richard, Jr. (Veracruz)
Walsh, Sman James A. (Veracruz)
Wilkinson, Ensign Theodore S., Jr (Veracruz)
Zuiderveld, Hospital Apprentice 1st Class William (Veracruz)

HAITI 1915

†Butler, Maj. Smedley D. (Fort Rivière)
†Daly, Gy. Sgt. Daniel J. (Fort Liberté)
Gross, Pvt. Samuel (Fort Rivière)
Iams, Sgt. Ross L. (Fort Rivière)
Ostermann, 1st Lt. Edward A. (Fort Liberté)
Upshur, Capt. William P. (Fort Liberté)

DOMINICAN REPUBLIC 1916

Glowin, Cpl. Joseph A. (Guayacanas)
Williams, 1st Lt. Ernest C. (San Francisco de Macoris)
Winans, 1st Sgt. Roswell (Guayacanas)

HAITI 1919-1920

Button, Cpl. William R. (Grande Rivière)
Hanneken, Sgt. Herman H. (Grande Rivière)

NICARAGUA 1927-1933

Schilt, 1st Lt. Christian F. (Quilali)
Truesdell, Cpl. Donald I., (Constancia)

THE MEDAL IN PEACETIME 1865-1940

1865-1870

Bates, Sman Richard (Eastport, Maine)
Brown, Capt. of the Afterguard John (Eastport, Maine)
Burke, Sman Thomas (Eastport, Maine)
Carey, Sman James (NOR)
†Cooper, QM John (Mobile, Ala)
Du Moulin, Aprentice Frank (New London, Conn)
Halford, Coxswain William (Sandwich Islands)
†Mullen, BM Patrick (NOR)
Robinson, Capt. of the Hold John (Pensacola Bay, Fla)
Robinson, Capt. of the Afterguard Thomas (New Orleans, La)
Stacy, Sman William B. (Cape Haiten, Haiti)
Taylor, Sman John (New York, NY)

1871-1898

MARINES

Morris, Cpl. John (Villefranche, France)
Steward, Cpl. James A. (Villefranche, France)

NAVY

Ahern, Watertender William (NOR)
Anderson, Coxswain William (NOR)
Atkins, Ship's Cook Daniel (NOR)
Auer, Ord. Sman Apprentice John F. (Marseille, France)
Barrett, 2d Class Fireman Edward (Calao Bay, Peru)
Belpitt, Capt. of the Afterguard W. H. (Foochow, China)
Benson, Sman James (NOR)
Bradley, Lman Alexander (Cowes, England)
Buchanan, Apprentice David M. (New York, NY)
Cavanaugh, Fireman 1st Class Thomas (Cat Island–Nassau)
Chandron, Sman Apprentice August (Alexandria, Egypt)
Connolly, Ord. Sman Michael (Halifax Harbor, Nova Scotia)
Corey, Lman William (New York, NY)
Costello, Ord. Sman John (Philadelphia, Pa)
Courtney, Sman Henry C. (Washington Navy Yard, DC)
Cramen, BM Thomas (Washington Navy Yard, DC)
Creelman, Lman George W. (Norfolk, Va)
Davis, Ord. Sman John Toulon, France)
Davis, Lman Joseph H. (Norfolk, Va)
Dempsey, Sman John (Shanghai, China)
Deneef, Capt. of the top Michael (Para, Brazil)
Denham, Sman Austin (Greytown, Nicaragua)
Eilers, GM Henry A. (Fort McHenry, Md)
Elmore, Lman Walter (Mediterranean Sea)
Enright, Lman John (Ensenada, Mexico)
Everetts, GM 3d Class John (NOR)
Fasseur, Ord. Sman Isaac L. (Callao, Peru)
Flannagan, BM John (Le Havre, France)
Fowler, QM Christopher (Point Zapotitlan, Mexico)
Gidding, Sman Charles (New York, NY)
Gillick, BM Matthew (Marseilles, France)
Handran, Sman John (Lisbon, Portugal)
Harrington, 1st Class Fireman David (NOR)
Hayden, Apprentice John (New York, NY)
Hill, Chief QG George (Greytown, Nicaragua)
Hill, Capt. of the Top William L. (Newport, RI)
Holt, QG George (Hamburg, Germany)
Horton, Capt. of the Top James (NOR)
Jardine, Fireman 1st Class Alexander (Cat Island–Nassau)
Johnson, Sman John (Greytown, Nicaragua)
Johnson, Cooper William (Mare Island, Calif)
Kersey, Ord. Sman Thomas (New York, NY)
King, Ord. Sman Hugh (Delaware River, NJ)
Kyle, Lman Patrick J. (Port Mahon, Minorca)
Lakin, Sman Thomas (Mare Island, Calif)
Laverty, 1st Class Fireman John (Callao, Peru)
Lejeune, Sman Emile (Port Royal, SC)
Low, Sman George (New Orleans, La)
Lucy, 2d Class Boy John (Castle Garden, NY)
McCarton, Ship's Printer John (Coaster's Harbor Island, RI)
Maddin, Ord. Sman Edward (Lisbon, Portugal)
Magee, 2d Class Fireman John W. (NOR)
Manning, QM Henry J. (Newport, RI)
Matthews, Capt. of the Top Joseph (NOR)
Miller, BM Hugh (Alexandria, Egypt)
Millmore, Ord. Sman John (Monrovia, Liberia)
Mitchell, Lman Thomas (Shanghai, China)
Moore, BM Francis (WashingtonNavy Yard, DC)
Moore, Sman Philip (Genoa, Italy)
Morse, Sman William (Rio de Janeiro, Brazil)
Noil, Sman Joseph B. (Norfolk, Va)
Norris, Lman J. W. (New York, NY)
O'Conner, Sman James F. (Norfolk, Va)
Ohmsen, Master-at-Arms August (NOR)
O'Neal, BM John (Greytown, Nicaragua)
Osborne, Sman John (Philadelphia, PA)
Osepins, Sman Christian (Hampton Roads, Va)
Parker, BM Alexander (Mare Island, Calif)
Pile, Ord. Sman Richard (Greytown, Nicaragua)
Regan, Ord. Sman Patrick (Coquimbor, Chile)
Rouning, Ord. Sman Johannes (Hampton Roads, Va)
Russell, Sman John (Genoa, Italy)
Ryan, Ord. Sman Richard (Norfolk, Va)
Sadler, Capt. of the Top William (Coaster's Harbor Island, RI)
Sapp, Sman Isacc (Villefranche, France)
Simpson, 1st Class Fireman Henry (Monrovia, Liberia)
Smith, Sman James (Greytown, Nicaragua)
Smith, Sman John (Rio de Janeiro, Brazil)
Smith, Sman Thomas (Para, Brazil)
Sullivan, BM James F. (Newport, RI)
Sweeney, Ord. Sman Robert (Hampton Roads, Va)
Second award (New York, NY)
Sweeney, Lman William (Norfolk, Va)
Taylor, QM Richard H. (Apia, Samoa)
Thayer, Ship's Cpl. James (Norfolk, Va)
Thompson, Sman Henry (Mare Island, Calif)
Thornton, Sman Michael (Boston, Mass)
Tobin, Lman Paul (Hamburg, Germany)
Trout, 2d Class Fireman James M. (Montevideo, Uruguay)
Troy, Chief BM Jeremiah (Newport, RI)
Turvelin, Sman Alexander H. (Toulon, France)
Weisbogel, Capt. of the Mizzen Top Albert (NOR)
Second award (NOR)
Weissel, Ship's Cook Adam (Newport, RI)
Williams, Sman Antonio (NOR)
Williams, Carpenter's Mate Henry (NOR)
Williams, Capt. of the Hold Louis (Honolulu, Hawaii)
Second award (Callao, Peru)
Willis, Coxswain George (Greenland)
Wilson, Boilermaker August (NOR)

1899-1911

ARMY

Gaujot, Capt. Julien E. (Aqua Prieta, Mex)

MARINES

Helms, Sgt. John H. (Montevideo, Uruguay)
Pfeifer, Pvt. Louis F. (NOR)

NAVY

Behne, Fireman 1st Class Frederick (NOR)
Behnke, Sman 1st Class Heinrich (NOR)
Bjorkman, Ord. Sman Ernest H. (NOR)
Boers, Sman Edward W. (San Diego, Calif)
Bonney, Chief Watertender Robert E. (NOR)
Breeman, Sman George (NOR)
Bresnahan, Watertender Patrick F. (NOR)
Brock, Carpenter's Mate 2d Class George F. (San Diego, Calif)
Cahey, Sman Thomas (NOR)
Clary, Watertender Edwward A. (NOR)
Clausey, Chief GM John J. (San Diego, Calif)
Corahorgi, Fireman 1st Class Demetri (NOR)
Cox Chief GM Robert E. (Pensacola, Fla)
Cronan, BM Willie (San Diego, Calif)
Davis, QM 3d Class Raymond E. (San Diego, Calif)
Fadden, Coxswain Harry D. (NOR)
Floyd, Boilermaker Edward (NOR)
Fredericksen, Watertender Emil (San Diego, Calif)
Girandy, Sman Alphonse (NOR)
Gowan, BM William H. (Coquimbo, Chile)
Grbitch, Sman Rade (San Diego, Calif)
Halling, BM 1st Class Luovi (NOR)
Hill, Ship's Cook 1st Class Frank E. (San Diego, Calif)
Holtz, Chief Watertender August (NOR)
Johannessen, Chief Watertender Johannes J. (NOR)
King, Watertender John (NOR)
Second award (NOR)
Klein, Chief Carpenter's Mate Robert (NOR)
Lipscomb, Watertender Harry (NOR)
Monssen, Chief GM Mons (NOR)
Mullin, Sman Hugh P. (Hampton Roads, Va)
Nelson, Machinist's Mate 1st Class Oscar F. (San Diego, Calif)
Nordstrom, Chief Boatswain Isidor (NOR)
Peters, BM 1st Class Alexander (NOR)
Quick, Coxswain Joseph (Yokohama, Japan)
Reid, Chief Watertender Patrick (NOR)
Roberts, Machinist's Mate 1st Class Charles C. (NOR)
Schepke, GM 1st Class Charles S. (NOR)
Schmidt, Sman Otto D. (San Diego, Calif)
Shacklette, Hospital Steward William S. (San Diego, Calif)
Snyder, Chief Electrician William E. (Hampton Roads, Va)
Stanton, Chief Machinist's Mate Thomas (NOR)
Stokes, Chief Master-at-Arms John (Jamaica)
Stupka, Fireman 1st Class Loddie (NOR)
Teytand, QM 3d Class August P. (NOR)
Walsh, Chief Machinist Michael (NOR)
Westa, Chief Machinist's Mate Karl (NOR)
Wheeler, Shipfitter 1st Class George H. (Coquimbo, Chile)

1915-1916

Cary, Lt. Cmdr. Robert W. (NOR)
Crilley, Chief GM Frank W. (Honolulu, Hawaii)
Jones, Cmdr. Claud A. (Santo Domingo)
*Rud, Chief Machinist's Mate George W. (Santo Domingo)
Smith, Chief Watertender Eugene P. (NOR)
Smith, GM 1st Class Wilhelm (NOR)
Trinidad, Fireman 2d Class Telesforo (NOR)
Willey, Machinist Charles H. (Santo Domingo)

1920-1940

ARMY

Greely, Maj. Gen. Adolphus W. (Various)
Lindbergh, Capt. Charles A. (New York City–Paris, France)

MARINES

Smith, Pvt. Albert J. (Pensacola, Fla)

NAVY

Badders, Chief Machinist's Mate William (Portsmouth, NH)
Bennett, Machinist Floyd (North Pole)
Breault, Torpedoman 2d Class Henry (NOR)
Byrd, Cmdr. Richard E., Jr. (NorthPole)
*Cholister, BM 1st Class George R. (Off Virginia coast)
*Corry, Lt. Cmdr. William M., Jr. (Hartford, Conn)
Crandall, Chief BM Orson L. (Portsmouth, NH)
*Drexler, Ensign Henry C. (NOR)
Eadie, Chief GM Thomas (Provincetown, Mass)
Edwards, Lt. Cmdr. Walter A. (Sea of Marmara, Turkey
Huber, Machinist's Mate William R. (Norfolk, Va)
*Hutchins, Lt. Carlton B. (Off California coast)
McDonald, Chief Metalsmith James H. (Portsmouth, NH)
Mihalowski, Torpedoman 1st Class John (Portsmouth, NH)
Ryan, Ensign Thomas J. (Yokohama, Japan)

WORLD WAR I 1914-1918

ARMY

Adkinson, Sgt. Joseph B. (Bellicourt, France)
Allex, Cpl. Jake (Chipilly Ridge, France)
Allworth, Capt. Edward C. (Clery-le-Petit, France)
Anderson, 1st Sgt. Johannes S. (Consenvoye, France)
*Baesel, 2d Lt. Albert E. (Ivoiry, France)
Barger, Pvt. Charles D. (Bois-de-Bantheville, France)
*Barkeley, Pvt. David B. (Pouilly, France)
Barkley, Pfc. John L. (Cunel, France)
Bart, Pvt. Frank J. (Medeah Ferme, France)
*Blackwell, Pvt. Robert L. (St. Soupplers, France)
*Bleckley, 2d Lt. Erwin R. (Binarville, France)
Bronson, 1st Lt. Deming (Eclisfontaine, France)
Call, Cpl. Donald M. (Varennes, France)
*Chiles, Capt. Marcellus H. (Le Champy Bas. France)
*Colyer, Sgt. Wilbur E. (Verdun, France)
*Costin, Pvt. Henry G. (Bois-de-Consenvoye, France)
*Dilboy, Pfc. George (Belleau, France)
Donaldson, Sgt. Michael A. (Sommerance-Landres-et-St.

Georges Road, France)
Donovan, Lt. Col. William J. (Landres-et-St. Georges, France)
Dozier, 1st Lt. James C. (Montbrehain, France)
*Dunn, Pvt. Parker F. (Grand-Pre, France)
Edwards, Pfc. Daniel R. (Soissons, France)
Eggers, Sgt. Alan L. (Le Catelet, France)
Ellis, Sgt. Michael B. (Exermont, France)
Forrest, Sgt. Arthur J. (Remonville, France)
Foster, Sgt. Gary E. (Montbrehain, France)
Funk, Pfc. Jesse N. (Bois-de-Bantheville, France)
Furlong, 1st Lt. Harold A. (Bantheville, France)
Gaffney, Pfc. Frank (Ronssoy, France)
*Goettler, 1st Lt. Harold E. (Binarville, France)
Gregory, Sgt. Earl D. (Bois-de-Consenvoye, France)
Gumpertz, 1st Sgt. Sydney G. (Bois-de-Forges, France)
*Hall, Sgt. Thomas L. (Montbrehain, France)
Hatler, Sgt. M. Waldo (Pouilly, France)
Hays, 1st Lt. George P. (Greves Farm, France)
*Heriot, Cpl. James D. (Vaux-Andigny, France)
Hill, Cpl. Ralyn M. (Donnevoux, France)
Hilton, Sgt. Richmond H. (Brancourt, France)
Holderman, Capt. Nelson M. (Binarville, France)
Johnston, Sgt. Harold I. (Pouilly, France)
Karnes, Sgt. James E. (Estrees, France)
Katz, Sgt. Phillip C. (Eclisfontaine, France)
Kaufman, 1st Sgt. Benjamin (Argonne Forest, France)
Latham, Sgt. John C. (Le Catelet, France)
*Lemert, 1st Sgt. Milo (Bellicourt, France)
Loman, Pvt. Berger (Consenvoye, France)
*Luke, 2d Lt. Frank, Jr. (Murvaux, France)
Mallon, Capt. George H. (Bois-de-Forges, France)
Manning, Cpl. Sidney E. (Breuvannes France)
McMurtry, Capt. George G. (Charlevaux, France)
*Mestrovitch, Sgt. James I. (Fismette, France)
Miles, Capt. L. W. (Revillon, France)
*Miller, Maj. Oscar F. (Gesnes, France)
Morelock, Pvt. Sterling (Exermont, France)
Neibaur, Pvt. Thomas C. (Landres-et-St. Georges, France)
O'Neil, Sgt. Richard W. (Ourcq River, France)
*O'Shea, Cpl. Thomas E. (Le Catelet, France)
Parker, 2d Lt. Samuel I. (Soissons, France)
Peck, Pvt. Archie A. (Argonne Forest, France)
*Perkins, Pfc. Michael J. (Belieu Bois, France)
*Pike, Lt. Col, Emory J. (Vandières, France)
Pope, Cpl. Thomas A. (Hamel, France)
Regan, 2d Lt. Patrick (Bois-de-Consenvoye, France)
Rickenbacker, 1st Lt. Edward V. (Billy, France)
Robb, 1st Lt. George S. (Sechault, France)
*Roberts, Cpl. Harold W. (Montrebeau Woods, France)
Sampler, Cpl. Samuel M. (St. Etienne, France)
Sandlin, Sgt. Willie (Bois-de-Forges, France)
*Sawelson, Sgt. William (Grand-Pre, France)
Schaffner, 1st Lt. Dwite H. (Bourevilles, France)
Seibert, Sgt. Lloyd M. (Epinonville, France)
*Skinker, Capt. Alexander R. (Cheppy, France)
Slack, Pvt. Clayton K. (Consenvoye, France)
*Smith, Lt. Col. Fred E. (Binarville, France)
Talley, Sgt. Edward R. (Ponchaux, France)
Thompson, Maj. Joseph H. (Apremont, France)
Turner, Cpl. Harold L. (St. Etienne, France)
Turner, 1st Lt. William B. (Ronssoy, France)
*Valente, Pvt. Michael (Ronssoy, France)
Van Iersel, Sgt. Ludovicus M. (Mouzon, France)
Villepigue, Cpl. John C. (Vaux-Andigny, France)
Waaler, Sgt. Reidar (Ronssoy, France)
Ward, Pvt. Calvin J. (Estress, France)
West, 1st Sgt. Chester H. (Bois-de-Cheppy, France)
Whittlesey, Maj. Charles W. (Argonne Forest, France)
*Wickersham, 2d Lt. J. Hunter (Limey, France)
*Wold, Pvt. Nels (Cheppy, France)
Woodfill, 1st Lt. Samuel (Cunel, France)
York, Cpl. Alvin C. (Chatel-Chehery, France)

MARINES

† Cukela, Sgt. Louis (Villers-Cotterets, France)
† Janson, Gy. Sgt. Ernest A. (Château-Thierry, France)
† Kelly, Pvt. John J (Blanc Mont Ridge, France)
*† Kocak, Sgt. Matej (Villers-Cotterets, France)
*† Pruitt, Cpl. John H. (Blanc Mont Ridge, France)
Robinson, Gy. Sgt. Robert G. (Pittham, Belgium)
*# Stockham, Gy. Sgt. Fred W. (Bois-de-Belleau, France)
* Talbot, 2d Lt. Ralph (France & Pittham, Belgium)

NAVY

Balch, Pharmacist's Mate 1st Class John H. (Vierzy & Somme-Py, France)
Boone, Lt. Joel T. (Vierzy, France)
Bradley, Cmdr. Willis W., Jr. (NOR)
Cann, Sman Tedford H. (NOR)
Covington, Ship's Cook 3d Class Jesse W. (NOR)
Graves, Sman Ora (NOR)
Hammann, Ensign Charles H. (Pola,Aegean Sea)
Hayden, Hospital Apprentice 1st Class David E. (Thiaucourt, France)
*Ingram, GM 1st Class Osmond K. (NOR)
Izac, Lt. Edouard V. M. (German submarine U-90)
Lyle, Lt. Cmdr. Alexander G. (French Front)
MacKenzie, Chief BM John (NOR)
Madison, Lt. Cmdr. James J. (NOR)
McGunigal, Shipfitter 1st Class Patrick (NOR)
Ormsbee, Chief Machinist's Mate Francis E., Jr. (Pensacola, Fla)
*Osborne, Lt.(j.g.) Weedon E. (Bouresche, France)
Petty, Lt. Orlando H. (Bois-de-Belleau, France)
Schmidt, Chief GM Oscar, Jr. (NOR)
Siegel, BM 2nd Class John O. (NOR)
Sullivan, Ensign Daniel A. J. (NOR)
Upton, QM Frank M. (NOR)

† Also received army Medal of Honor for same action.
# Received army medal only.

WORLD WAR II
1939-1945

ARMY

Adams, SSgt. Lucian (St. Die, France)
Anderson, TSgt. Beaufort T. (Okinawa)
*Antolak, Sgt. Sylvester (Cisterna di Littoria, Italy)
Atkins, Pfc. Thomas E. (Villa Verde Trail, Philippines)
*Baker, Lt. Col. Addison E. (Ploesti, Rumania)
*Baker, Pvt. Thomas A. (Saipan, Mariana Islands)
Barfoot, TSgt. Van T. (Carano, Italy)
Barrett, Pvt. Carlton W. (St. Laurent-sur-Mer, France)
*Beaudoin, 1st Lt. Raymond O. (Hamelin, Germany)
Bell, TSgt. Bernard P. (Mittelwihr, France)
Bender, SSgt. Stanley (La Lande, France)
*Benjamin, Pfc. George, Jr. (Leyte, Philippines)
Bennett, Cpl. Edward A. (Heckhuscheid, Germany)
Bertoldo, MSgt. Vito R. (Hatten, France)
Beyer, Cpl. Arthur O. (Arloncourt, Belgium)
*Bianchi, 1st Lt. Willibald C. (Bagac, Philippines)
Biddle, Pfc. Melvin E. (Soy, Belgium)
Bjorklund, 1st Lt. Arnold L. (Altavilla, Italy)
Bloch, 1st Lt. Orville E. (Firenzuola, Italy)
Bolden, SSgt. Paul L. (Petit-Coo, Belgium)
Bolton, 1st Lt. Cecil H. (Mark River, Holland)
Bong, Maj. Richard I. (Borneo & Leyte, Philippines)
*Booker, Pvt. Robert D. (Fondouk, Tunisia)
*Boyce, 2d Lt. George W. G., Jr. (Afua, New Guinea)
Briles, SSgt. Herschel F. (Scherpenseel, Germany)
Britt, Lt. Maurice L. (Mignano, Italy)
*Brostrom, Pfc. Leonard C. (Dagami, Philippines)
Brown, Capt. Bobbie E. (Aachen, Germany)
Burke, 1st Lt. Francis X. (Nuremberg, Germany)
*Burr, 1st Sgt. Elmer J. (Buna, New Guinea)
Burr, SSgt. Herbert H. (Dorrmoschel, Germany)
Burr, Capt. James M. (Wurselen, Germany)
*Butts, 2d Lt. John E. (Normandy, France)
Calugas, Sgt. Jose (Culis, Philippines)
*Carey, SSgt. Alvin P. (Plougastel, France)
*Carey, TSgt. Charles F., Jr. (Rimling, France)
*Carswell, Maj. Horace S., Jr. (South China Sea)
*Castle, Brig. Gen. Frederick W. (Germany)
*Cheli, Maj. Ralph (Wewak, New Guinea)
Childers, 2d Lt. Ernest (Oliveto, Italy)
Choate, SSgt. Clyde L. (Bruyères, France)
*Christensen, 2d Lt. Dale E. (Driniumor River, New Guinea)
*Christian, Pvt. Herbert F. (Valmonotone, Italy)
*Cicchetti, Pfc. Joseph J. (South Manila, Philippines)
Clark, TSgt. Francis J. (Kalborn, Luxembourg, & Sevenig, Germany)
Colalillo, Pfc. Mike (Untergriesheim, Germany)
*Cole, Lt. Col. Robert G. (Carentan, France)
Connor, Sgt. James P. (Cape Cavalaire, France)
Cooley, SSgt. Raymond H. (Lumboy, Philippines)
Coolidge, TSgt. Charles H. (Belmont-sur-Buttant, France)
*Cowan, Pfc. Richard E. (Krinkelter Wald, Belgium)
Craft, Pfc. Clarence B. (Okinawa)
*Craig, 2d Lt. Robert (Favoratta, Sicily).
*Crain, TSgt. Morris E. (Haguenau, France)
*Craw, Col. Demas T. (Port Lyautey, French Morocco)
Crawford, Pvt. William J. (Altavilla, Italy)
Crews, SSgt. John R. (Lobenbacherhof, Germany)
Currey, Sgt. Francis S. (Malmedy, Belgium)
Dahlgren, Sgt. Edward C. (Oberhoffen, France)
Dalessondro, TSgt. Peter J. (Kalterherberg, Germany)
Daly, Lt. Michael J. (Nuremberg, Germany)
Davis, Capt. Charles W. (Guadalcanal)
*DeFranzo, SSgt. Arthur F. (Vaubadon, France)
*DeGlopper, Pfc. Charles N. (La Fière, France)
*Deleau, Sgt. Emile, Jr. (Oberhoffen, France)
Dervishian, TSgt. Ernest H. (Cisterna, Italy)
*Diamond, Pfc. James H. (Mintal, Philippines)
*Dietz, SSgt. Robert H. (Kirchain, Germany)
Doolittle, Lt. Col. James H. (Over Japan)
Doss, Pfc. Desmond T. (Okinawa)
Drowley, SSgt. Jesse R. (Bougainville Island)
Dunham, TSgt. Russell E. (Kayserberg, France)
*Dutko, Pfc. John W. (Ponte Rotto, Italy)
Ehlers, SSgt. Walter D. (Goville, France)
*Endl, SSgt. Gerald L. (Anamo, New Guinea)
Erwin, SSgt. Henry E. (Koriyama, Japan)
*Eubanks, Sgt. Ray E. (Noemfoor Island, Dutch New Guinea)
Everhart, TSgt. Forrest E. (Kerling, France)
*Femoyer, 2d. Lt. Robert E. (Merseburg, Germany)
Fields, 1st Lt. James H. (Rechicourt, France)
Fisher, 2d Lt. Almond E. (Grammont, France)
*Fournier, Sgt. William G. (Guadalcanal)
*Fowler, 2d Lt. Thomas W. (Carano, Italy)
*Fryar, Pvt. Elmer E. (Leyte, Philippines)
Funk, 1st Sgt. Leonard A., Jr. (Holzheim, Belgium)
*Galt, Capt. William W. (Villa Crocetta, Italy)
*Gammon, SSgt. Archer T. (Bastogne, Belgium)
Garcia, Ssgt. Marcario (Grosshau, Germany)
Garman, Pvt. Harold A. (Montereau, France)
Gerstung, TSgt. Robert E. (Berg, Germany)
*Gibson, Technician 5th Grade Eric G. (isola Bella, Italy)
*Gonzales, Pfc. David M. (Villa Verde Trail, Philippines)
*Gott, 1st Lt. Donald J. (Saarbrucken, Germany)
*Grabiarz, Pfc. William J. (Manila, Philippines)
Gregg, TSgt. Stephen R. (Montelimar, France)
*Gruennert, Sgt. Kenneth E. (Buna, New Guinea)
Hal, SSgt. George J. (Anzio, Italy)
*Hall, Technician 5th Grade Lewis (Guadalcanal)
*Hallman, SSgt. Sherwood H. (Brest, France)
Hamilton, Maj. Pierpont M. (Port Lyautey, French Morocco)
*Harmon, Sgt. roy W. (Casaglia, Italy)
*Harr, Cpl. Harry R. (Maglamin, Philippines)
*Harris, 2d Lt. James L. (Vagney, France)
*Hastings, Pfc. Joe R. (Drabenderhohe, Germany)
Hawk, Sgt. John D. (Chambois, France)
Hawks, Pfc. Lloyd C. (Carano, Italy)
*Hedrick, TSgt. Clinton M. (Lembeck, Germany)
Hendrix, Pvt. James R. (Assenois, Belgium)
*Henry, Pvt. Robert T. (Luchem, Germany)
Herrera, Pfc. Silvestre S. (Mertzwiller, France)
Horner, SSgt. Freeman V. (Wurselen, Germany)
Howard, Lt. Col. James H. (Oschersleben, Germany)
Huff, Cpl. Paul B. (Carano, Italy)
*Hughes, 2d Lt. Lloyd H. (Ploesti, Rumania)
*Jachman, SSgt. Isadore S. (Flamerge, Belgium)
*Jerstad, Maj. John L. (Ploesti, Rumania)
*Johnson, Pvt. Elden H. (Valmontone, Italy)
Johnson, Col. leon W. (Ploesti, Rumania)
*Johnson, Sgt. Leroy (Limon, Philippines)
Johnson, Sgt. Oscar G. (Scarperia, Italy)
Johnston, Pfc. William J. (Padiglione, Italy)
*Kandle, 1st Lt. Victor L. (La Forge, France)
Kane, Col. John R. (Ploesti, Rumania)
Karaberis, Sgt. Christos H. (Guignola, Italy)
Kearby, Col. Neel E. (Wewak, New Guinea)
*Keathley, SSgt. George D. (Mt. Altuzzo, Italy)
*Kefurt, SSgt. Gus (Bennwihr, France)
*Kelley, SSgt. Jonah E. (Kesternich, Germany)
*Kelley, Pvt. Ova A. (Leyte, Philippines)
Kelly, Cpl. Charles E. (Altavilla, Italy)
*Kelly, Cpl. John D. (Fort du Roule, France)
Kelly, Cpl. Thomas J. (Alemert, Germany)
Kerstetter, Pfc. Dexter J. (Galiano, Philippines)
*Kessler, Pfc. Patrick L. (Ponte Rotto, Italy)
*Kimbro, Technician 4th Grade Truman (Rocherath, Belgium)
*Kiner, Pvt. Harold G. (Palenberg, Germany)
*Kingsley, 2d Lt. David R. (Ploesti, Rumania)
Kisters, Sgt. Gerry H. (Gagliano, Sicily)
Knappenberger, Pfc. Alton W., (Cisterna di Littoria, Italy)
*Knight, 1st Lt. Jack L. (Loi-kang, Burma)
*Knight, ist Lt. Raymond L. (Northern Po Valley, Italy)
*Krotiak, Pfc. Anthony L. (Balete Pass, Philippines)
*Lawley, 1st Lt. William R., Jr. (Over Europe)
Laws, SSgt. Robert E. (Pangasinan Province, Philippines)
Lee, ist Lt. Daniel W. (Montreval, France)
*Leonard, 1st Lt. Turney W. (Kommerscheidt, Germany)
*Lindsey, Capt. Darrell R. (L'Isle Adam Bridge, France)
Lindsey, TSgt. Jake W. (Hamich, Germany)
*Lindstrom, Pfc. Floyd K. (Mignano, Italy)
*Lloyd, 1st Lt. Edgar H. (Pompey, France)
*Lobaugh, Pvt. Donald R. (Afua, New Guinea)
Logan, Sgt. James M. (Salerno, Italy)
Lopez, Sgt. Jose M. (Krinkelt, Belgium)
Mabry, Lt. Col. George L., Jr. (Hurtgen Forest, Germany)
MacArthur, Gen. Douglas (Bataan Peninsula, Philippines)
McCall, SSgt. Thomas E. (San Angelo, Italy)
McCarter, Pvt. Lloyd G. (Corregidor, Philippines)
McGaha, MSgt. Charles L. (Lupao, Philippines)
McGarity, TSgt. Vernon (Krinkelt, Belgium)
*McGee, Pvt. William D. (Mulheim, Germany)
*McGill, Sgt. Troy A. (Los Negros Islands)
Mac Gillivary, Sgt. Charles A. (Woelfling, France)
*McGraw, Pfc. Francis X. (Schevenhutte, Germany)
*McGuire, Maj. Thomas B., Jr. (Luzon, Philippines)
McKinney, Pvt. John R. (Tayabas Province, Philippines).
*McVeigh, Sgt. John J. (Brest, France)
*McWhorter, Pfc. William A. (Leyte, Philippines)
*Magrath, Pfc. John D. (Castel d'Aiano Italy)
*Mann, Pfc. Joe E. (Best, Holland)
*Martinez, Pvt. Joe P. (Attu, Aleutian Islands)
*Mathies, Sgt. Archibald (Over Europe)
*Mathis, 1st Lt. Jack W. (Vegesack, Germany)
Maxwell, Technician 5th Grade Robert D. (Besancon, France)
*May, Pfc. Martin O. (Ie Shima, Ryukyu Islands)
Mayfield, Cpl. Melvin (Cordillera Mountains, Philippines)
Meagher, TSgt. John (Ozato, Okinawa)
Merli, Pfc. Gino J. (Sars la Bruyère, Belgium)
*Merrell, Pvt. Joseph F. (Lohe, Germany)
*Messerschmidt, Sgt. Harold O. (Radden, France)
*Metzger, 2d Lt. William E., Jr. (Saarbrucken, Germany)
Michael, 1st Lt. Edward S. (Over Germany)
*Michael, 2d Lt. Harry J. (Neiderzerf, Germany)
*Miller, SSgt. Andrew (Woippy, France-Kerprich Hemmersdorf, Germany)
Mills, Pvt. James H. (Cisterna di Littoria, Italy)
*Minick, SSgt. John W. (Hurtgen, Germany)
*Minue, Pvt. Nicholas (Medjez-el-Bab, Tunisia)
*Monteith, 1st Lt. Jimmie W., Jr. (Collesville-sur-Mer, France)
Montgomery, 1st Lt. Jack C. (Padiglione, Italy)
*Moon, Pvt. Harold H., Jr. (Pawig, Philippines)
Morgan, 2d Lt. John C. (Over Europe)
*Moskala, Pfc. Edward J. (Kakazu Ridge, Okinawa)
*Mower, Sgt. Charles E. (Capoocan, Philippines)
*Muller, Sgt. Joseph E. (Ishimmi, Okinawa)
*Munemori, Pfc. Sadao S. (Seravezza, Italy)
Murphy, 2d Lt. Audie L. (Holtzwihr, France)
*Murphy, Pfc. Frederick C. (Saarlautern, Germany)
Murray, 1st Lt. Charles P., Jr. (Kaysersberg, France)
*Nelson, Sgt. William L. (Djebel Dardys, Tunisia)
Neppel, Sgt. Ralph G. (Birgel, Germany)
Nett, Lt. Robert P. (Cognon, Philippines)
Newman, 1st Lt. Beryl R. (Cisterna, Italy)
*Nininger, 2d Lt. Alexander R., Jr. (Abucay, Philippines)
*O'Brien, Lt. Col. William J. (Saipan, Mariana Islands)
Ogden, 1st Lt. Carlos C. (Fort du Roule, France)
*Olson, Capt. Arlo L. (Volturno River, Italy)
*Olson, Sgt. Truman O. (Cisterna di Littoria,italy)
Oresko, MSgt. Nicholas (Tettington, Germany)
*Parrish, Technician 4th Grade Laverne (Binalonan, Philippines)
*Pease, Capt. Harl, Jr. (Rabaul, New Britain)
*Peden, Technician 5th Grade Forrest E. (Biesheim, France)
*Pendleton, SSgt. Jack J. (Bardenberg, Germany)
*Peregory, TSgt. Frank D. (Grandcampe, France)
*Perez, Pfc. Manuel, Jr. (Fort William McKinley, Philippines)
*Peters, Pvt. George J. (Fluren, Germany)
*Peterson, SSgt. George (Eisern, Germany)
*Petrarca, Pfc. Frank J. (New Georgia, Solomon Islands)
*Pinder, Technician 5th Grade John J., Jr. (Colleville-sur-Mer, France)
Powers, Pfc. Leo J. (Cassino, Italy)
*Prussman, Pfc. Ernest W. (Les Coates, France)
*Pucket, 1st Lt. Donald D. (Ploesti, Rumania)
*Ray, 1st Lt. Bernard J. (Hurtgen Forest, Germany)
*Reese, Pvt. James W. (Mt. Vassillio, Sicily)
*Reese, Pfc. John N., Jr. (Manila, Philippines)
*Riordan, 2d Lt. Paul F. (Cassino, Italy)
Robinson, 1st Lt. James E., Jr. (Untergriesheim, Germany)
Rodriguez, Pvt. Cleto (Manila, Philippines)
*Roeder, Capt. Robert E. (Mt. Battaglia, Italy)
*Roosevelt, Brig. Gen. Theodore, Jr. (Normandy, France)
Ross, Pvt. Wilburn K. (St. Jacques, France)
Rudolph, TSgt. Donald E. (Munoz, Philippines)
Ruiz, Pfc. Alejandro R. (Okinawa)
*Sadowski, Sgt. Joseph J. (Valhey, France)
*Sarnoski, 2d Lt. Joseph R. (Buka Area, Solomon Islands)
*Sayers, Pfc. Foster J. (Thionville, France)
Schaefer, SSgt. Joseph E. (Stolberg, Germany)
Schauer, Pfc. Henry (Cisterna di Littoria, Italy)
Scott, Lt. Robert S. (New Georgia, Solomon Islands)
Shea, 2d Lt. Charles W. (Mt Damiano, Italy)
*Sheridan, Pfc. Carl V. (Weisweiler, Germany)
*Shockley, Pfc. William R. (Villa Verde Trail, Philippines)
Shomo, Maj. William A. (Luzon, Philippines)
*Shoup, SSgt. Curtis F. (Tillet, Belgium)
Silk, 1st Lt. Edward A. (St. Pravel, France)
Siogren, SSgt. John C. (San José Hacienda, Philippines)
Slaton, Cpl. James D. (Oliveto, Italy)
*Smith, Pvt. Furman L. (Lanuvio, Italy)
Smith, Sgt. Maynard H. (Over Europe)
Soderman, Pfc. William A. (Rocherath, Belgium)
*Specker, Sgt. Joe C. (Mt. Porchia, Italy)
Spurrier, SSgt. Junior J. (Achain, France)
*Squires, Pfc. John C. (Padiglione, Italy)
*Stryker, Pfc. Stuart S. (Wesel, Germany)
*Terry, 1st Lt. Seymour W. (Okinawa)
*Thomas, Pfc. William H. (Zambales Mountains, Philippines)
Thompson, Sgt. Max (Haaren, Germany)
*Thorne, Cpl. Horace M. (Grufflingen, Belgium)
*Thorson, Pfc. John F. (Dagami, Philippines)
Tominac, 1st Lt. John J. (Saulx de Vesoul, France)
*Towle, Pvt. John R. (Oosterhout, Holland)
Treadwell, Capt. Jack L. (Nieder-Wurzbach, Germany)
*Truemper, 2d Lt. Walter E. (Over Europe)
*Turner, Sgt. Day G. (Dahl, Luxembourg)

Turner, Pfc. George B. (Philipsbourg, France)
Urban, Capt. Matt (Renouf & St. Lo, France, & Meuse River, Belgium)
*Valdez, Pfc. Jose F. (Rosenkrantz, France)
*Van Noy, Pvt. Junior (Finschafen, New Guinea)
*Vance, Lt. Col. Leon R., Jr. (Wimereaux, France)
*Viale, 2d Lt. Robert M. (Manila, Philippines)
*Villegas, SSgt. Ysmael R. (Villa Verde Trail, Philippines)
Vlug, Pfc. Dirk J. (Limon, Philippines)
Vosler, TSgt. Forrest T. (Bremen, Germany)
Wainwright, Gen. Jonathan M. (Philippines)
*Walker, Brig. Gen. Kenneth N. (Rabaul, New Britain)
*Wallace, Pfc. Herman C. (Prumzurley, Germany)
Ware, Lt. Col. Keith L. (Sigolsheim, France)
*Warner, Cpl. Henry F. (Dom Butgenbach, Belgium)
*Waugh, 1st Lt. Robert T. (Tremensucli, Italy)
Waybur, 1st Lt. David C. (Agrigento, Sicily)
*Weicht, Sgt. Ellis R. (St. Hippolyte, France)
*Wetzel, Pfc. Walter C. (Birken, Germany)
Whiteley, 1st Lt. Eli (Sigolsheim, France)
Whittington, Sgt. Hulon B. (Grimesnil, France)
Wiedorfer, Pvt. Paul J. (Chaumont, Belgium)
*Wigle, 2d Lt. Thomas W. (Monte Frassino, Italy)
Wilbur, Col. William H. (Fedala, French Morocco)
*Wilkin, Cpl. Edward G. (Siegfried line, Germany)
*Wilkins, Maj. Raymond H. (Rabaul, New Britain)
*Will, 1st Lt. Walter J. (Eisern, Germany)
*Wilson, Technician 5th Grade Alfred L. (Bezange la Petite, France)
Wise, SSgt. Homer L. (Magliano, Italy)
*Woodford, SSgt. Howard E. (Tabio, Philippines)
*Young, Pvt. Rodger W. (New Georgia, Solomon Islands)
Zeamer, Capt. Jay, Jr. (Buka Area, Solomon Islands)
*Zussman, 2d Lt. Raymond (Noroy le Bourg, France)

COAST GUARD

*Munro, Signalman 1st Class Douglas A. (Point Cruz, Guadalcanal)

MARINES

*Agerholm, Pfc. Harold C. (Saipan, Marian Islands)
*Anderson, Pfc. Richard B. (Roi Island, Marshall Islands)
*Bailey, Maj. Kenneth D. (Guadalcanal)
Basilone, Sgt. John (Guadalcanal)
*Bauer, Lt. Col. Harold W. (Solomon Islands Area)
*Bausell, Cpl. Lewis K. (Peleliu Island)
*Berry, Cpl. Charles J. (Iwo Jima)
*Bonnyman, 1st Lt. Alexander, Jr. (Tarawa)
*Bordelon, SSgt. William J. (Tarawa)
Boyington, Maj. Gregory (Central Solomons Area)
*Bush, Cpl. Richard E. (Okinawa)
*Caddy, Pfc. William R. (Iwo Jima)
*Cannon, 1st Lt. George H. (Sand Island, Midway Islands)
Casamento, Cpl. Anthony (Guadalcanal)
Chambers, Lt. Col. Justice M. (Iwo Jima)
*Cole, Sgt. Darrell S. (Iwo Jima)
*Courtney, Maj. Henry A., Jf. (Okinawa Shima)
*Damato, Cpl. Anthony P. (Engebi Island, Marshall Islands)
DeBlanc, Capt. Jefferson J. (Kolombangara Island, Solomon Islands)
Dunlap, Capt. Robert H. (Iwo Jima)
*Dyess, Lt. Col. Aquilla J. (Namur Island, Marshall Islands)
*Edson, Col. Merritt A. (Guadalcanal)
*Elrod, Capt. Henry T. (Wake Island)
*Epperson, Pfc. Harold G. (Saipan Island, Mariana Islands)
*Fardy, Cpl. John P. (Okinawa Shima)
*Fleming, Capt. Richard E. (Midway)
Foss, Capt. Joseph J. (Guadalcanal)
*Foster, Pfc. William A. (Okinawa Shima)
Galer, Maj. Robert E. (Solomon Islands Area)
*Gonsalves, Pfc. Harold (Okinawa Shima)
*Gray, Sgt. Ross F. (Iwo Jima)
*Gurke, Pfc. Henry (Bougainville Island)
*Hansen, Pvt. Dale M. (Okinawa Shima)
*Hanson, 1st Lt. Robert M. (Bougainville Island & New Britain Island)
Harrell, Sgt. William G. (Iwo Jima)
*Hauge, Cpl. Louis J., Jr. (Okinawa Shima)
*Hawkins, 1st Lt. William D. (Tarawa)
Jackson, Pfc. Arthur J. (Peleliu Island)
Jacobson, Pfc. Douglas T. (Iwo Jima)
*Julian, Sgt. Joseph R. (Iwo Jima)
*Kinser, Sgt. Elbert L. (Okinawa Shima)
*Kraus, Pfc. Richard E. (Peleliu Island)
*La Belle, Pfc. James D. (Iwo Jima)
Leims, 2d Lt. John H. (Iwo Jima)
Lucas, Pfc. Jacklyn H. (Iwo Jima)
*Lummus, 1st Lt. Jack (Iwo Jima)
*McCard, Gy. Sgt. Robert H. (Saipan, Mariana Islands)
McCarthy, Capt. Joseph J. (Iwo Jima)
*McTureous, Pvt. Robert M., Jr. (Okinawa)
*Martin, 1st Lt. Harry L. (Iwo Jima)
*Mason, Pfc. Leonard F. (Guam)
*New, Pfc. John D. (Peleliu Island)
*Owens, Sgt. Robert A. (Cape Torokina, Bougainville Island)
*Ozbourn, Pvt. Joseph W. (Tinian Island, Mariana Islands)
Paige, Sgt. Mitchell (Guadalcanal)
*Phelps, Pvt. Wesley (Peleliu Island)
*Phillips, Pvt. George (Iwo Jima)
Pope, Capt. Everett P. (Peleliu Island)
*Power, 1st Lt. John V. (Namur Island, Marshall Islands)
*Roan, Pfc. Charles H. (Peleliu Island)
Rouh, 1st Lt. Carlton R. (Peleliu Island)
*Ruhl, Pfc. Donald J. (Iwo Jima)
*Schwab, Pfc. Albert E. (Okinawa Shima)
Shoup, Col. David M. (Betio Island, Tarawa)
Sigler, Pvt. Franklin E. (Iwo Jima)
Skaggs, Pvc. Luther, Jr. (Guam)
Smith, Maj. John L. (Solomon Islands Area)
Sorenson, Pvt. Richard K. (Namur Island Marshall Islands)
*Stein, Cpl. Tony (Iwo Jima)
Swett, 1st Lt. James E. (Solomon Islands Area)
*Thomas, Sgt. Herbert J. (Koromokina River, Bougainville Island)
*Thomason, Sgt. Clyde (Makin Island)
*Timmerman, Sgt. Grant F. (Saipan, Mariana Islands)
Vandergrift, Maj. Gen. Alexander A. (Guadalcanal)
Walsh, 1st Lt. Kenneth A. (Solomon Islands Area)
*Walsh, Gy. Sgt. William G. (Iwo Jima)
Watson, Pvt. Wilson D. (Iwo Jima)
Williams, Cpl. Hershel W. (Iwo Jima)
Wilson, Capt. Louis H., Jr. (Fonte Hill, Guam)
*Wilson, Pfc. Robert L. (Tinian Island, Mariana Islands)
*Witek, Pfc. Frank P. (Guam)

NAVY

Antrim, Lt. Richard N. (Makassar, Netherlands East Indies)
*Bennion, Capt. Mervyn S. (Pearl Harbor, Hawaii)
*Bigelow, Watertender 1st Class Elmer C. (Corregidor Island, Philippines)
Bulkeley, Lt. Cmdr. John D. (Philippines)
Bush, Hospital Apprentice 1st Class Robert E. (Okinawa)
*Callaghan, Rear Adm. Daniel J. (Savo Island, Solomon Islands)
*Cromwell, Capt. John P. (Truk Island)
*David, Lt. (j.g.) Albert L. (French West Africa)
*Davis, Cmdr. George F. (Lingayen Gulf, Philippines)
*Dealey, Cmdr. Samuel D. (Sulu Sea, Borneo)
*Evans, Cmdr. Ernest E. (Samar, Philippines)
Finn, Lt. John W. (Kaneohe Bay, Hawaii)
*Flaherty, Ensign Francis C. (Pearl Harbor, Hawaii)
Fluckey, Cmdr. Eugene B. (Coast of China)
Fuqua, Capt. Samuel G. (Pearl Harbor, Hawaii)
Gary, Lt. (j.g.) Donald A. (Kobe, Japan)
*Gilmore, Cmdr. Howard W. (Southwest Pacific)
Gordon, Lt. Nathan G. (Bismarck Sea)
Hall, Lt. (j.g.) William E. (Coral Sea)
*Halyburton, Pharmacist's Mate 2d Class William D., Jr. (Okinawa Shima)
*Hammerberg, BM 2d Class Owen F. P. (Pearl Harbor, Hawaii)
Herring, Lt. Rufus G. (Iwo Jima)
*Hill, Chief Boatswain Edwin J. (Pearl Harbor, Hawaii)
*Hutchins, Sman 1st Class Johnnie D. (Lae, New Guinea)
*Jones, Ensign Herbert C. (Pearl Harbor, Hawaii)
*Keppler, BM 1st Class Reinhardt J. (Solomon Islands)
*Kidd, Rear Adm. Isaac C. (Pearl Harbor, Hawaii)
*Lester, Hospital Apprentice 1st Class Fred F. (Okinawa Shima)
McCampbell, Cmdr. David (Philippine Sea)
McCandless, Cmdr. Bruce (Savo Island, Solomon Islands)
McCool, Lt. Richard M., Jr. (Okinawa)
O'Callahan, Cmdr. Joseph T. (Kobe, Japan)
O'Hare, Lt. Edward H. (Raboul, New Britain)
O'Kane, Cmdr. Richard H. (Formosa Strait)
*Parle, Ensign John J. (Sicily, Italy)
*Peterson, Chief Watertender Oscar V. (NOR)
Pharris, Lt. Jackson C. (Pearl Harbor, Hawaii)
Pierce, Pharmacist's Mate 1st Class Francis J. (Iwo Jima)
*Powers, Lt. John J. (Coral Sea)
Preston, Lt. Arthur M. (Wasile Bay, Halmahera Island)
Ramage, Cmdr. Lawson P. (Pacific)
*Reeves, Radio Electrician Thomas J (Pearl Harbor, Hawaii)
*Ricketts, Lt. Molton E. (Coral Sea)
*Rooks, Capt. Albert H. (Java, Indonesia)
Ross, Machinist Donald K. (Pearl Harbor, Hawaii)
Schonland, Lt. Cmdr. Herbert E. (Savo Island, Solomon Islands)
*Scott, Rear Adm. Norman (Savo Island, Solomon Islands)
*Scott, Machinist's Mate 1st Class Robert R. (Pearl Harbor, Hawaii)
Street, Cmdr. George L. III (Quelpart Island, Korea)
*Tomich, Chief Watertender Peter (Pearl Harbor, Hawaii)
*Van Valkenburgh, Capt. Franklin (Pearl Harbor, Hawaii)
*Van Voorhis, Lt. Cmdr. Bruce A. (Greenwich Island, Solomon Islands)
Wahlen Pharmacist's Mate 2d Class George E. (Iwo Jima)
*Ward, Sman 1st Class James R. (Pearl Harbor, Hawaii)
*Williams, Pharmacist's Mate 3d Class Jack (Iwo Jima)
*Willis, Pharmacist's Mate 1st Class John H. (Iwo Jima)
Young, Cmdr. Cassin (Pearl Harbor, Hawaii)

THE KOREAN WAR
1950-1953

AIR FORCE

*Davis, Maj. George A., Jr. (Sinuiju-Yalu River Area)
*Loring, Maj. Charles J., Jr. (Sniper Ridge, N. Korea)
*Sebille, Maj. Louis J. (Hanchang)
*Walmsley, Capt. John S., Jr. (Yangdok)

ARMY

Adams, Sfc. Stanley T. (Sesim-ni)
*Barker, Pvt. Charles H. (Sokkogae)
*Bennett, Pfc. Emory L. (Sobangsan)
Bleak, Sgt. David B. (Minari-gol)
*Brittin, Sfc. Nelson V. (Yonggong-ni)
*Brown, Pfc. Melvin L. (Kasan)
Burke, 1st Lt. Lloyd L. (Chong-dong)
*Burris, Sfc. Tony K. (Mundung-ni)
*Charlton, Sgt. Cornelius H. (Chipo-ri)
*Collier, Cpl. Gilbert G (Tutayou)
*Collier, Cpl. John W. (Chindong-ni)
*Coursen, 1st Lt. Samuel S. (Kaesong)
*Craig, Cpl. Gordon M. (Kasan)
Crump, Cpl. Jerry K. (Chorwon)
Dean, Maj. Gen. William F. (Taejon)
*Desiderio, Capt. Reginald B. (Ipsok)
Dodd, 2d Lt. Carl H. (Subuk)
*Duke, Sfc. Ray E. (Mugok)
*Edwards, Sfc. Junior D. (Changbong-ni)
*Essebagger, Cpl. John, Jr. (Popsudong)
*Faith, Lt. Col. Don C., Jr. (Hagaru-ri)
*George, Pfc. Charles (Songnae-dong)
*Gilliland, Pfc. Charles L. (Tongmang-ni)
*Goodblood, Cpl. Clair (Popsudong)
*Hammond, Cpl. Lester, Jr. (Kumwha)
*Handrich, MSgt. Melvin O. (Sobuk San Mountain)
*Hanson, Pfc. Jack G. (Pachi-dong)
*Hartell, 1st Lt. Lee R. (Kobangsan-ni)
Harvey, Capt. Raymond (Taemi-Dong)
*Henry, 1st Lt. Frederick F. (Am-Dong)
Hernandez, Cpl. Rodolfo P. (Wontong-ni)
Ingman, Cpl. Einar H., Jr. (Maltari)
*Jecelin, Sgt. William R. (Saga)
*Jordan, Pfc. Mack A. (Kumsong)
*Kanell, Pvt. Billie G. (Pyongyang)
*Kaufman, Sfc. Loren R. (Yongsan)
*Knight, Pfc. Noah O. (Kowang-San)
Kouma, Sfc. Ernest R. (Agok)
*Krzyzowski, Capt. Edward C. (Tondul)
*Kyle, 2d Lt. Darwin K. (Kamil-ni)
Lee, MSgt. Hubert L. (Ip-o-ri)
*Libby, Sgt. George D. (Taejon)
*Long, Sgt, Charles R. (Hoeng-song)
*Lyell, Cpl. William F. (Chup'a-ri)
*McGovern, 1st Lt. Robert M. (Kamyangjan-ni)
*Martinez, Cpl. Benito (Satae-ri)
*Mendonca, Sgt. Leroy A. (Chich-on)
Millett, Capt. Lewis L. (Soam-Ni)
Miyamura, Cpl. Hiroshi H. (Taejon-ni)
Mize, Sgt. Ola L. (Surang-ni)
*Moyer, Sfc. Donald R. (Seoul)
*Ouellette, Pfc. Joseph R. (Yongsan)
*Page, Lt. Col. John U. D. (Chosin Reservoir)
*Pendleton, Cpl. Charles F. (Choo Gung-Dong)
*Pililaau, Pfc. Herbert K. (Pia-ri)
Pittman, Sgt. John A. (Kujang-dong)
*Pomeroy, Pfc. Ralph E. (Kumhwa)
*Porter, Sgt. Donn F. (Mundung-ni)
*Red Cloud, Cpl. Mitchell, Jr. (Chonghyon)
Rodriguez, Pfc. Joseph C. (Munye-ri)
Rosser, Cpl. Ronald E. (Ponggilli)
*Schoonover, Cpl. Dan D. (Sokkogae)
Schowalter, 1st Lt. Edward R., Jr. (Kumhwa)
*Shea, 1st Lt. Richard T., Jr. (Sokkogae)
*Sitman, Sfc. William S. (Chipyong-ni)
*Smith, Pfc. David M. (Yongsan)
*Speicher, Cpl. Clifton T. (Minari-gol)
Stone, 1st Lt. James L. (Sokkogae)
*Story, Pfc. Luther H. (Agok)
*Sudut, 2d Lt. Jerome A. (Kumhwa)
*Thompson, Pfc. William (Haman)
*Turner, Sfc. Charles W. (Yongsan)
*Watkins, MSgt. Travis E. (Yongsan)
West, Pfc. Ernest E. (Sataeri)
Wilson, MSgt. Benjamin F. (Hwach'on-Myon)
*Wilson, Pfc. Richard G. (Opari)
*Womack, Pfc. Bryant H. (Sokso-ri)
*Young, Pfc. Robert H. (Kaesong)

MARINES

*Abrell, Cpl. Charles G. (Hangnyong)
Barber, Capt. William E. (Chosin Reservior)
*Baugh, Pfc. William B. (Koto-ri to Hagaru-ri)
Cafferata, Pvt. Hector A., Jr. (Chosin Reservoir)
*Champagne, Cpl. David B. (Korea)
*Christianson, Pfc. Stanley (Seoul)
Commiskey, 2d Lt. Henry A., Sr. (Yongdungp'o)
*Davenport, Cpl. Jack A. (Songnae-Dong)
Davis, Lt. Col. Raymond G. (Hagaru-ri)
Dewey, Cpl. Duane E. (Panmunjon)
*Garcia, Pfc. Fernando L. (Korea)
*Gomez, Pfc. Edward (Hill 749)
*Guillen, SSgt. Ambrosio (Songuch-on)
*Johnson, Sgt. James E. (Yudam-ni)
*Kelly, Pfc. John D. (Korea)
*Kelso, Pfc. Jack W. (Korea)
Kennemore, SSgt. Robert S. (Yudam-ni)
*Littleton, Pfc. Herbert A. (Chungchon)
*Lopez, 1st Lt. Baldomero (Inchon)
McLaughlin, Pfc. Alford L. (Korea)
*Matthews, Sgt. Daniel P. (Vegas Hill)
*Mausert, Sgt. Frederick W., III (Songnap-yong)
*Mitchell, 1st Lt. Frank N. (Hansan-ni)
*Monegan, Pfc. Walter C., Jr. (Sosa-ri)
*Moreland, Pfc. Whitt L. (Kwagch'i-Dong)
Murphy, 2d Lt. Raymond G. (Korea)
Myers, Maj. Reginald R. (Hagaru-ri)
*Obregon, Pfc. Eugene A. (Seoul)
O'Brien, 2d Lt. George H., Jr. (Korea)
*Phillips, Cpl. Lee H. (Korea)
*Poynter, Sgt. James I. (Sudong)
*Ramer, 2d Lt. George H. (Korea)
*Reem, 2d Lt. Robert D. (Chinhung-ni)
*Shuck, SSgt. William E., Jr. (Korea)
Simanek, Pfc. Robert E. (Korea)
Sitter, Capt. Carl L. (Hagaru-ri)
*Skinner, 2d Lt. Sherrod E., Jr. (Korea)
Van Winkle, SSgt. Archie (Sudong)
*Vittori, Cpl. Joseph (Hill 749)
*Watkins, SSgt. Lewis G. (Korea)
Wilson, TSgt. Harold E. (Korea)
*Windrich, SSgt. William G. (Yudam-ni)

NAVY

*Benford, Hospital Corpsman 3d Class Edward C. (Korea)
Charette, Hospital Corpsman 3d Class William R. (Korea)
*Dewert, Hospital Corpsman Richard D. (Korea)
*Hammond, Hospital Corpsman Francis C. (Korea)
Hudner, Lt.(j.g.) Thomas J., Jr. (Chosin Reservior)
*Kilmer, Hospital Corpsman John E. (Korea)
*Koelsch, Lt.(j.g.) John K. (North Korea)

THE VIETNAM WAR
1964-1973

AIR FORCE

*Bennett, Capt. Steven L. (Quang Tri)
Day, Maj. George E. (North Vietnam)
Dethlefsen, Capt. Merlyn H. (North Vietnam)
Fisher, Maj. Bernard F. (A Shau)
Fleming, 1st Lt. James P. (Duc Co)
Jackson, Lt. Col. Joe M. (Kham Duc)
*Jones, Lt. Col. William A. III (Dong Hoi, N. Vietnam)
Levitow, Airman 1st Class John L. (Long Binh)
*Sijan, Capt. Lance P. (North Vietnam)
Thorsness, Maj. Leo K. (North Vietnam)
*Wilbanks, Capt. Hilliard A. (Da Lat)
Young, Capt. Gerald O. (Khe Sanh)

ARMY

*Adams, Maj. William E. (Kontum Province)
*Albanese, Pfc. Lewis (Phu Muu-2)
Anderson, SSgt. Webster (Tam Ky)
*Ashley, Sfc. Eugene, Jr. (Lang Vei)
Baca, Sp4c. John P. (Phuoc Long Province)
Bacon, SSgt. Nicky D. (Tam Ky)
Baker, Pfc. John F., Jr. (South Vietnam)
*Barnes, Pfc. John A. III (Dak To)
Beikirch, Sgt. Gary B. (Kontum Province)
*Belcher, Sgt. Ted (Plei Jrang)
*Bellrichard, Pfc. Leslie A. (Kontum Province)
Benavidez, SSgt. Roy P. (Cambodia)
*Bennett, Cpl. Thomas W. (Pleiku Province)
*Blanchfield, Sp4c. Michael R. (Binh Dinh Province)
Bondsteel, SSgt. James L. (An Loc Province)
*Bowen, SSgt. Hammett L., Jr. (Binh Duong Province)
Brady, Maj. Patrick H. (Chu Lai)
*Bryant, Sfc. William M. (Long Khanh Province)
Bucha, Capt. Paul W. (Phuoc Vinh)
*Buker, Sgt. Brian L. (Chau Doc Province)
Cavaiani, SSgt. Jon R. (Quang Tri Province)
*Crescenz, Cpl. Michael J. (Hiep Duc Valley)
*Cutinha, Sp4c. Nicholas J. (Gia Dinh)
*Dahl, Sp4c. Larry G. (An Khe)
Davis, Sgt. Sammy L. (Cai Lay)
*Devore, Sp4c. Edward A., Jr. (Saigon)

Dix, SSgt. Drew D. (Chau Doc Province)
*Doane, 1st Lt. Stephen H. (Hau Nghia Province)
Dolby, Sp4c. David C. (South Veitnam)
Donlon, Capt. Roger H. C. (Nam Dong)
Dunagan, Capt. Kern W. (Quang Tin Province)
*Durham, 2d Lt. Harold B., Jr. (South Vietnam)
*English, SSgt. Glenn H., Jr. (Phu My)
*Evans, Sp4c. Donald W., Jr. (Tri Tam)
Evans, Sgt. Rodney J. (Tay Ninh Province)
Ferguson, CWO Frederick E. (Hue)
*Fernandez, Sp4c Daniel (Cu Chi)
Fitzmaurice, Sp4c. Michael J. (Khe Sanh)
*Fleek, Sgt. Charles C. (Binh Duong Province)
Foley, Capt. Robert F. (Quan Dau Tieng)
*Folland, Cpl. Michael F. (Long Khanh)
*Fournet, 1st Lt. Douglas B. (A Shau Valley)
*Fous, Pfc. James W. (Kien Hoa Province)
*Fratellenico, Cpl. Frank R. (Quang Tri Province)
Fritz, Capt. Harold A. (Binh Long Province)
*Gardner, 1st Lt. James A. (My Canh)
*Gertsch, SSgt. John G. (A Shau' Valley)
*Grandstaff, Sgt. Bruce A. (Pleiku Province)
*Grant, 1st Lt. Joseph X. (South Vietnam)
*Guenette, Sp4c. Peter M. (Quan Tan Uyen)
Hagemeister, Sp4c. Charles C. (Binh Dinh Province)
*Hagen, 1st Lt. Loren D. (South Vietnam)
*Hartsock, SSgt. Robert W. (Hau Nghia Province)
*Harvey, Sp4c. Carmel B., Jr. (Binh Dinh Province)
Herda, Pfc. Frank A. (Dak To)
*Hibbs, 2d Lt. Robert J. (Don Dien Loke)
*Holcomb, Sgt. John N. (Quan Loi)
Hooper, Sgt. Joe R. (Hue)
*Hosking, MSgt. Charles E., Jr. (Phuoc Long Province)
Howard, Sfc. Robert L. (Laos)
Ingalls, Sp4c. George A. (Duc Pho)
Jacobs, 1st Lt. Jack H. (Kien Phong Province)
Jenkins, Pfc. Don J. (Kien Phong Province)
Jennings, SSgt Delbert O. (Kim Song Valley)
Joel, Sp5c. Lawrence (War Zone D)
Johnson, Sp5c. Dwight H. (Dak To)
*Johnston, Sp4c. Donald R. (Tay Ninh Province)
*Karopczyc, 1st Lt. Stephen E. (Kontum Province)
*Kawamura, Cpl. Terry T. (Camp Radcliff)
Kays, Pvt. Kenneth M. (Thua Thien Province)
*Kedenburg, Sp5c. John J. (Laos)
Keller, Sgt. Leonard B. (Ap Bac)
Kinsman, Pfc. Thomas J. (Vinh Long)
Lambers, Sgt. Paul R. (Tay Ninh Province)
Lang, Sp4c. George C. (Kien Hoa Province)
*Langhorn, Pfc. Garfield M. (Pleiku Province)
*LaPointe, Sp4c. Joseph G., Jr. (Quang Tin Province)
*Lauffer, Pfc. Billy L. (Bong Son)
*Law, Sp4c. Robert D. (Tinh Phuoc Thanh)
*Lee, Pfc. Milton A. (Phu Bai)
*Leisy, 2d Lt. Robert R. (Phuoc Long Province)
Lemon, Sp4c Peter C. (Tay Ninh Province)
*Leonard, Sgt. Matthew (Suoi Da)
Liteky, Capt. Angelo J. (Phuoc Lac)
Littrell, Sfc. Gary L. (Kontum Province)
*Long, Sgt. Donald R. (South Vietnam)
*Lozada, Pfc. Carlos J. (Dak To)
Lucas, Lt. Col. Andre C. (FSB Ripcord)
Lynch, Sp4c. Allen J. (My An-2)
McCleery, Sgt. Finnis D. (Quang Tin Province)
*McDonald, Pfc. Phill G. (Kontum City)
*McKibben, Sgt. Ray (Song Mao)
*McMahon, Sp4c. Thomas J. (Quang Tin Province)
McNerney, 1st Sgt. David H. (Polei Duc)
*McWethy, Sp5c. Edgar L., Jr. (Binh Dinh Province)
Marm, 2d Lt. Walter J., Jr. (Ia Drang Valley)
*Michael, Sp4c. Don L. (South Vietnam)
Miller, SSgt. Franklin D. (Kontum Province)
*Miller, 1st Lt. Gary L. (Binh Duong Province)
Molnar, SSgt. Frankie Z. (Kontum Province)
Monroe, Pfc. James H. (Bong Son)
Morris, SSgt. Charles B. (South Vietnam)
*Murray, SSgt. Robert C. (Hiep Duc)
*Nash, Pfc. David P. (Giao Duc)
Novosel, CWO Michael J. (Kien Tuong Province)
*Olive, Pfc. Milton L. III (Phu Cuong)
*Olson, Sp4c. Kenneth L. (South Vietnam)
Patterson, Sgt. Robert M. (La Chu)
Penry, Sgt. Richard A. (Binh Tuy Province)
*Peterson, Sp4c. Danny J. (Tay Ninh Province)
*Pierce, Sgt. Larry South (Ben Cat)
*Pitts, Capt. Riley L. (Ap Dong)
Port, Pfc. William D. (Que Son Valley)
*Poxon, 1st Lt. Robert L. (Tay Ninh Province)
*Pruden, SSgt. Robert J. (Quang Ngai Province)
*Rabel, SSgt. Laszlo (Binh Dinh Province)
Ray, 1st Lt. Ronald E. (Ia Drang Valley)
*Roark, Sgt. Anund C. (Kontum Province)
Roberts, Sp4c. Gordon R. (Thua Thien Province)
*Robinson, Sgt. James W., Jr. (South Vietnam)
Rocco, Sfc. Louis R. (Katum)
Rogers, Lt. Col. Charles C. (Fishook, Cambodian border)
*Rubio, Capt. Euripedes (Tay Ninh Province)
*Santiago-Colon, Sp4c. Hector (Quang Tri Province)

*Sargent, 1st Lt. Ruppert L. (Hau Nghia Province)
Sasser, Pfc. Clarence E. (Dinh Tuong Province)
Seay, Sgt. William W. (Ap Nhi)
*Shea, Pfc. Daniel J. (Quang Tri Province)
*Sims, SSgt. Clifford C. (Hue)
*Sisler, 1st Lt. George K. (Laos)
*Skidgel, Sgt. Donald South (Song Be)
*Smith, SSgt. Elmelindo R. (South Vietnam)
Sprayberry, 1st Lt. James M. (South Vietnam)
*Steindam, 1st Lt. Russell A. (Tay Ninh Province)
*Stewart, SSgt. Jimmy G. (South Vietnam)
Stone, Sgt. Lester R., Jr. (LZ Liz)
*Stout, Sgt. Mitchell W. (Khe Gio Bridge)
*Stryker, Sp4c. Robert F. (Loc Ninh)
Stumpf, Sp4c. Kenneth E. (Duc Pho)
Taylor, 1st Lt. James A. (Que Son)
Thacker, 1st Lt. Brian M. (Kontum Province)
*Warren, 1st Lt. John E., Jr. (Tay Ninh Province)
*Watters, Maj. Charles J. (Dak To)
*Wayrynen, Sp4c Dale E. (Quang Ngai Province)
Wetzel, Pfc. Gary G. (Ap Dong An)
*Wickam, Cpl. Jerry W. (Loc Ninh)
*Willett, Pfc. Louis E. (Kontum Province)
Williams, 2d Lt. Charles Q. (Dong Xoai)
*Winder, Pfc. David F. (South Vietnam)
Wright, Sp4c. Raymond R. (Ap Bac)
*Yabes, 1st Sgt. Maximo (Phu Hoa Dong)
*Yano, Sfc. Rodney J. T. (Bien Hoa)
*Yntema, Sgt. Gordon D. (Thong Binh)
*Young, SSgt. Marvin R. (Ben Cui)
Zabitosky, SSgt. Fred W. (Laos)

MARINES

*Anderson, Pfc. James, Jr. (South Vietnam)
*Anderson, LCpl. Richard A. (Quang Tri Province)
*Austin, Pfc. Oscar P. (Da Nang)
*Barker, LCpl. Jedh C. (Con Thien)
Barnum, Lt. Harvey C., Jr. (Ky Phu)
*Bobo, 2d Lt. John P. (Quang Tri Province)
*Bruce, Pfc. Daniel D. (Quang Nam Province)
*Burke, Pfc. Robert C. (Quang Nam Province)
*Carter, Pfc. Bruce W. (Quang Tri Province)
Clausen, Pfc. Raymond M. (South Vietnam)
*Coker, Pfc. Ronald L. (Quang Tri Province)
*Connor, SSgt. Peter South (Quang Ngai Province)
*Cook, Capt. Donald G. (Phuoc Tuy Province)
*Creek, LCpl. Thomas E. (Cam Lo)
*Davis, Sgt. Rodney M. (Quang Nam Province)
*De La Garza, LCpl. Emilio A., Jr. (Da Nang)
*Dias, Pfc. Ralph E. (Que Son Mountains)
*Dickey, Pfc. Douglas E. (South Vietnam)
*Foster, Sgt. Paul H. (Con Thien)
Fox, 1st Lt. Wesley L. (Quang Tri Province)
*Gonzalez, Sgt. Alfredo (Hue)
*Graham, Capt. James A. (South Vietnam)
*Graves, 2d Lt. Terrence C. (Quang Tri Province)
Howard, SSgt. Jimmie E. (Nui Vu)
*Howe, LCpl. James D. (South Vietnam)
*Jenkins, Pfc. Robert H., Jr. (FSB Argonne)
*Jimenez, LCpl. Jose F. (Quang Nam Province)
*Johnson, Pfc. Ralph H. (Quan Duc Valley)
*Keith, LCpl. Miguel (Quang Ngai Province)
Kellogg, SSgt. Allan J., Jr. (Quang Nam Province)
Lee, Capt. Howard V. (Cam Lo)
Livingston, Capt. James E. (Dai Do)
McGinty, SSgt. John J. III (Song Ngam Valley)
*Martini, Pfc. Gary W. (Bihn Son)
*Maxam, Cpl. Larry L. (Cam Lo)
Modrzejewski, Capt. Robert J. (Song Ngam Valley)
*Morgan, Cpl. William D. (Laos)
*Newlin, Pfc. Melvin E. (Quang Nam Province)
*Noonan, LCpl. Thomas P., Jr. (A Shau Valley)
O'Malley, Cpl. Robert E. (An Cu'ong-2)
*Paul, LCpl. Joe C. (Chu Lai)
*Perkins, Cpl. William T., Jr. (Quang Tri Province)
Peters, Sgt. Lawrence D. (Quang Tin Province)
*Phipps, Pfc. Jimmy W. (An Hoa)
Pittman, LCpl. Richard A. (DMZ)
Pless, Capt. Stephen W. (Quang Ngai)
*Prom, LCpl. William R. (An Hoa)
Reasoner, 1st Lt. Frank S. (Da Nang)
*Singleton, Sgt. Walter K. (Gio Linh)
*Smedley, Cpl. Larry E. (Quang Nam Province)
*Taylor, SSgt. Karl G., Sr. (South Vietnam)
Vargas, Capt. Jay R. (Dai Do)
*Weber, LCpl. Lester W. (Quang Nam Province)
*Wheat, LCpl. Roy M. (Quang Nam Province)
*Williams, Pfc. Dewayne T. (Quang Nam Province)
*Wilson, Pfc. Alfred M. (Quang Tri Province)
*Worley, LCpl. Kenneth L. (Bo Ban)

NAVY

Ballard, Hospital Corpsman 2d Class Donald E. (Quang Tri Province)
*Capodanno, Lt. Vincent R. (Quang Tin Province)

*Caron, Hospital Corpsman 3d Class Wayne M. (Quang Nam Province)
*Estocin, Lt. Cmdr. Michael J. (Haiphong, N. Vietnam)
Kelley, Lt. Thomas G. (Kien Hoa Province)
Kerrey, Lt.(j.g.) Joseph R. (Nha Trang Bay)
Lassen, Lt.(j.g.) Clyde E. (North Vietnam)
‡McGonagle, Cmdr. William L. (Eastern Mediterranean)
Norris, Lt. Thomas R. (Quang Tri Province)
*Ouellet, Sman David G. (Mekong River)
*Ray, Hospital Corpsman 2d Class David R. (Quang Nam Province)
*Shields, Construction Mechanic 3d Class Marvin G. (Dong Xoai)
Stockdale, Capt. James B. (Hanoi, N. Vietnam)
Thornton, Petty Officer Michael E. (South Vietnam)
Williams, BM 1st Class James E. (Mekong River)

‡Six Day War, 1967

Total medals awarded:

AIR FORCE	16
ARMY	2,342
COAST GUARD	1
MARINES	300
NAVY	744
UNKNOWN SOLDIERS	9
	3,412

Total number of recipients
(Total medals minus double awards)   3,394

Possibly the most colorful of all the men who have worn the Medal of Honor, Lieutenant Colonel Gregory "Pappy" Boyington (overleaf) had the full support of the men he personally chose to fly with him in what he called the "Black Sheep" squadron.

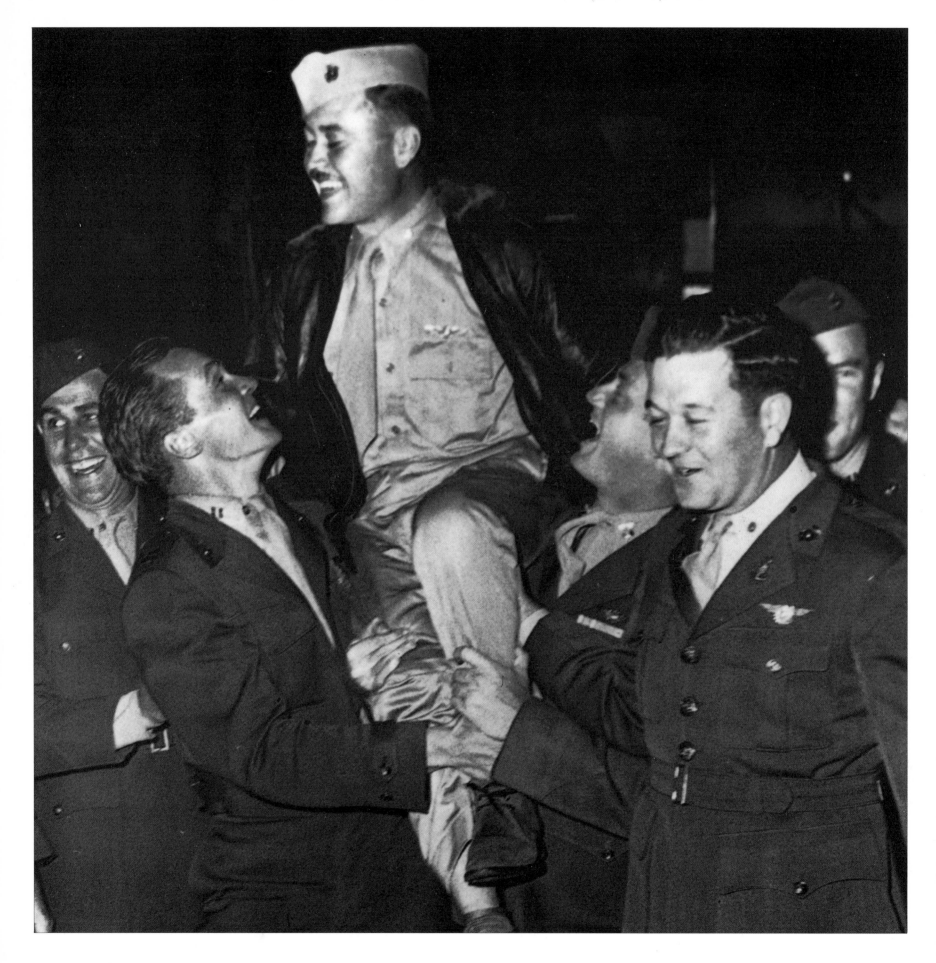